Defending the West

# DEFENDING THE WEST

## JAMES GOW

polity

First published in 2005 by Polity Press

Polity Press
65 Bridge Street
Cambridge CB2 1UR, UK

Polity Press
350 Main Street
Malden, MA 02148, USA

ISBN: 0-7456-3234-3
ISBN: 0-7456-3235-1 (paperback)

A catalogue record for this book is available from the British Library.

Typeset in 10.5 on 12 pt Times NR
by Graphicraft Limited, Hong Kong
Printed and bound in Great Britain by MPG Books Ltd,
Bodmin, Cornwall

For further information on Polity, visit our website: www.polity.co.uk

# CONTENTS

# PREFACE

Every book makes a journey. This one has taken a winding road, to make a fairly direct journey. As long ago as 1992, while contributing to a project for the David Davies Memorial Institute, then an independent institute in London (it is now associated with the University of Wales, Aberystwyth – perhaps its spiritual home). I was a minor participant in that project, drafted in by Lawry Freedman, a more important contributor, to furnish detail on the Yugoslav conflict, which was blighting the European landscape at that stage. The project was on humanitarian intervention, a popular theme during the 1990s and one that related to the use of force in international life. Surrounded by events in a changing world, I inadvertently saw something that I thought was special. I realized that the statement issued in January that year by the first ever summit meeting of the Heads of State and Government of the UN Security Council, redefining the terms of its primary business, dealing with threats to international peace and security, had a tremendous implication for international relations. This was a moment at which the world's leaders – at least their executive – had realized something that many academic observers and theorists appeared not to have registered – and indeed only recognized slowly over the next few years: there had been a seismic shift in terms of the way the world worked, in terms of its most basic international rules and in the foundation on which the rules and the workings were based – the quality of sovereignty. I discuss this in the course of this book.

This insight led to the development of the International Peace and Security Programme, based in the School of Law at King's College London, but a joint enterprise with the Department of War Studies at

King's. Lawry Freedman – a key figure throughout these developments – was the operational marriage broker. Rein Müllerson was, for want of a better term, the marriage partner – a former Olympic athlete, a former legal adviser to the Soviet leader Mikhail Gorbachev and a former Estonian foreign minister. This 'former' person was also a 'future' person. We shared an interest in the radical transformation taking place and in the implications of these changes at the legal–political boundary, the diplomatic–security interface and the frontiers of a new era. That programme, which took its first cohort of Masters students in 1997, has been one of the most privileged and exciting of the experiments since 1992. This book owes much to the intelligence, industry and enthusiasm of all the students who have studied with us at King's. Discussing their dissertations with them once the exam season has passed has been the best part of my job over those years – always intriguing, ever adventurous and uniquely challenging. Many of these great students have taken their cue from the programme to sail close to the conceptual and empirical wind, rarely if ever falling the wrong side of it. While the book is mine – it has to be because so many of them would be uncomfortable with the crucial parts of the argument here – I treasure their engagement and influence in developing the ideas and material here.

Material that would eventually be transformed into parts of this book were further developed during periods spent as a visiting scholar at the Woodrow Wilson International Center for Scholars, Washington, DC; the Institute for War and Peace Studies at Columbia University; and the Liechtenstein Research Program on Self-Determination at the Center of International Studies, in the Woodrow Wilson School, Princeton University. It was at Princeton that it became clear to me that the logical corollary of redefining 'threats to international peace and security' was to redefine the right to self-defence. While at Princeton I was able to write and develop an article published by *Security Dialogue* in September 2000, called 'A Revolution in International Affairs?' That article built a helical structure of revolutions in sovereignty, the protection of order in the international system and, most crucially – and radically – the right to self-defence. Passages in chapter 7 draw on that article, which is where the conceptual gap created by redefining threats to peace and security was first identified. The logic was that self-defence had to change.

This was a dangerous suggestion, I discovered over the years. It seemed to make my colleagues and audience uncomfortable when first presented in a seminar at Princeton. It certainly worried the reviewers of the article for *Security Dialogue*, some of whom judged it to be dangerous, while others presumably found it dangerous to the extent that they deemed offering any comment at all to be close to condoning it. I am more than grateful, therefore, to Pavel Baev, then editor of the journal, who stuck with the article (and the quest for reviewers who would actually review it, rather than dismiss it because of the message). That process, including the subsequent responses in the journal, sharpened the thinking over the years. The atmosphere of 'danger' persisted through to drafting the present volume and the comments of those who kindly read it for me, including one anonymous reader who was intrigued by the argument, but wondered if it was a 'dangerous fantasy'. It is not, but this comment was one of many for which I am indebted to that reader. It is one that has found its way into the final manuscript, juxtaposed with the more relevant 'needed reality'.

My original conception of what the book would be began when I realized how three separate strands of work over the past decade came together under the title *Defending the West*. I was sure that there was no book that linked the three themes I had been working on and considering. These were the nature and scope of international order, the evolution of Euroatlantic security arrangements and concerns, and the conceptual gap regarding the scope of the right to self-defence that had been opened up once the UN Security Council had radically defined the meaning of 'threats to international peace and security'. Bringing these together, I believed, was essential. The changes required in self-defence required prior understanding of changes in international order, including the action of the UN Security Council, as well as developments in the nature and scope of arrangements for defence of the West after the Cold War. This is what I have done in the present volume.

The book has had a long and winding route thus far, and was not always straightforward. For example, I was discussing the book on the eve of the attacks on Virginia and New York on 11 September 2001, but had a problem explaining the case because there was a lack of familiarity not only with issues of order, but with Usama bin Ladin and his al-Qa'ida network. Indeed, I sent an email the day after meeting one person perhaps, I admit, a little immaturely saying something along the lines of 'do you know who and what I mean now?' From that point onwards, the book should have been done in no time, were it not for the bureaucratic clamp of contemporary academic life. For a two-year period the book was largely on hold.

A chance to work on the book, in Berlin in August 2002, occurred against the backdrop of changes in the world that made a conceptual problem – aligning the right to self-defence with the transformation of 'threats to international peace and security' – a practical and policy one. The attacks on the twin towers and subsequent American and international responses had begun to change the scope of the right to self-defence. But it was a process begun, but not ended and not properly understood. The book now had to be written against a moving target – with increasing discussion of US-led action against Iraq a major part of that context.

By the time I was able to return to the book, major combat operations of the Iraq campaign of 2003 were over. But many issues needed to be addressed, including the need to acknowledge a right to pre-emptive self-defence and to set appropriate boundaries for it.

How to accommodate issues in the book was a big challenge. By this stage, the book was due to go into a series of short volumes dealing with twenty-first century-themes. It was a major effort to prepare a manuscript short enough to fit the series. In the end, that proved to be too much and I failed the challenge. Although the manuscript was submitted in that form, feedback came in the autumn: it was clear that a new phase was required, expanding parts of the book and restructuring it. The result is a volume almost twice the length, with seven chapters not five – and one in which some aspects, such as the theoretical prism of Constructivist Realism, the meaning of the West and the concept of self-defence have all been developed. The book is now one where the necessity and even inevitability of a shift to acknowledge the right to pre-emptive self-defence are undeniable, as well as one where the value of Constructivist Realism is confirmed.

Having come this far, I can only affirm the conviction that this book makes a case for what is unavoidable. Any weaknesses or flaws in it are, of course, as the ritual goes, my responsibility, as are, I trust, its strengths. That said, there are so many people to whom I owe thanks. These must begin with the tremendous, supportive, imaginative, high-calibre students with whom I have had the pleasure of exploring the issues considered in this book and others at the forefront of international change and at the barriers of law and politics in international society. That exploration has been in two contexts – the MA International Peace and Security in the School of Law at King's College London, and all the 'school' or 'college' of research students whom I have supervised. The 'plant', which is this book, is mine, but they were the nourishing earth in which it could prosper.

As well as all those bright-spark students, I have a number of other debts to acknowledge. I acknowledge these in the hope that I am not overlooking someone, somewhere – but I am sure that inevitably I shall. Against this, there are some who would be impossible to forget – without the continuous encouragement and intellectual challenge of Rachel Kerr, Chris Mackmurdo and Ivan Zveržhanovski the book might not be at all and in any case would certainly be worse. Pavel Baev's significant role has already been noted. Without the spur of publication he provided, the book would not have emerged. And thanks are also due to Andrea Drugan and Louise Knight at Polity, who also contributed spurs to publication. The list of others who helped me is long and, in some ways, varied – and sometimes the help might be largely forgotten by those involved, I suspect, while others will no doubt wish it had been. So, in no necessary order, thanks go to: Ilfana Vali, Monica Zazzer, Vesko Popovski, Rein Müllerson, Adam Roberts, Mats Berdal, Jan Willem Honig, Lawry Freedman, Mike Clarke, Abdoolkarim Vakil, Mark Barnhill, Paul Cornish, Barrie Paskins, Matthew Rycroft, Jonathan Marshall, Rahul Roy Choudery, Justin Morris, Sabrina Ramet, Marie Gillespie, Andrew Hoskins, Stuart Croft, Wolfgang Danspeckgrüber, Dick Ullman, Michael Doyle, Aaron Friedman, Sam Wells, Bob Ponichterra, John Lampe, Marty Sletzinger, John Ikenberry, Richard Crampton, Eliot Cohen, Dennis Pluchinsky (and a colleague of his whose name I have shamefully forgotten), Steve Hill, Robert Jervis, Jack Snyder, Richard Betts and the late Warren Zimmermann. In addition, the Bernerd Foundation and the Marchmont Trust provided financial support for related work, which found its way into the present volume. Finally, there are personal thanks to those who sustain book-writing spiritually. Franz and Petra helped revive a flagging battery. Peter and Dušica were supportive as ever. There would be nothing without Milena. And there would be less without my Dad and my Mum, who died along my way to writing this book. She would appreciate my final acknowledgement being to regret that there are individuals and groups in the world who make the need to alter the scope of self-defence necessary.

The research for this volume was partly conducted under the auspices of the ESRC's New Security Challenges Programme, ESRC Award RES-223-25-0063 'Shifting securities: news cultures before and beyond the Iraq crisis 2003', held jointly by Dr Marie Gillespie, Dr Andrew Hoskins and the author.

# ABBREVIATIONS

| | |
|---|---|
| ARRC | Allied Command Europe Rapid Reaction Corps |
| CJTF | Combined Joint Task Forces |
| CSCE | Conference on Security and Co-operation in Europe |
| DCI | Defence Capabilities Initiative |
| EAPC | Euro-Atlantic Partnership Council |
| ESD | European Security and Defence |
| ICC | International Criminal Court |
| IFOR | Implementation Force (Bosnia) |
| ISG | Iraq Survey Group |
| ITEC | information, technology, electronics and communication |
| KFOR | Kosovo Force |
| LoC | Line of Control |
| NACC | North Atlantic Co-operation Council |
| OAU | Organization of African Unity |
| OCSE | Organization for Security and Co-operation in Europe |
| PfP | Partnership for Peace |
| RIIA | Royal Institute of International Affairs |
| RUSI | Royal United Services Institute |
| SFOR | Stabilization Force (Bosnia) |
| UBL | Usama bin Ladin |
| UNPROFOR | UN Protection Force (Bosnia) |
| WEU | Western European Union |
| WMD/I | Weapons of Mass Destruction or Impact |
| WTO | World Trade Organization |

# 1 INTRODUCTION

Defending the West matters. It matters to me, as an educated white middle-class male – a prime (though second- or third-order) beneficiary of the liberal democratic system. It matters to Western governments and organizations, of course. And it matters to others who might not benefit so obviously.

It matters to Zahbia,[1] a middle-class Asian woman in Manchester, England, seeking to make her way as an individual, balancing elements of family tradition and professional development. It matters to Mohammed, an investment banker in Lisbon, Portugal, seeking to promote not only business, but also inter-communal harmony and the future security of and success of young people. It matters to Emel, a German-Turk in New York City, editing a gossip magazine and making her way in the vibrant city where cultures meet and flow both side by side and together, where, despite the best of will, things could not be the same after 11 September 2001. It matters to David, working in a major international hotel in Berlin, where the absence of international travellers has meant fewer big conventions and so massively reduced trade – and so bonuses and tips. Defending the West matters to all these people.

It also matters to Hasan, a blue-collar Asian male, working in industrial engineering in the English Midlands, whose job is threatened because suicide-mass murderers flew civilian passenger aircraft into buildings in New York City, and Virginia, USA. As a result, internationally, major airlines were hit with a seismic downturn in business, revealing underlying structural flaws in the industry – and that meant tens of thousands of direct job losses. Each of those job losses probably meant between one and five further job losses in local communities, wherever the airlines operated; and it meant that airlines cut back or completely countermanded orders for new aircraft. And without orders for new aircraft, the manufacturers and the maintenance firms do not need the parts that are produced by Hasan's and his fellow workers' labour.

Defending the West also matters to Humaira, a Gujerati Muslim, working in international high fashion in a major Western city, whose colleagues tried to make clear that they did not mean her, when making broad (albeit misjudged) condemnations of those who shared her faith and some aspects of her culture; both Humaira and her colleagues were affected by the downturn in wealthy international travellers, from all parts of the world, stopping off to spend; and Humaira was threatened by the way her colleagues and others not of her faith and culture scrutinized her.

Defending the West also matters to Tunji, managing a factory in New Jersey which uses modern methods and so never has more than four or five days of material at one time, as the others will be shipped quickly and cheaply as needed; it matters to Gianni, the truck driver who delivers those parts, but who is doing less driving as the flow of parts from the docks is slowed; it matters to Johnnie, working on the dock, as there is less throughput of imported parts; it matters to all of them because the increased time frames and increased costs, owing to additional security inspections, have meant that output from the factory Tunji manages has declined, as a result of falls in demand – themselves the result of both unreliability, when supplies are not available, and general uncertainty and insecurity among the buying public.

Defending the West also matters to Prashanthi, an Australian of Indian descent, working in financial investment risk analysis in Sydney. On the one hand, security challenges are her work and therefore mean business for her. On the other, the impact of security challenges diminishes confidence, and when confidence falls, the economy sinks and business collapses. Without business and investment, there is no need for her job, while less enlightened elements of the New South Wales population might actually blame her.

And defending the West matters to Murielle, and her family and friends, who might be tourists visiting the Tour Eiffel in Paris as an explosive-laden aircraft crashes into it for both destructive and propaganda effect, or working in the City of London as a 2,000 pound truck bomb destroys the Bank of England and much in its vicinity, unravelling the UK's financial system and large parts of its international counterpart, or living in almost any major city as a caesium or uranium device – a radioactive 'dirty' bomb – is used, generating cancers, genetic mutation and infertility for several kilometres around, affecting hundreds of thousands, perhaps millions, of people.

And, whoever you are, by chance reading this, defending the West matters to you – even if you are someone seeking to defeat the West. Defending the West matters despite the manifold imperfections of the West – indeed, it matters because of those defects, because of its fallibility, and because of its vital capacity to embrace error and slowly to correct itself. Defending the West is, perhaps, the biggest challenge of the twenty-first century. The two starting points for addressing that challenge are an understanding of 'the West' as a label and identification of the key, contentious question at the core of any serious discussion of defending the West – pre-emptive self-defence. The former is handled in later sections of this introductory chapter, while the latter, the key question, is posed in the following section.

*Extract from here*

## Pre-Emption: Real Need or Dangerous Fantasy?

UK Prime Minister Tony Blair sought to set a 'new style' for British politics and for his own leadership when he addressed the UK House of Commons Liaison Committee in July 2002. In the course of this session he also raised two issues, both in response to questions on Iraq, that offered the prospect of changes in international affairs that would be far more substantial and important than any changes in British politics, though they would also constitute a 'new style'. One concerned proaction to bring about 'regime change' in Iraq, if possible, and, certainly, to stop Iraq's potential to use Weapons of Mass Destruction – the only question was how this was to be done. The other suggested a radical change in the concept of self-defence. The events of 11 September 2001 had made it clear, he said, that there could be no sense in waiting for something to happen before responding – it would be better to act first.[2]

This chimed with statements from US Defense Secretary Donald Rumsfeld, urging a doctrine of 'pre-emptive' action, reflected in the US National Security Doctrine.[3] It also chimed with an earlier declaration (made in passing) by UK Secretary of State for Defence Geoff Hoon that the legal framework had been changed and would be again, if circumstances dictated.[4] Hoon's statement reflected the considerable change that had already taken place regarding the concept of self-defence, as well as pre-figuring even greater change to come. This is probably the most radical change in international society for over 300 years, reflecting an inevitable seismic change in the Western, liberal approach to the use of force and the protection traditionally offered, in legal, political and security terms, by the rights pertaining to sovereignty. Yet, while there has been limited discussion over the legality and the wisdom of action regarding Iraq, there has been no sense of the vast change in the notion of self-defence that occurred after 11 September, nor of the logic that requires further change, if the West, in particular, and all who benefit from international order, generally, are to be defended. To be sure, the change raises a series of questions which have to be addressed – including the practical 'how' part of the equation noted by Blair. But the change involved is necessary. The need therefore is to understand the altered parameters of self-defence as a legal-political-security concept, rather than to continue unaware of change, or to be distracted with debate over whether change is appropriate or not – debate that could create dangerous delays at moments where timely, perhaps immediate, action is required. International order has already changed, and the definition and needs of defence have already changed. But the concept of self-defence has not been changed with the times and so needs to be modernized and made appropriate to twenty-first-century conditions. Facing the threats and challenges that confront the US, the UK and others demands pre-emption.

Sharp – mostly negative – discussion of pre-emption marked discourse around the world in late 2002 and early 2003, mostly concerning the US National Security Doctrine of September 2002 and looming action over Iraq.[5] The US-led military operations against Iraq in spring 2003 were not really pre-emption. They were, at root, in legal terms, an enforcement action. They were about persistent non-compliance with international legal obligations and defaulting on the terms on which international military action against Iraq had ceased in 1991. But, even though the armed action against Iraq was not pre-emptive self-defence, it could have been. Iraq was judged to be a threat, on different levels. First, it posed a threat in terms of its anti-Western position (perhaps the only regime to celebrate September 11 publicly). Secondly, its continuing pursuit of chemical, biological and, crucially, nuclear weapons with which to challenge the West could not be dismissed. Thirdly, there was also the more contentious and debatable issue of its harbouring and fostering links with al-Qa'ida, and the prospect of potential collusion with it.[6] The group that had turned 11 September 2001 into the event known as September 11, or 9/11,[7] had some links with Baghdad – though Washington, DC, and other capitals even including London, held different views on the significance of those links.[8] And, finally, perhaps the core of the problem was Saddam Hussein himself, Iraq's uncompromising, irredeemable leader, whose personality, defined by obsession with the worst of weapons and pitiless violence, made him the real threat. The combination of personality, rogue state and potential collaboration with al-Qa'ida was such that pre-emption was relevant, even if it was not actually the basis for action – although the US implicitly allowed that this might be a complementary reason. Without the compliance framework, the same action would have been necessary. And it would have to have been just as pre-emptive self-defence.

Necessity and power are not sufficient, if the essence of the West is to be retained. The point should not be to say that pre-emptive action is against the rules, as so many politicians and commentators did in the context of Iraq, nor that the rules do not matter, which appeared to be the position of some, such as US Secretary of Defense Donald Rumsfeld, who stated the raw case for pre-emption. While the necessity of action has to be recognized, it is important also to preserve the Western ethos in doing so. Where the law is anachronistic, it needs to be changed, rather than set aside.

The traditional concept of self-defence, embedded in customary international law and politics, and in Article 51 of the United Nations Charter, has to change. For the twenty-first century, defending the West – and international society as a whole – needs a shift to embrace pre-emptive self-defence. But that shift to pre-emptive self-defence, while vital, needs to be founded on recognition of rules. That means an adjustment of the rules to define the acceptable terms for pre-emption.

Pre-emption is highly controversial. It worries many people as a matter of principle – especially experts and political activists. And it is a matter of concern to ordinary people, folded in with a range of fears about peace and stability in the world and worries about apparent or potential misuse of American military power. To many of those who reject pre-emption, it was a dark spectre, advocated by what were thought to be dangerous fantasists of American imperialism. At the same time, to many of them the idea that rules were being broken was of vital importance and gave great energy to concerns and protests – including the large-scale protests involving millions of people in different countries in the run-up to the Iraq operations in 2003. However, there is no point arguing that the rules do not permit pre-emptive action. And there is equally no point at the other end of the spectrum in believing that the rules do not matter. The rules do matter. But

they can and have to change to accommodate the new realities of
international security. The crux of this is to understand the evolutionary character of international law and its relationship to politics –
politics, practice and precedent contribute to the maintenance and the
development of international humanitarian law. Pre-emption without
attention to the rules would indeed be dangerous, as many ordinary
people, as well as political activists, believed. But the need for pre-
emption was real and necessary. The dangerous fantasy, as I shall
argue ultimately in this volume, is not to articulate pre-emption, but
rather to believe either that its adoption is not a genuine imperative,
or that its advocacy can be sustained without attention to changing
the rules. The real issue is not whether to change the scope of the
right to self-defence to accommodate pre-emption, but what the parameters of that change must be.

Defending the West requires a change to the rules. Those rules have
developed intrinsically with Western values over more than 300 years
and especially in the second half of the twentieth century. There are
three levels of defending the West: defence from physical threats;
defence from chaos and instability; and defence of values. Integrating
the three levels creates a puzzle. The riddle is how to reconcile the
need to change the rules in order to make the first and second levels
of defence possible without losing the values, including respect for
rules in a law-based society, that constitute the third level. Defence
against physical attack and, to a considerable extent, defence against
instability, can be achieved by power and action. But to do this
without reference to lawfulness and legitimacy will corrode the values
on which the West is based. There must be attention to the rules. This
does not mean preventing necessary action simply because the existing rules do not allow for a particular kind of action – for example,
intrusive intervention, or pre-emptive self-defence. It means the rules
must change, if the West is to survive. But necessary change is also a
test of the West – how to change in order to protect both its physical
self and its values without forsaking those self-same values?

Defending the West matters to Humaira, Hasan and all the others
on three levels. The first of these is physical attacks on Western countries that might hit them or their families directly, and if not, would
have knock-on effects. The second involves the way in which the
ripple-effect of disruption and instability in some other part of the
world threatens their livelihood and well-being. And the final level
comprises the undermining of openness and the liberal values that
allow them to grow as individuals, within living, multivalent communities. The West has to be understood primarily in terms of values, not

geography, and those values have to be defended along with socio-political stability and both persons and property, which means that ultimately it is a shared sense of security, of that which needs to be defended, that defines the West.

# Defining the West: Delineating the West

That which needs to be defended – the West – is, of course, a construction. It is a phenomenon created by factors such as geography, history, culture, politics, religion, philosophy and identity. While it would not be impossible to seek through rigorous logic to pin down a narrow definition of the West, this might also be unsatisfactory when considering defence of the West. There are key features that can be described as being generally applicable to the content of the West – especially their co-occurrence. To take this approach, as can be seen below, is to offer a soft definition of the West, but one that is defensible, both in intellectual terms for the present purpose and (because of that purpose) for those engaged in the practice of defending the West. Thus, the West has fuzzy edges for security purposes and is ultimately to be defined in terms of other- and self-perception of security. The West to be defended is a construction emerging from the interaction of those who believe themselves to be part of that which is threatened or part of the collectivity that must participate in protecting the West. Those interactions include the political discourse of security and practical and operational security commitments. This sense of the West is somewhat more flexible and open than that offered by Samuel Huntington, who nonetheless provides an excellent discussion of the West and its complements and competitors – indeed it would be hard to produce a better or more condensed reading of that which has fed into and constitutes the West. However, Huntington's context for the use of that term is a little more problematic and leads him to miss reflexivity as one of the essential qualities of 'the West' whatever its content,[9] as discussed below. This is one of the reasons to recognize the need for a flexible and inclusive approach to definition of the West (while acknowledging that ultimately any such terms will always of necessity be exclusive[10]). However, this less than rigid definition of 'the West' has to take account of the major features that can be generally described as characterizing the West.

The starting point for discussion of the West must be geography. The label, after all, refers to a point of the compass. As has been pointed out, definition of the West in these terms has a contingent, even arbitrary character.[11] While north and south, in conventional usage, can be seen as fixed points because of identification of distinctive polar regions, there is no equivalent for east and west.[12] While there is a point at which the only way is south (and conversely another where the only way is north), given the globe that is the earth, anything that is west of something is also east of something else. In this context, the lack of fixity in the term West is clear historically by different contrasts. The first was the Western and Eastern Christian Churches after the schism in 285. This was followed by the contrast of 'the West' with the Orient, meaning predominantly the Islamic-based Ottoman Empire until the twentieth century. For that century, East and West came to mean primarily the contrast between communist power in the Soviet Union and, after 1945, its satellites to the east of Europe, and the liberal democratic countries, to the West. This opposition of West and East was embedded, after 1948, in the Cold War. Of course, through those periods there were always other 'Orients' and 'Easts', those that embraced India or China and their neighbours. While 'the West' in each of these contexts retained a degree of fixity geographically, there was always a degree of flux, depending on the other determinants of that which constituted 'the West'.

Among the other determinants of 'the West', Roman Catholic and later Protestant Christianity is generally seen as being a core element. Indeed, the root of using the term 'West' is surely the third-century split in the Christian Church and so the parameters for East and West are formed by Europe. However, in any conventional contemporary sense, the West expands beyond Europe and embraces multi-faith, multi-cultural societies, even if these are based in part on a core tradition derived from the role of the Western Christian churches. It is also relevant to acknowledge the place of Islamic culture in the West, either through Moorish or Ottoman presence on the continent, whether in southern Europe, in terms of the former, or in terms of Central and Eastern Europe, regarding the latter.

Another element traditionally regarded as defining the West is 'culture'. This culture is generally taken to be the history of the arts in Europe, from their classical roots through to the modern art of the twentieth century, whether painting and sculpture, music and the literary arts, or, perhaps the most important of all in terms of cultural and civilizational hallmarks, architecture. This is the point made by the late Lord Clark in his imperious landmark study *Civilisation*. He quotes the nineteenth-century critic John Ruskin, who posited that 'great nations' have autobiographies written in 'three manuscripts' – deeds, words and art, but of the three only the last is trustworthy, before adding his own interpretation of that same message to bolster Ruskin's. Clark writes: 'If I had to say which was telling the truth about society, a speech by a Minister of Housing or the actual buildings put up in his time, I should believe the buildings.'[13] Little can be guaranteed to last forever, but among the potentially most durable elements of any culture can be found its buildings and its artefacts. Indeed, while civilization broadly is the process by which humans have come to master their environment, initially for basic survival and material need, it is the refinement in particular cultures within the pattern of civilization to the point of refinement for its own sake and purely for the spiritual satisfaction that it brings that has salience and which lasts. Indeed, Clark, who recognizes that he cannot define civilization in the abstract, produces a volume (and a set of films that went with the book) that are a history of art in Western Europe. Thus, his civilization, even as a history of Western art, does not include North America, which had, by the time he wrote, in many ways become the most active spring of artistic and other cultural development. Thus, while there is clearly a cultural history of something that is the West, it is marked by change and evolution. This is true both in terms of shifting *loci* of salient creativity and in terms of absorbing different influences, changing the shape and content of whatever the form is, whether Moorish architecture in Spain, or Polynesian culture in the painting of Paul Gauguin.

This same pattern of adaptation and flux is equally true of most of the other features that could be attributed, at one time or another, or in one way or another, to the West. These include the rule of law, the importance of languages, pluralism and representative political bodies, secular features such as the relative separation of faith and state, and, above all, a focus on the individual. Huntington points out that any of these might appear in any context, that none is perfect in any Western context, but that it is the combination of them that marks out the distinctiveness of the West.[14]

Perhaps the greatest hallmark of the Western way, though often overlooked, both in analysis and in practice, is the sense of fallibility and self-correction. Of course, there have been moments of presumed infallibility in the West, including the Spanish Inquisition and the Third Reich. But it is the sense of fallibility and so of testing knowledge theoretically and empirically, coupled with – or because of – a focus on the individual rather than the collective, that ultimately makes the West different. It is the openness to enquiry and the space allowed for individual intellectual development that has been a spur to the evolution of the West. This is the case whether in terms of art and high culture, or politics and liberties, or, indeed, the natural scientific investigation that led to the technological mastery that underpinned what William H. McNeill celebrated as *The Rise of the West*.[15] In his magisterial analysis, McNeill demonstrated the growth of Western technical culture in relation to the emergence and dominance of Western power.

The focus on individualism, rather than collectivism, that marks out the West is at the core of the values and culture on which Western societies depend, whatever the defects in practice over time. This core value gives rise to the way in which others manifest themselves in Western societies – whether artistic creativity, scientific enquiry, the rule of law, or pluralist and representative politics, where change is assumed on the grounds that no rulers can be perfect, omniscient or comprehensive. All of this constitutes values that both represent and generate Western power. In the twentieth century, the core of the ideological conflict between the West and the communists was that of the individual versus the collective. To a large extent the same is true in terms of the conflict that came to dominate the globe in the early twenty-first century – the 'clash' between the Islamist ideology coupled with political violence sponsored by the al-Qa'ida network of Usama bin Ladin (UBL) and its affiliates, and the West, with America as the bull's eye.[16]

# Defining the West: Defending the West

'Clash' theories have been an important element in discussion of international peace and security since the mid-1990s. This discourse has involved concepts of civilization, culture, ideology, modernity and political violence, often used un-reflexively and based on potentially dangerous assumptions. The main proponent of this type of argument, Huntington, argued that world order, following the Cold War conflict between Western liberal democracy and Soviet communism, was being re-made by a clash of civilizations.[17] On the whole, what Huntington meant was broad religiously labelled groups, with relatively low common denominators. However, the diversity within each tradition almost automatically undermined this notion of civilization clashes.

Nonetheless, the thesis proved to be provocative and attractive, at the same time, to different audiences (as might well have been intended, it can be presumed, from an author who had already had two big ideas in his career – military professionalism and political order and political change[18] – and who was searching for a third). The emergence of al-Qa'ida played to Huntington's theme, with UBL's movement laying claim to the name of Islam and seeking to persuade Muslims to reject the West. Whether this division amounts to a 'Clash of Civilizations', I doubt. Rather, I would judge it is a clash between civilization and anti-civilization. This assumes less that 'civilization' is Western than that it is a process in which human groups master their environment and their mutual relations, as already noted.[19] The numerous cultures of the human social world are the various manifestations of this process – they are the specifics, the arenas in which values and practices are communicated and negotiated implicitly – that is, how the environment is mastered differs. Hence differences in cuisine are differences of culture, but different cuisines are equally aspects of civilization. In this sense, Huntington's much vaunted thesis, aside from its specific empirical weaknesses, falls conceptually: civilization is not 'culture writ large',[20] as he argues; rather, it is the collective process and phenomenon, which has myriad specific cultural manifestations. Contrary to Huntington, culture is civilization writ small and specific. And also contrary to Huntington, it is inherent in the civility of civilization that, even if a plurality of them were accepted (and this is debatable, at best), clashes would be inimical.

And yet there is perhaps something to Huntington's analysis. There is a clash of armed ideologies and worldviews. It is a clash between those who embrace modernity (and even postmodernity) and those who are anti-modern; between those who embrace ideas of individualism and openness, and those who advocate collectivism and insularity; and between those who embrace the Western-dominated international state system and international society, and those who reject the state system and seek an ideologically defined realm. This analysis assumes that Christopher Coker's notions of 'post-Atlantic' and 'post-Western' fall into line with the judgement that any sense of 'cultural' or 'civilizational' clash is predicated on the understanding that this means 'a distinctive mode of existence' not an 'ideal'.[21] There is not a clash of civilizations, but there is a clash. It is a clash between ideologies, political-security forces and between civilization and anti-civilization. It is a clash between modernity and the political-religious Luddites of Islamism, who would return to the seventh century, apparently corrupting a great faith along the way.[22]

The use of 'Islamist' indicates a particular ideology, claiming to derive from the teachings of the Prophet, but reflecting a particularly narrow view of Islam, politics and the world, in which modernity is a corrupting force and in which the representatives of modernity – including Muslims contaminated by it – are enemies.[23] This ideology is distinguished from Islam, which, like other religions or international social movements, has considerable variety within it. Adoption of the ideology does not necessarily connote a commitment to political violence, such as using terrorist means. Those who do adopt violent means are only a minority even among those who accept this apparently radical version of the faith. Indeed, one of the central issues for Islam in the Islamist trend is the degree to which it indicates diversity of opinion and debate, while the proponents of Islamism seek to monopolize the truth and promote only one view of the world. However, even within Islamism, there is a division, reflecting different interpretations of the faith. This difference is between those who regard violence as being unacceptable, given that the Prophet teaches that it is wrong to harm any of God's creatures whether among the *umma* – the human faithful – or not, and those who regard the infidels as not being God's creatures, and so legitimate targets.

There is an important political dimension to this because the brand of Islamist extremism in question is founded on discontent and anti-Western sentiment. Countries might be *ipso facto* Islamic, but concern might justifiably emerge in the West if Islamist pressures in a country were to shape that country's exterior policy – as was the potential in Algeria, for example. The potential success of the Front Islamique du Salut in the 1990s might have resulted in a situation where the use of chemical weapons against southern Europe became conceivable. This might be either as an act of coercion (to gain a political response) or as an act of destabilization (the presence of significant Arab communities in France and Spain would put internal stress on those societies and their character as political communities). Indeed, one of the biggest challenges to stability for the West concerns social cohesion. The impact of violent Islamist action in one Western state, above all within the EU, would have undoubted impact on others, including the prospect of further terrorist activity. One point of this, from the perspective of the Islamist terrorists, would be to mobilize support among co-religionists, no matter what their ethnic, cultural or political background otherwise, and to foster internal tensions. Given the effect of modern communications in conjunction with images as messages, it would take little to spread the impact among alleged-kin communities in a world of transnational communities that have homes or links in at least two countries. While the benefits of inter-communal mixing and interaction can be immense, if mis-manipulated by those seeking to bring down the West, the result might be to create social fissures, or to make them more acute. This could happen simultaneously in many countries, placing pressure on governments at both the national and institutional level. Thus, there is an imperative for Western governments to acknowledge the role of various cultural inputs, including Islam, historically, as well as the relevance of that kind of input in the contemporary cultural and political environment. Above all, there is a need to balance problems of security – dealt with in the final chapter – with those of inclusion and openness, focused around promotion and protection of the individual and concomitant values. Recognizing that this is essential to the West is also relevant in managing reactions to Western power. This means, above all, American power, because it is the US which, no matter whether its role in the world is actually beneficial or harmful, is the focus for jaundiced rejection of that which is American and Western.[24]

America sits at the political core of the West in the early twenty-first century and has done so for much of the previous century. Western Europe occupies its historical and cultural wealth. Other 'settler' communities around the globe, who emerged from emigration from Europe, are its flag-bearers. But the West is not necessarily exclusive. Indeed, much of that which makes the West has made it dynamic and open, in terms of culture and values, as well as politics, finance and business. It has the potential to be universal in some aspects – and some in the West seek to achieve this. However, it is clear that the benefits of the Western way, and above all the American way, are attractive almost everywhere they go, if the success of fast food and films, on the popular cultural hand, and democracy, on the political hand, are fair measures.

Of course, acceptance and consumption of Western products does not mean being part of a wholly shared realm. Indeed, as Huntington astutely points out, given the moment at which he was writing, it is possible to drink Coca Cola, watch Hollywood films and wear jeans while planning how to blow up an American airliner. Nonetheless, at a broader level, there are common bonds which, while not necessarily absolute and certainly not irrespective of cultural specificities, cannot be set aside, and create shared interests in a system predicated on the openness characteristic of the West. Economic, cultural, political and security concerns are shared broadly by most governments around the world – and virtually all of them depend on webs of interaction that rest on international stability, which webs and the layers of stability on which they rest are the product, effectively, of Western achievement.

The West is a way of life. At its core is a set of values predicated on openness – the core value. The West, it should be understood, is interpreted as a non-geographic label. This is in contrast to the somewhat facile approach taken by some who ask how, for example, a geographical region can be 'compared' to Islam as a religion. Sets of values might be compared – although a comparison between Islam and the West is additionally problematic. This is because Islam is part of the West. This is true whether it is Western Christianity's reaction to the emergence of Islamic faith around 700, the historical impact of Islamic-oriented cultures in Europe (such as the grandeurs of Granada, or the Turkish baths and cuisine of Central Europe), or the contemporary role of various Muslim communities in Western societies. For example, there are over 30 million Muslims living in the European Union's Member States – potential not necessarily harnessed for the greatest strengthening effect by European political leaders to date. Rather, the West is defined primarily as a set of values, founded on qualities such as openness, fallibility, individual rights, tolerance and self-limitation. These values are not geographically specific and may be wholly or partially relevant to politics, economics, society or ethics. Because of this, Western states depend on a stable order and openness. These qualities constitute material interest and values (and the latter themselves constitute an interest), which must be preserved and promoted through security policy.

During the Cold War, European security was at the core of Western defence. However, the parameters of European security have changed, as has Europe's position within the world. With the end of the Cold War, there has been adjustment not only in the European relationship with the US, but also with reference to relationships in its more immediate neighbourhood. EU Europe has a clear concern with the evolution of non-EU Europe around its periphery, especially regarding the transition of former communist countries in Central and Eastern Europe. EU Europe also has a growing role and concern as an actor around the Mediterranean. These are both contexts in which the EU and its Member States might have responsibilities, which could require the use of armed forces in the twenty-first century. These are likely to be responsibilities which others much of the time would find less compelling to tackle.

Since the end of the Cold War, other regions, not part of a 'geographic' west, but clearly attached to it in terms of politics and values, have perhaps gained greater importance. While Europe and North America constitute the core of the West, whatever it means, the definitional scope should be larger. Australia and New Zealand, always part of the West, are implicated in the growing importance of the Asian Pacific. As well as the Australasian countries, the economically and politically Western-oriented and interdependent countries of Asia, above all Japan (which has had to emerge from a post-1945 shell), are also part of the Western sphere. They are at the frontiers of key developments, including a good number of the major security challenges for the twenty-first century. These include violent statehood and ideological clashes, with an international terrorist dimension, in Indonesia and the Philippines; political upheaval or nuclear threat on the Korean peninsula; nuclear confrontation in South Asia; and developments regarding China. Although a geographical contradiction, Asia – or in other ways Africa – can be seen as part of the West. However, despite this, and the reality that Australia has probably become the closest and most reliable ally of the US, the political and economic weight of the West will remain focused on the Euroatlantic region. So too will the dynamic discussion of interests and values, and evolutionary adjustments to the historic alliance between the US and a variety of European countries (hence the focus of chapter 5).

Some have suggested that a Euroatlantic parting of the ways might be inevitable. In a striking and important contribution, Robert Kagan has argued that radically different cultures of power and the use of force have determined and will determine the future of the relationship between the Americans and Europeans.[25] This is a strong argument, rightly recognizing continuity between US Administrations in this respect, where others might focus on surface differences. And the analysis captures a strong flavour of 'postmodern' approaches to international problems. But it misses the complexity and variety of approaches to power by each of the European countries, let alone the more obvious variety between them. Above all, it misses two all-important points: that there is more to the relationship than power, even for the US – values and legitimacy are vital; and that common bonds, forged through various patterns of interaction, identity and values, create shared interests. Cases such as Kosovo and Iraq, or the emergence of non-state 'rogue' actors in the 1990s, despite differences of emphasis, have impelled a radically new approach towards protection of the state because it was in the joint interest of Western – and other states that value stability and order – to do so. As the former Yugoslavia demonstrated, a question for one or some will become a question for all, requiring engagement, if it is not treated as such anyway. I have shown this elsewhere.

> The Yugoslav War moved from being an important question for stability and security and a test of the then CSCE's brand new Conflict Prevention Centre, to being a test of the future of EU Common Foreign

and Security Policy; from that it moved to being a test of UN diplomacy and UN peacekeeping; from that it became a test of European, Transatlantic and East–West relations and post-Cold War co-operative security; and, finally, it became a test of NATO credibility and with that of international and particularly American credibility.[26]

In a sense, this is the descriptive summary in one case of this process of interaction, cross-relevance, and, ultimately, the value of a Constructivist Realist analysis, which is explored in chapter 2.

For most Europeans, a complete transatlantic divorce is unthinkable and undesirable. It is something which, on the whole, the majority of European states fear. The World Trade Organization (WTO), for example, makes it clear that there can be substantial differences of orientation between the US and its friends and partners in Europe on crucial questions. In particular, in the context of the WTO, there was (and surely remains) concern in parts of Europe that advanced media and technological innovations may well present a cultural challenge to Europeans and others in a world market led and dominated by the US. Behind this there is an even greater sense that unrestrained trade in these areas would also consolidate US domination of all high frontier information capabilities – thus placing European states in a position of complete dependency on the US. In principle, there may be no difficulty with this so long as the US and the Europeans have a reliable relationship. If, however, there are signs that there could be areas in which the relationship might be questioned (as was the case over the former Yugoslavia and Iraq), a complete dependency would be a strategic black hole, meaning that Europeans would need an alternative. Although European strategic thinkers might need to consider transatlantic divorce, realistically, it seems likely that European engagement will be in partnership with the United States.[27] It seems, moreover, that at the Cold War core of the security West, the US and Europe will 'hang together or hang separately'.[28] And, with Russia the only alternative for the former also a likely complement, the US and Europe might well both be in partnership with Russia as well as with the NATO-led deployments of IFOR, SFOR and KFOR in the former Yugoslavia.

Shared values and common bonds drive US–European relations, so defining the West is largely a question of who shares those values and interests that need to be protected, of who is 'on-board' for developments to offer defence and whom such developments threaten. How to understand that question and the discussion that there is about it is an aspect of defining the West. This concerns less the important process of discussion of how difficult it is and debate on working out the parameters of change, but the key issue of whether or not the need for the change is seen and the need to be offered protection by it is understood. Do you feel the need to be defended, or do you see these changes as the pretexts for American imperial action notionally against 'terrorism' but really as excuses for manifestations of military power, destruction and subjugation – a different form of 'terror'? In a sense, this provides an 'us' and 'them' answer – the West and the rest. In practice, some of the lines are not always distinctly drawn. As suggested above, this is not a problem, as such. The West is defined by openness and adaptability – and in terms of security this is vitally important. It is being part of the world generated by Western dynamism and values and depending on stability in the international system in order to benefit from those qualities. In line with the West's openness, inclusion and exclusion depend on involvement and interaction and commitment to shared values and interests. This, ultimately, is not the political West, nor is it the cultural or religious West. It is the security West – what it is and who is part of it has no hard and necessary boundary. It means entanglement in a web of activity and values and a need for openness and interaction in the international system – those things that the West needs to be prepared to protect and secure, either through inclusion or, where necessary, intervention. The West, as a political-security phenomenon based on shared values and interests, is also a social construction. In many ways, given the focus on values and interests, the definition of the West is perhaps best signalled by the question 'Who requires defending?' Whatever the answer, that is 'the West'. Somewhat axiomatically, defending the West defines the West.

## The Book

This reflexive understanding of the West as based on values and approaches and openness – and above all on an imperative to maintain shared security – is the point of departure for the remainder of this study. Although conceivably it could be, given the title, this book is not really about strategy and operations, other than in the broadest and highest-level sense – even though there is something to say about the use of flexible, dynamic strategy and tactics, using manoeuvre warfare and exploitation of success. Such a book might also address the practical and operational security and intelligence approaches to protecting the West. This 'how to' book would be another volume altogether. The present book builds the case for changing the rules regarding the right to self-defence to accommodate pre-emption. This is essential to defending the West against disruption of stability in the international system, as well as to acting to stop attacks by a group such as al-Qa'ida. For the present volume distinctively to argue, as it does, that defence of the West requires a new interpretation of the political and legal right to self-defence and recognition of partnership, a novel theoretical prism is required to complement that change. This is 'Constructivist Realism', which is outlined in chapter 2. This method of investigation and interpretation recognizes both the constitutive nature of attitudes to interest and power, and necessity in the construction and attribution of value. This approach allows analysis to escape the confines of traditional Realism, to accommodate change and to permit interpretation and understanding of the structural and empirical challenges that confront the West in the twenty-first century – which other ways of seeing cannot. Armed with that theoretical lens, chapter 3 addresses the character of the international order on which states, above all if they are Western-oriented, depend. And it introduces the notion of stratified stability, which matches the constructed character of international order and permits theoretically guided empirical investigation of the real state and non-state threats and challenges to that order. That array of physical and stability threats is the subject of chapter 4. Having established the theoretical framework, an understanding of international order and awareness of the threats that confront it and the West, in chapters 5–7 I address the approaches that the West needs to take for self-protection. The first of these chapters, using the Constructivist Realist perspective, tackles the evolution and transformation of Western joint security arrangements, notably NATO and the European Union, from their Cold War origins to the adaptive, enlarging, stability and partnership-focused policies of the post-Cold War period. Having shown the contemporary historical evolution, I argue in chapter 6 that partnership, predicated on fostering peace, security and stability, should be understood as one of two key planks of the approaches taken by the West to defence. This is proactive, preventive and, where necessary, security and state building, addressing the challenges of instability and in some cases physical threat that confront the West. However, there are circumstances in which partnership, either alone or at all, will not be sufficient or most appropriate. These other situations will require defence – and that might well need to be pre-emptive. This is the culminating topic of the final chapter, which argues that pre-emption is unavoidable, where governments have evidence or interpretation of threats and challenges and can identify armed action that might be necessary fully to allow self-defence. However, to acknowledge that this is appropriate is not enough. The essence of the West, as well as requiring prudence in international diplomacy, requires that an adjustment to the rules governing self-defence is introduced, given the changing contours of the key concepts of necessity, immediacy and proportionality. The changes to pre-emption and to new rules are not optional – they are essential to the defence of the West. These changes will address the conceptual gap that emerged at the beginning of the 1990s, when the UN Security Council redefined the term 'threats to international peace and security', moving it away from a state-to-state focus and acknowledging that non-state actors and phenomena required attention. The Security Council's authority to deal with these threats under Chapter VII of the UN Charter is one of two instruments governing the use of armed force in international law and international politics. The other is self-defence. That pillar was left behind. The events of September 11, in particular, turned identification of and attention to a conceptual gap, which could be posited intellectually, into a pressing and pre-eminent policy priority. Conceptually and practically, both pre-emption and a change to the rules are ineluctable. The only question is what the reasonable boundaries of change will be, in the end. The world is a wonderful but dangerous place, where the West and what it means, as well as Humaira, Hasan and so on, and you (almost certainly), and I (certainly), all need to be defended.

# 2 THEORY

To a large extent, understanding the issues involved in defending the West needs new ways of thinking and seeing. Traditional theoretical prisms in international relations are not appropriate to the twenty-first-century international security environment. They are not capable of grasping the nature of order and the nature of the problems to be confronted. One of the essential elements to define in any approach to defending the West, aside from the notion of the West itself (see above), is how to think about tackling Western security. In terms of the theoretical context, a new term is required, to capture and explain the framework for the changes necessary in order to protect the West and its values from a range of threats, risks and challenges: Constructivist Realism.[1] Beginning with an understanding that order and the concepts that go with it are socially constructed – that is, they emerge from social interaction and discourse – it is my view that new constructions, including ideas of defence, may be developed over time to match circumstances. However, adopting this approach is to reject Alexander Wendt's view that Constructivism is necessarily or uniquely a Liberal approach to international affairs.[2] Rather, it is to contend that Constructivism can be applied equally in Realist and other approaches. From this point of departure, the need for and value of Constructivist Realism can be discerned.

## Realism and the Rest

Realism has dominated theoretical understanding of international politics since 1945 and, arguably, dominated it implicitly throughout history. The term Realism appeared as a label in the wake of the Cold War and at the birth of the Cold War, when Hans J. Morgenthau coined 'political realism'.[3] Part of a long tradition dating back to Thucydides and embracing Machiavelli and Hobbes, the label itself is a product of the twentieth-century development of International Relations as a field of study, or discipline. Realism, in essence, focuses on the maximization of power and the pursuit of material self-interest. States (conventionally understood as the prime actors) are deemed to have interests, the pursuit of which can best be accomplished through maximization of power *vis à vis* others, who have equivalent (and therefore competing) interests. While traditional Realists see this as a 'natural' phenomenon, Neo-Realists tend to see it as a structural problem – because other actors behave in this way, any one actor must do so, or pay the price. The primary interest is physical security, on which all others are built. And security is a function of power – hence the need to maximize power. Proponents of Realism regard it as the only rational approach to political life in the international sphere. While the author of political Realism as such, Hans J. Morgenthau,[4] held a more refined and sophisticated view that recognized the importance of values, for the most part, his disciples have focused on the maximization of brute power.

One of the main problems with Realism is that it is unrealistic. The world is more complex than most Realist positions can allow, with a range of factors interacting, making interests multiple and varied – and often contradictory. Part of that complexity is also that all political actors do not have the same motivation – some are not necessarily out to vanquish others simply to augment material power. However, in favour of Realism, it would be foolish to believe naively that no political actor has malign intentions. This was the message of E. H. Carr,[5] considered as part of the twentieth-century canon of Realism. His point, empirically and more modestly based on the experience of the twenty-year period between the two world wars, was that some actors might have bad intentions and that it would have been (and would be) prudent and realistic to recognize this and to make appropriate arrangements. In laying out this position, Carr was responding to what he termed the 'Utopian' or 'Idealist' (also cast as 'Liberal' or 'Universalist', at times) approach that had dominated the period bridging the two world wars. This view embraced the hopes of those such as US President Woodrow Wilson that the world could be based on rules and observance of them, fostering peaceful relations between countries and peoples. The rise of Fascist Italy, Imperial Japan and Nazi Germany had shown that good will and good wishes were not enough where others did, indeed, have the will to maximize power.

Among the advantages Realism and its variants have over competitors is relative coherence – Realists and their opponents generally agree on the use of the term 'realism' and on that which the term constitutes. In contrast, the range of opposing ideas contains lexical and conceptual overlap, depending on the particular writer or approach being taken. One reason for this might well be that most of the relevant labels have been imposed, in part at least, *ex post facto* and by others. Terms such as 'Idealist', 'Liberal' and 'Utopian' tended to be imposed by others writing critically about the dominance of ideas associated with those labels in the period between the First and Second World Wars – for example, E. H. Carr challenged what he described as the Utopian views that had prevailed following the horrors of the 1914–18 war. These had included the positions of the US President at the time, Woodrow Wilson, who had a major influence, promoting the ending of empire and the right to self-determination, as well as the founding of the League of Nations. This 'Liberal' world was intended to be one in which the scourge of war was attenuated by the emergence of what have often been called 'liberal institutions'. The League was a prominent example of this – a body which would espouse the theory of collective security and create an array of institutions to embrace states, as well as subjecting them to law and eliminating conflicts between them. The history of that inter-war period, in various ways, confirmed that, against the hopes of those promoting the League, their slogan 'law not war' could not hold in the given framework – as Chris Brown has pointed out, 'the only way in which "law" could be maintained was *by* "war"'.[6]

International Relations as a dedicated field of study, or discipline, only emerged in the early twentieth century, and primarily as a reaction to the First World War. The first chair of international relations was established at the University of Wales Aberystwyth in 1919. It was established thanks to the benevolence of David Davies, with a largely 'liberal' mission. That chair was established as the League of Nations was being formed and the Paris peace conferences were cementing the peace in 1919. In the spirit of the creation of the League, the early study of international relations was focused on how law, in particular, as an institution could end war. The solution to war, it seemed, was to make it illegal.

At the core of an array of Liberal and Idealist theories is an assumption that values are more important than matter. Where Realists might believe in original sin, their Liberal counterparts are more likely to focus on redeeming qualities of human nature. In this view of the world human nature is not inherently selfish and competitive in absolute terms. On the contrary, peaceful relations between individuals are the norm, given the chance, and this translates into the potential for peaceful and co-operative relations among states and other actors, all of which entail the possibility of developing a consolidated community of shared values, of which peace is the primary one.[7]

Probably the most important author in the 'peace' camp historically is Immanuel Kant, who devised a formula for what he called 'perpetual peace'.[8] Kant is often cited in the canon of Liberal or Idealist thought. While Kant was undoubtedly liberal, the degree to which the Idealist tag fits might be questioned. Kant's vision of the world was to be empirically built, sovereign individual by sovereign individual, until the collectivity of individuals who formed a state, based of necessity in his formulation on a republican constitution, join a federation of states – itself a form of democracy among states extending from that democracy to be found among individuals within them. For Kant, peace was not something that could be achieved by an agreement signed by governments overnight. It could certainly not be signed by princes and the like – they were the corrupt leaders who, acting in their selfish personal interest, took the ordinary person to war. The assumption in Kant's view was that the people would not choose the awfulness of war if they were free to decide. The republican constitution was the framework for this. While the republic retained the right to use force in self-defence, should some unscrupulous remnant of the monarchical system disrupt the peace, the Kantian theory held that over time the people, that is, the individuals acting through the republic, would not countenance their own losses through war. This position was to be consolidated by the 'pacific federation' of states, in which an agreement would be signed to secure the rights of each state without prejudice to others. This would be an entirely voluntary arrangement, which Kant believed would build incrementally into perpetual peace as more and more states became republics, the republics acted in the interests of their sovereign individuals, and a 'universal community' came to be formed. For Kant, peace is achievable, but war remains until the 'universal community' is accomplished.

To reach that point, several Kantian views play an important role. The most important of these are the concepts of 'conscience' and 'publicity'. Kant was deeply sceptical of the world of diplomacy, resting as it did in particular in his time (if not at others) on secret treaties and forms of dissembling. Publicity was the counter to this. By 'publicity' Kant did not mean anything to do with advertising or promotion, as the term might most commonly be understood in the twenty-first century. He meant doing only that which you could say openly and which, linked to the other concept, you could do with good conscience. This element of Kant, perhaps more than anything else, renders him an Idealist – albeit one with his feet firmly on the ground, who is mapping out how to improve on the human and social lot in a world of insecurity and war. He is not saying this is how it is, necessarily; rather, this is how it could be. He is idealistic in aspiration, but actually quite realistic, at least in the common-sense version of that term (but maybe also that of political theory too).

The introduction of 'universal' by Kant leads to another of the areas of confusion in the literature on international relations theory and the lexicon of terms used. Kant is certainly a Universalist in so far as his theory is intended to apply to all peoples and states once accomplished. He would not, however, have countenanced the imposition of values deemed abstractly to be universal on those who had not chosen themselves to adopt those values. So, for example, given the essentially voluntary nature of his worldview, he probably would not have favoured any form of international intervention, such as the 'humanitarian intervention' by NATO countries in Kosovo, or even action authorized on behalf of the international community by the UN Security Council.

At the same time, the term Universalist, sometimes used as a rough synonym for 'Liberal' or 'Idealist', can be applied to other theories that are radically different in their character. For example, Marxism at core is a 'Universalist' theory, in that it seeks to explain all situations.[9] Marxists, by identifying the relationship between power and ownership with the means of production as the core mechanism of history and change, are projecting an explanation that applies to all. However, in contrast to anything Idealist, that theory is founded entirely in a materialist conception of the world. It is the relationship of one group to another in terms of material – that which is produced – which counts. There is no room whatsoever for ideals of any kind in this interpretation.[10]

Rationalism and Revolutionism present similar difficulties as terms. Martin Wight, in one of the classic studies of international relations theory,[11] uses these two terms in addition to Realism. While his use of Realism coincides with that which might be generally recognized by Realists and their critics, his use of Rationalism and Revolutionism presents problems. For example, Wight places Kant among the Revolutionists. Yet Kant is decidedly anti-revolutionary – his approach is not to overturn the order radically and completely, but to transform it in an evolutionary, rather than revolutionary, manner. At the same time, Kant is a supreme rationalist. The achievement of perpetual peace, should it be managed, would come through a rational approach. Thus the use of these terms can at times be overlapping and confusing.

Rationalism, in Wight, is used to refer largely to a class of scholarship often otherwise dubbed 'Groatian', or the 'English School'. The approach reflected here is generally (and generally seen to be) somewhere between Realism and Idealism and counts among its traditional heritage the work of Hugo Grotius and, in its international relations era classical form, Hedley Bull.[12] To this extent, one of the key authors in the field, Bull, can sometimes be seen as a Realist and at others as a Liberal.[13] This is possible because his way of seeing international politics has common ground, at its core, with both those more prominent schools of thought. The term 'anarchy', which permeates Neo-Realism, forms a core part of Bull's key idea – the sublime oxymoron 'anarchical society'.[14] However, the other part of that equation has resonance with Liberalism, as it focuses squarely on the basic mutual rules that transform 'anarchy' as the absence of overarching government into a 'society' based on mutual recognition of basic rules. The most basic of those rules concerns sovereign rights: by recognizing each other as the incumbents of sovereign rights, states agree not to interfere in each other's internal affairs, leaving each state to decide on that which happens within its borders. This basic rule ensures society – an arrangement based on the mutual recognition of rules – at the same time as it serves to define anarchy among states at the international level. In reality, this is perhaps the most realistic (not Realist) approach to understanding international relations, although it is largely overlooked in much US coverage of the field.[15]

The 'society of states' approach has potential overlap with other approaches, such as Pluralism, or Interdependence, where the variety of actors and interactions and their interrelationships are stressed.[16] This alternative to straightforward Realism to some extent straddles the Realist–Idealist divide, recognizing that there is variety at play, with self-help assisted and constrained in different ways by a variety of pressures and interactions – including norms – and the same, in reverse, for Idealism. It could be argued that Social Constructivism, or just Constructivism,[17] also comes close to the 'society of states' position – and that, because it emerged in the North American context, which dominated discussion around the world, it perhaps offers a better route to a more nuanced interpretation of international relations than either a stereotype of Realism or Idealism could offer. In reality, it has some potential to bridge gaps between Realism and the various approaches that engage with it, seeking to refute it or at least to qualify it. However, this is not really the approach that its main proponents have taken. They have engaged with Realism, not so much as a potential bridge (even where they claim to do so), but as part of the opposition to its dominance. This somewhat ideological approach has devalued the potential of a Constructivist approach to a large extent. However, the potential of hitching Constructivism to Realism, rather than using it to oppose Realism, has eminent potential in the twenty-first-century security environment, as I shall argue in the following section. Constructivism can be and should be just as much, or more, an ally of Realism than it is an opponent.

## Constructivist Realism

While various proponents of Idealist views have tilted at Realism, as have those of Socialist, Marxist, Critical and other perspectives, the reality of International Relations, an academic subject, dominated by US scholars, has been that each has confirmed the status of Realism as the primary ideology in the field. In doing so, each has confirmed the failure of any competitor to supplant it, simply by pitching criticism and analysis against it. While narrow Realism might not fit the world as such, given that there is more to life than material interest and benefit, if nothing else, there can be little doubt that material interest and benefit, including security, constitute a necessary part of the equation. In practice, elements of both Realism and Idealism play a part. This is recognized by those who implicitly, or explicitly, embrace elements of each, beginning with the Dutch international lawyer Hugo Grotius, who saw the inevitability of brute power, but also saw the importance and possibility of rules in tempering it and developing into and beyond the 'international society' identified by Hedley Bull.[18]

The basis of Bull's international society – that which makes a society, rather than anything else – is mutual recognition of rules, crucially, as the base of everything else, the quality of sovereignty and the rules that pertain to it. This, in a sense, is a form of social construction. Rules are the result of inter-subjective agreement, or alternatively of processes involving declaration or action, precedent and acceptance. Such processes may be formal, or they may come through custom and practice – in legal terms, for example, the rules might be treaties, or they might be customary law. At certain points, aspects of this inter-subjective process become so embedded, or reified, that the actors are not conscious of the process, or the prevalent interpretation it has produced.

The analytical strength of a Constructivist approach should be in understanding processes and dominant interpretations. However, the problem with the way in which Wendt introduced the approach to the International Relations repertoire is that he sought consciously to situate it in the Idealist tradition as a counter to Realism.[19] His focus was not on the mechanism and understanding of how interpretations of whatever kind emerged, but on how that understanding could be used to unpick Realism. As others writing in other fields, such as gender and nationalism, had done, Wendt sought to apply Constructivist analysis to show that Realism was not scientific, material and necessary, but social, cultural and contingent; that it was, in some sense, an invention, not an inevitability. However, following George Schöpflin's challenge to those applying Constructivism to nationalism, the only reasonable response to this might be: 'So what? That does not make it any less real.'[20]

The point, for some,[21] in Constructivism has been ideological: because reality is constructed, the fallacious reasoning seems to be, this means that it can be re-constructed in whichever way a particular author or group wishes. This, indeed, is one of the hopes that Wendt, who did most to raise the profile of Constructivism, holds.[22] However, Wendt's approach is regarded as being shallow and too engaged in seeking a dialogue with Realism by some other proponents of Constructivism, who take a more strongly Reflectivist position.[23] This means that (in a similar manner to Critical and Postmodern theorists) they reject arguing on the same ground as the Realists – and indeed their 'Rationalist' counterparts in Liberalism and elsewhere. This view takes a purely and avowedly normative approach, in which there is no independent reality that can be tested by Positivist Scientific rationality. 'Facts' are not established through empirical testing (although some concessions might be made for the physical world), but are socially agreed.[24] This is misguided, though, as the real analytical strength of Constructivism is in identifying the social process – and that applies equally to Realism, Idealism and any other school of thought, or practice. Any product of social construction (and there should be no confusion here with social engineering, or even ideological manipulation) is still 'real' in two senses: in its underpinnings and in the way it is felt or perceived. That Realism is constructed does not make it arbitrary, or necessarily wrong. Indeed, while a sceptical approach is important as a check on the merit of any interpretation, it is probably fair to judge that Realism, although socially constructed, has remained dominant, as a function of inter-subjective processes, precisely because it builds on something 'real' – the need for security and viability and the relevance of power in securing them.

The majority of students of international relations using a Constructivist approach have been opposed to Realism – and indeed to Idealism and other traditions and schools of thought. Constructivist Realism, therefore, represents, I believe, a radical step in the appreciation of international politics. The term is unique and meaningful,[25] but it is not necessarily the first attempt to deploy Constructivism while acknowledging merit in Realism. By referring to 'interactions' Wendt, in popularizing the notion of Social Constructivism in the study of international relations and seeking avowedly to present a normative-driven, Idealist challenge to Realism, nonetheless acknowledges that he is a 'realist' to the extent that his focus is on the state.[26] This is a deeply qualified nod to Realism – one that is considerably outweighed by the overall aim of undoing and revising the dominant Realist position. A more notable example is that of the 'Copenhagen' Constructivists Barry Buzan, Ole Weaver and Jaap de Wilde, who go some way towards taking a similar position to Constructivist Realism, but fall short of doing so.

Although their purpose and primary focus is the broadening of the security agenda, while also setting boundaries to its expansion, the approach they take is both avowedly Constructivist and openly Realist. It is Constructivist to the extent that they view 'securitization' as 'an essentially inter-subjective process', which means that in all but the most immediate and extreme cases, threats could not be objectively identified.[27] It is Realist to the extent that they seek to identify their position as 'post-sovereign realism'.[28] However, their attention to the social processes that determine security seems ultimately driven by the same desire to temper the Realist predicament. By taking a partly Constructivist approach, they maintain, 'it will sometimes be possible to maneuver the interaction among actors and thereby curb security dilemmas'.[29] The reflexively engaged use of Constructivism, even with a foothold in Realism, makes clear that their ultimate agenda is a similar desire to use the power of knowledge and understanding to tame and change the Realist beast to that expressed by Wendt. In the end, their mission is to change Realism, if not eventually to transform security relations and remove that concept's dominance. It is not to situate Realism in an inter-subjective context, where the soundness of their analysis on the constituted and changeable character of Realism makes clear that Realism is not necessarily an inherent or 'natural' position, whatever its strengths and merits.

Acknowledging that Realism is neither natural, nor as fixed as its proponents and its critics would maintain, is to recognize it for the social construction that it is. However, this does not invalidate it, as both Realists and some of their opponents have proposed. In addition, the Constructivist perspective can enhance Realism, permitting it greater variety and flexibility, as well as allowing legitimate scope to values and other elements than power. As Sabrina Ramet has argued, albeit from an avowedly Idealist position, there is a need to avoid simplistic and reified interpretations of the international environment, such as the archetypal 'Othering' of Realists and Idealists by each other in international relations theory and caricature.[30] The reality of the world is complex, and a sensitive, composite theoretical approach, recognizing both the necessity of rules and the importance of change, is apposite – hence the framework of 'Constructivist Realism' introduced here.

Constructivist Realism as a notion actually only confirms that which Realism always was in many ways. The focus on material aspects in traditional realism while giving an apparent *a priori* foundation to a scientific approach is actually more important as a focal point for the attribution of value – the conventional Realists and Neo-Realists are right to focus on the material to a large extent, but not because it necessarily has independent and intrinsic force. Rather, the material counts because that is where value is attributed. To acknowledge that Realism is socially constructed is absolutely not to say that it is merely invention for the sake of it. The construction of value around the material is what counts.[31]

While the roots of Realism lie in assumptions about human nature, the Neo-Realist modification of it, which has become hegemonic in theoretical terms, places the burden of assumption on structure. In the model set out by Kenneth Waltz,[32] it is inevitable that states are in competition in a world of anarchy, as each can only depend on self-help. However, the attempt to create inevitability and predictability through emphasis on the state and the structure that binds states into an insecure pattern of competition and self-help fails in a world where threats and challenges entail more flux, can be perceived only dimly and certainly do not fall into any particular regular pattern. This is not to say that there is no element of structure in the contemporary and future environment. There is. Structure emerges precisely from processes of construction. In the contemporary environment, a complex pattern of relationships, a function of the behaviour of states as the primary agents in international life, is and has to be structured by the imperative of stability in the international system (this and the corresponding threats are developed in more detail in the following chapters).

Waltzian Neo-Realism adapts more traditional versions of the concept to include economic dimensions of power as well as purely military. This is a move that makes sense, in grand strategic terms, if we recall that military might needs to be paid for ultimately and that research and development to stay ahead in a self-help system is not cheap. It also differs, as already noted, in its emphasis on the structure of the international system. Waltz argues that while states (qualified by sovereignty) may differ in terms of political, ideological and constitutional character, their foreign policies and international behaviour are very similar – the United States and the Soviet Union during the Cold War might be taken to exemplify the point. The reason for this is the international system, which gives states no real alternative. This does not mean that the detail of policy positions will not be different, or that states will not try to push ideological preferences at the margins. It does mean, however, that the scope for such action will probably be limited to the margins, while the main thrust of activity will be the same, in a mirror effect. This is because each state, dictated by the structure of its relationship with the other (or others), is bound to act so as not to let the others gain an advantage, as a baseline, and to seek to gain an advantage, if possible. In contrast to traditional Realism, it is not necessarily the nature of the states themselves that dictates this relationship, but their mutual relationships, which mean that they can ill afford to lose out. The key to this structured relationship is statehood. States have this relationship with each other, not with any other entity.

The logic of structured interaction dictating behaviour in the international system, gleaned at least in part from observation of the Cold War power division in international society, could make sense. In the post-Cold War context, Neo-Realist state-centricity was a more problematic phenomenon. Already criticized by commentators for the narrow focus on the state, three main challenges arose, as an apparent de-emphasis on the state emerged – although, to be clear, this did not mean that the state had ceased to be relevant at all. The first of these concerned the perceived shift in the locus of armed conflict from the state level to the sub-state level – a Realist focus on the state could not significantly inform analysis of a world characterized by intra-state conflict. The second involved the impact of non-state actors apart from the participants in internal conflicts. The third concerned the emergence of an apparently new approach to the protection offered by sovereign rights.

The problem of intra-state conflict, which was not new but gained greater attention with the decline of the Cold War, could not be accounted for by reference to Neo-Realism and the emphasis on structured state relations. As there were various attempts to grapple with the somewhat unhelpfully labelled 'ethnic conflicts',[33] Barry Posen made the sensible effort to apply a Realist approach to the actors in non-state armed conflicts.[34] The essential point in doing this was to register that the protagonists in such an armed conflict, or indeed prior to the outbreak of war, were structured in the same kind of relationship as they would be if they were states. While Posen to some extent appeared not to have mastered the shift in a wholly comfortable manner, the trajectory certainly made sense. This can be confirmed by reference to a similar shift that could be introduced regarding the second trinity of Carl von Clausewitz. Circumstances at the end of the Cold War also seemed to lead some scholars to assume that Clausewitz was also redundant in a world where states were less important – or at least where they were not the most immediately apparent focus for armed conflict.[35] However, the triangulation of government or state, armed forces and people could easily be translated to political leadership or political community, armed forces and supporters, validating the eternal wisdom of Clausewitz's insight into the harmony required for strategic success in war.[36] The logic of this applied to the attempt by Posen to relocate the logic of Realism to the level of participants in intra-state conflict. However, while the logic was there, it did mean a shift away from the state level at the core of the Waltzian model.

That shift did not, however, remove the importance of the state wholly either. In fact, statehood remained central to armed conflict. These were statehood clashes. The issues at their heart concerned control of existing states and how they should be run. They involved the absence of central enforcing authority in such states. Or they were about the redistribution of territory, populations and resources within, or across, the boundaries of existing states, and with the aim of changing the contours or the status of borders as the purpose of at least one of the belligerents.[37] Thus, while the structured relationship required of states in Neo-Realist theory did not apply in many important cases, *as such*, a *quasi* state and structure position emerged, and the state retained central importance as the prime actor and so the prime focus for study in international life.

The second and third challenges to the Neo-Realist model were more problematic, although they both, in the end, also served to confirm the continuing relevance of the state as the nodal point of analysis of international politics. In addition to sub-state actors in internal armed conflicts, other non-state actors emerged with salience on the international scene. Some of these were international and transnational bodies, often non-governmental, but in some cases sponsored by governments but having an independent character of their own beyond collective governmental sponsorship. The most striking example, as the twenty-first century began (and quite in contrast to other would-be benign bodies), was the al-Qa'ida network (discussed in chapter 4). At the same time, there were other forces in international life that, while given meaning in social contexts, were somewhat independent of them. These included – by no means exclusively – environmental degradation, in particular the much discussed global warming, and the effects of a highly integrated global financial system (again, matters of relevance in later chapters, where issues of order and threat are discussed more fully). The sum of growing international concern over and attention to these issues led to the third trend, the changing approach to state sovereignty. Each of these issues did not mean the end of state relevance. Indeed, the point was that they confirmed the continuing centrality of the state, once the surface of issues was broken and a little perspective added, because the reason any of these issues arose at all was that they impacted on particular states, groups of states, state capacities, or the concept and meaning of the state. In the end, an array of non-state actors and phenomena gained increasing attention because they affected the state, in one way or another. And, most strikingly of all, the changed approach to the protection offered traditionally under the scheme of mutual recognition of sovereign rights was relevant only where the needs of states and of international society as a whole were to reinforce the state in one way or another. The only way to achieve this and to preserve the order and stability upon which states generally depended in an integrated and interdependent world was by overriding the traditional protection offered by sovereignty in the system. The traditional rules of the sovereignty arrangement were amended in order to preserve the position of the state, generally, rather than to undermine it. (Once again, this is a topic developed in later chapters.) States required stability in international order. If that order was absent and the solution lay in taking action within or across borders in order to protect states and their order, then this had to happen.

While the state remained paramount, confirming one part of the Waltzian position, interpreting state behaviour on an assumption of structure became less pertinent. This is not to say that where traditional state-to-state relations were involved the structured relationship would not be of continuing importance. However, in many ways, the key threats and challenges could not be addressed by this approach. While the analysis of structure could conceivably be applied to political communities in the same way as the Clausewitzian trinity could be translated to them, this was not possible with regard to the variety of other non-state actors and issues, or the problem of stability in the international system.

This problem arises over the position taken by authors such as John Mearsheimer.[38] Mearsheimer argues for the continuing relevance of Realism. He posits five theses that confirm its status. First, he writes that states continue to be the dominant actors and that they operate under conditions of anarchy. Secondly, he reports that great powers always have an offensive military capacity. Thirdly, he suggests that no state can be completely sure about the intentions of any other state towards it. Fourthly, great powers accord importance to their survival. And fifthly, he asserts that states are relatively rational actors, capable of devising strategies to ensure their survival. These are reasonable propositions, in and of themselves, with regard to describing aspects of statehood in international life. His projection from this is also reasonable. This is that no one can know what the alignment of states and power might be by the third decade of the twenty-first century – although much ought to be discernible if the Neo-Realist project were informing understanding as successfully as its logic of structure would claim. The unknowable elements of the future are perhaps more likely not to correspond with the images of a return to the past, which he raises in a scenario where US forces might be withdrawn from Germany and East Asia, giving rise to the resurgence of Germany and Japan as great powers underpinned by military force, than Mearsheimer seems to allow.

More saliently, what his approach cannot accommodate is the real set of problems that any state, including a great power, has to face. Governments and their agencies in Washington, DC, London, Madrid, Rome, Berlin, Paris, Canberra, Tokyo and so forth could be expected to be paying attention to each other and even more so to a variety of other states in the system. However, the threats and challenges that dominated perhaps 80 or 90 per cent of the policy agenda in the 1990s and the first years of the 2000s were not covered by the Mearsheimer position. These were the disruption of international order and the statehood system by intra-state conflicts, such as that in the Yugoslav lands, and the operations of clandestine networks, with a prime mission not only to wreak destruction on US and Western targets, to the extent that this was possible, but more importantly to use those attacks and other activity to disrupt and destabilize international order in general, and Western societies in particular. In one specific example, the Realist model had no provision for the September 11 attacks, which Constructivist and empirical approaches might – and in the broadest terms empirically did.[39] In terms of the Neo-Realist model, states, while still central to the practice and study of international politics, as Mearsheimer correctly identifies, could not have an equivalent to the structured relationship with other states at the heart of the theory with either a non-state actor or phenomenon, or with stability in the international system. Indeed, if any structural relationship were to be identified, this would need to be with stability in international order as a whole.

Structural Realism provided an *a priori* rationale for state behaviour. As far as it was accepted as an explanatory and guiding theory, in a world of states versus other states, it apparently could save having to discover empirically, at least to some extent, the nature and will of other states. Because it is assumed that states cannot know for sure the intentions of others, understanding how structure obliged them to act in certain ways could be inferred. However, once it is acknowledged that the nature of the most major threats and challenges is not from states, but from non-state sources, whether the need for stable order itself, or transnational or international ideological terrorist movements, then the logic of statist, structural Realism cannot apply. The new threats and challenges are fuzzy and hard to perceive. They have no equivalent to the *a priori* status of structurally bound states in Neo-Realism. While some threat from other states cannot be excluded, the challenge for policy makers, as well as for serious academics and for people in general, is to address the real questions – not to do so would be unrealistic, as well as negligent. Threats are not predominantly to be found in competitive state relations, as far as this represents the dominant position in the twenty-first century. And the kind of threat previously argued to be immanent in state relations cannot be immanent when consideration of threat involves stability threats, generally, and the actions of relatively nebulous non-state actors, more specifically. Like and unlike cannot be bound into an *a priori* relationship putatively defined by their own, shared nature, because their natures are different. Nor even are they immanent in the 'clash of civilizations' affirmed by Samuel Huntington, which at times implies quasi-immanence for the postulate. But in the end, even Huntington does not quite go so far as to suggest this – his argument is at times confused and his call for civilizations to pull together and to manage their relationships jointly to protect civilization against barbarism at the very end of the book renders this impossible.[40]

If there is no necessity, in terms of logical reasoning, that can be claimed for the mutual antipathy in, for example, al-Qa'ida's challenge to the West, or in the dependent correlation of states in the international system to a stable order, then the relevant interactions and relationships must be constitutive. Only a socially constructed approach, based on empirical understanding of the relevant structures or agents, can provide the perspective needed to tackle the real security problems in the contemporary world. In Neo-Realism the argument is that structure creates necessity for states. However, in the twenty-first-century security environment, that necessity is not applicable. The structure of state relations joins other factors in a pattern of contingencies. In the Constructivist Realist searchlight, necessity plays a notably different, but utterly essential role. Necessity lies at the core of the social construction of Realist understanding. The identification of threats and challenges, and of rogues and opponents, is not merely an arbitrary or entirely contingent matter. While the identification of threats involves a social process, that process is not without either empirical foundation or rationality. Indeed, state authorities might otherwise be deeply reluctant to take any kind of action, particularly the hard decisions involved in matters of security and the use of armed force. There is, then, a defining element of necessity at the core of both action by the relevant agents, responding to and redefining relevant structures, and the concept of Constructivist Realism. Structure is a product of construction – that is, the interaction of agents with each other and with structure. Structure through evolving processes of construction can change. Change will not come simply because somebody ideologically wants it. Change comes because it has to come. Necessity is the key because people act when they have to. That is the fundamentally Realist point. Necessity distinguishes Constructivist Realist theory from general Constructivism, as well as Reflectivist and other approaches based in social theoretical approaches. The patterns of social relations and inter-subjective relations that constitute international security are defined by necessity. That necessity might derive from material requirements, as in traditional versions of Realism. But it might equally derive from the sphere of values. And it might involve a combination of each. But in any case, it will not be founded contingently and arbitrarily. It will rest on need.

Constructivist Realism offers the prism needed to investigate, understand and gauge currents and developments in international politics. It enables and requires a focus on the empirical.[41] It does so even where there are problems of perception – where threats might exist, which might be unperceived, but nonetheless perceptible in principle (September 11 provides a concrete example of this), or where they are perceived by some, but remain imperceptible to others, who might well be sceptical. The attribution of value to the material is not to the exclusion of the attribution of value to the non-material. The theory embraces ideals and values, but does not admit them alone. Ideals make a contribution, but generally only where they reflect a perceived need. Values are an essential component both of reality and of that which needs to be secured. Values themselves need to be secured. And promotion of values is, or should be, *pace* Joseph Nye, part of the genuine Realist perspective.[42] Constructivist Realism is a notion that demonstrates its true value and utility when considering change and flux in the world – it allows for change and for revised approaches to change, but maintains a core focus on approaches to necessity in international security.

The value of recognizing the constructed character of Realism, as opposed to an essentialist material phenomenon to be discovered rather than created, is that it permits two things. The first is a more complex and subtle understanding (perhaps more in line with Morgenthau) that includes various strands, including the importance of values and rules (after all, the key point in maximizing power and security, apart from mere physical survival – which is at the root of the Realist construction – should be protection of these, without necessarily threatening others). The second is that it permits greater adaptability. Understanding of the world and of the rules operating in it can change as circumstances in it change. When this happens, adjustment is necessary. That adjustment is a social process, involving inter-subjective interaction. However, at its root will be the protection and promotion of physical security and values, and framing acceptable ways of dealing with threats to them. Cases such as Kosovo and Iraq, or the emergence of non-state 'rogue' actors in the 1990s, have impelled a radically new approach towards protection of the state because it was in the interest of Western states – and other states that value stability and order – to do so. Constructivist Realism permits this kind of adaptation.

# 3  ORDER

The West depends on a broader international order, to which it has been the primary contributor and in which it remains the primary stakeholder. The international society of states has its roots in Europe and is based on principles originally purposive in the European context, but later extended to the whole world and generally accepted. The emergence of that order over centuries, a structure emerging through different interactions of existing structure with values, interests and necessity, evolves and permits change. The underlying process at work here can be understood as Constructivist Realism. The present chapter considers what must be judged as radical shifts in international order that were recognized and occurred in the period after the end of the Cold War and continued into the twenty-first century. This revolutionary period of change was galvanized by the need for a new approach to the protection of states and international society broadly, to meet contemporary security circumstances. The key conceptual event was the redefinition of the term 'threat to international peace and security' by the UN Security Council in 1992. As will be seen in the present chapter, this reflected empirical changes that had already occurred and was a watershed that contributed to a continuing period of change. Among the implications of this shift was a revolutionary change in the approach to the fundamental principle, or quality, that makes international society possible: sovereignty. The need to uphold the principle of sovereignty was no longer a matter of protecting individual states from other states, but of protecting all states and their sovereign investment in international order, peace, security and stability from the disruptive acts, or effects, of particularly problematic states, non-state actors, phenomena and situations. Preserving order, under these conditions, was effectively defending the West. To explain these developments, the present chapter addresses the nature of order and change, and the particular changes that have taken place. It lays out the revolution regarding sovereignty that was manifest in the post-Cold War period, before developing a deeper understanding of the nature of order, using the concept of stratified stability, consistent with the prism of Constructivist Realism. It concludes by examining the ways in which changes in the 1990s were addressed by the UN Security Council, at the legal-political core of defining change, and the implications of those responses for sovereignty, order and defence of the West.

# The Post-Cold War Sovereignty Revolution

Something changed in the first half of the 1990s. This is attested by the volume and content of academic and political discussion. This literature was driven by and focused around major international events which presented complex practical, political and ethical challenges: the Kurds of northern Iraq, the Yugoslav War (particularly in Bosnia and Hercegovina), Somalia, Rwanda, Liberia and, in a different, but critical context, Libya.[1] Opinion was divided on the nature of the change.

The changes of the 1990s were a cause for debate. For many, there was a 'New World Order'; for an even greater legion of academic and political mimics, the correct label was 'New World Disorder'. The former school set the pace in the first two years of the decade, with US President George Bush as standard-bearer and his Secretary of State, James Baker, as chief foot soldier, treading new paths by the day.[2] Soon, though, the chorus of critics was asserting that the evidence all around – one conflict after another requiring attention, new states emerging – confirmed that order was in short supply.[3]

While both schools agreed that there had been a major change, they were diametrically opposed in their evaluations of that change. Much of this debate was conducted at a fairly superficial level. There were, though, some whose approach was a little more balanced and who were cautious in their judgement. Henry Kissinger, for example, was content to note that there had been a major change in discussing the idea of a new world order. But he would not rush beyond suggesting

that the new order was in 'a period of gestation', which would not
have a final form until sometime in the twenty-first century.[4]

Others, by the mid-point in the decade, had begun to recognize that
the disorder theorists had less of a case than the legion of parrots on
certain academic and political circuits insisted. Rather, there was an
affirmation of the world order established in 1945. There had been
change, but this had not heralded a new order, simply the old one
working in the way that its authors at the end of the Second World
War had wanted. (Indeed, one possible reading of George Bush's
nebulous vision of the 'New World Order' was that it really meant the
old one working – the crucial example being the UN-led action against
Iraq in 1990–1 which seemed as close as could be in the flawed real
world to the practical application of the theory of collective security.[5])
G. John Ikenberry typified the 'old order arrived' view: 'The task
today is not to discover or define some mythic new order but to
reclaim the policies, commitments and strategies of the old.'[6]

In truth, all views contained an element of some value. In one sense,
there was a perception of greater disorder (although not necessarily
the reality of it[7]) marked by armed hostilities. Yet each of those examples demonstrated that the mechanisms and values of the 1945
system – embodied in the United Nations – were becoming appropriate in a way which had not been possible during the Cold War
when balance of power politics froze the global body charged with the
maintenance of international peace and security. This was, of course,
in itself new. However, there is more to the changed world than a
reaffirmation of the UN order.

In one way, in particular, a new age was begun – although the precise
nature of this and its significance was not clearly understood by many
at the time or for a few years after. At the core of this change lay the
capacities and powers of the UN Security Council and crucially that
body's augmented interpretation of what could constitute a threat to
international peace and security. The Security Council, charged with
responsibility for defining and authorizing action to tackle threats to
international peace and security, redefined the scope of what constituted a threat (discussed more fully below). By doing so, it extended
the scope for what would otherwise be prohibited interference in the
internal affairs of the state under the UN Charter and the sovereignty
system that had developed over 300 years. The Security Council's
changed definition had radical implications for states, both as actors
collectively and as sovereign individual entities.

Evolutionary conditions had precipitated a revolution in the sovereignty principle. It is not entirely novel to posit the occurrence of a

revolution over the principle of sovereignty.[8] Dan Philpott suggests five such revolutions in history, counting the Peace of Westphalia as the first.[9] Then he adds the 'monarchical-republican' revolution, where the principle of sovereignty shifted from divine right to the will of the people, which would be broadly accepted as a revolution. He also dubs minority treaties in the nineteenth century and under the League of Nations, decolonization and the formation of the European Union as revolutionary changes. However, to apply the term revolution – understood here as the complete overturning of the old order – in these further instances is to overstate the case. Each of these three changed the application of sovereignty, but did not alter it intrinsically. Only the last major change – growing humanitarian intervention – even begins to question the condition and source of sovereignty, and it does so without identifying the alternative foundation for sovereignty. Humanitarianism is not the foundation for sovereignty, even though its relevance is greater in the context of radical change in the condition for exercising sovereign rights. That context is one in which the source of sovereignty has moved decisively from the popular to the international level and may be dubbed *equilibrant*. However, in order to identify the revolution in the sovereignty principle, it is necessary first to examine the concept.

Events in the 1990s transformed an international system that had evolved over a period of more than three centuries to ensure the security of states. That system, which culminated in the UN era at the end of the Cold War, was established on the basis of states qualified by sovereignty. Sovereignty has two aspects, internal and external. In terms of the latter, it is normally taken to connote freedom from outside interference: where the quality of sovereignty applies, no external actor may rightfully act without welcome. In terms of the former, it is the rights pertaining to supreme authority – the right to make the ultimate and defining decisions over a given territorial-political community. In sum, it is the right of a state not to be told what to do by others and to be able to decide what to do within its own boundaries.

The concept is vital in international affairs. It is the qualification of sovereign statehood that is 'a ticket of general admittance to the international arena'.[10] This is why those who do not have it so often seek it and those who have it seek to keep it – especially when weak in other ways. While it can be seen as having different aspects, including legal and political, these are not discrete versions of sovereignty, as some have held.[11] Nor has it ever made sense to talk of sovereignty's withering or becoming irrelevant.[12] Nor is it 'post-Westphalian' – at least in the 'end of sovereignty' sense that this term has been used.[13] And nor is it the old system working the way it was supposed to work, as some have suggested.[14] For all who consider international change in the 1990s to mean the end of sovereignty, it is salutary to note that many prominent analysts drew strong conclusions in this respect in the past.[15] It is more to the point to view sovereignty as an enduring quality that embraces and adapts to change.[16]

The key point that many miss regarding sovereignty is that it is a perpetual principle, the exact form, facts and incumbents of which may change or be redistributed over time. However, it remains because it is the key point of accountability. In both domestic and international terms, sovereignty confers not only ultimate rights, but also ultimate responsibilities.[17] Sovereignty furnishes the global structure in which states exist and into which new states may be born. But just as much as the new state gains rights on acquiring status, it also gets responsibilities.

Most scholars accept that a revolutionary shift occurred in the determinant of sovereignty when prescriptive, deist, monarchical sovereignty gave way to republican, self-determining, popular sovereignty. This process commenced with the American and French revolutions, was embedded in the aftermath of the First World War and was consolidated in the post-colonial age.[18] In this context, the external aspect of sovereignty did not change essentially from the Peace of Westphalia until the end of the twentieth century. The principle upon which sovereignty was based had changed in this time, but the international implications remained the same. The state was free to make decisions within its domestic jurisdiction and, crucially, was entitled to be free from external interference. While it can be argued that there were always exceptions to this principle and breaches of it,[19] these only served to confirm the principle. In the 1990s this changed in a revolutionary manner. While the notions of domestic jurisdiction and non-interference were not entirely removed, the sanctity that they had held as matters of principle was undone. Both notions became conditional on international accountability – not as a matter of fact, but as one of principle. Sovereignty was internationalized.

Internationalization of the sovereignty principle has incorporated expansion of the external dimension of sovereignty. The basic rule of international society – mutual recognition of sovereigns – has, in some sense, been expanded and with it the notions of domestic jurisdiction and non-interference have become conditional. The condition is that the exercise of sovereign rights within domestic jurisdiction does not cause a disturbance in international order. In numerous cases where this was the case, the UN Security Council using its formal powers under Chapter VII of the UN Charter to override the conventional sovereignty principle did so. The case of NATO action over Kosovo was to some extent *de facto* confirmation that this was likely to become a matter of state practice where the UN Security Council did not act fully. And the placing of both Kosovo and East Timor under the full authority of international transitional administrations authorized by the UN Security Council was the most blatant mark of internationalized sovereignty. Thus the condition for recognition of supreme authority over a polity was no longer based in the people, but in the state's not being a disruptive influence on international order.

Whereas the monarchical and popular versions of sovereignty had assumed external accountability only for external actions, this is no longer the case. If an internal matter affects other states in the international community, then either the UN Security Council, on behalf of the system as a whole, or the relevant affected states, cannot afford to have their own vested interest in a viable, stable order undermined, whether this is in terms of material or ideational interest. This confirms the notion that 'anarchy is what states make it'.[20] In a world that, for a variety of reasons (many linked to technological advance), has become smaller and more interdependent, the key issue for the majority of states has changed. It is no longer how to be free from external intervention, but how to keep the closely interwoven international order, upon which those states depend and in which they participate, free from disruption emanating from within states. International society has come to be based on strata of stability; disruption of that stability is harmful to those states which depend on it – as is discussed below.[21]

This revolution in the condition of sovereignty has been underscored by UN Secretary General Kofi Annan's declaration that there can no longer be 'sovereign impunity'.[22] The internationalization of sovereignty means the international accountability of sovereign states for grossly abusive exercise of sovereign rights. This does not mean an international audit of each state in each area of its responsibility. But it may well mean attention by states with an interest in order to those states whose conspicuous violation of sovereign rights disrupts international order.

Sovereign statehood remains the key to membership of international society and to the location of accountability in that society. However, whereas in the past the only sense in which states were accountable once recognized as 'sovereign' was if they were to transgress in the international sphere – for example, by carrying out a

military invasion of a neighbouring country – this is no longer necessarily the case. States may be accountable for those issues within
domestic jurisdiction that have adverse impact at the international
level. Sovereignty remains essential to defining international order
– but the exercise of sovereign rights within domestic jurisdiction
must not excessively disturb international order, either physically or
normatively. Thus, the contribution that a state makes to equilibrium
in the international state system has become the source of sovereignty, while the will of the people remains at a secondary level. Popular
sovereignty has been ousted as the primary qualification for statehood by *equilibrant* sovereignty. The principle upon which sovereignty
has come to be based is the degree to which it is a net contributor to
systemic and societal stability. This gives rise to the revolution in the
sovereignty principle. Non-interference and domestic jurisdiction were
the necessary conditions of sovereignty for which the source was the
people. Now, both characteristics are contingent on the necessary
condition of being a positive factor for stability in international order.
This discrete change in the principle of sovereignty transforms the
conditions for protection of overall order from disruption.

Paradoxically, it is the apparent disorder in the post-Cold War
international environment that confirms order. This is not only
confirmation of an old order, but of the initial phase of a new stage in
the evolution of international order. Just as entropy, as a measure
of disorder, confirms the existence of order in physics, so it does in
international affairs (see below). The degree of international involvement in a variety of problem situations around the globe in the last
decade of the twentieth century has paved the way for greater order in
the new millennium.

The international system evolves. Like the natural world, it evolves
in an uneven and random way, through the interaction of stable building blocks and accident. Order does not simply appear – and contrary
to nine out of ten thinkers on European security at the beginning of
the 1990s, it is not a matter of architecture and ideological assembly –
although human agency necessarily plays a role in shaping it. Order
emerges empirically through the interaction of stable structure and
chance. Stable structures do not emerge randomly by chance. Although
an element of contingent chance enters into the equation, they can
only emerge where the potential exists already. And in terms of the
human world, they can only emerge where potential, necessity and
human values and agency coincide. Stable structures emerge in layers.
As I will argue below, the accidental end of the Cold War has ushered
in a truly new era with an emerging new order in which the process

of evolution in international affairs can be identified, as well as an intrinsically revolutionary change and the nature of change in the international system itself, as interpreted through the Constructivist Realist prism. To describe this process, which became evident in the 1990s, and the nature of the order that has been emerging, I have adopted a term that captures both: stratified stability.[23]

## Stratified Stability: From Disorder to Order

Order is constructed empirically, through the interaction of something that exists already with something adding to it. Order is built unit on unit, layer on layer. One layer has to be in place before another can add to it. And only if one level is stable can any addition be secure. This is as true in international affairs as it is in nature. Stability and order are incremental and constructed – yet it cannot simply be designed or invented.[24] The probability, for example, that the order of atoms and molecules, which goes to make up an individual human being, would appear randomly is so infinitesimally small as to be all but impossible. Referring to the fate of the atoms which constitute an individual, Jacob Bronowski characterized common bewilderment: 'How madly improbable that they should come to this place at this instant and form me.'[25] He added, however, that this, of course, is not the way things happen. Rather, he argues, order in the physical world is built in layers. In the following paragraphs, I shall outline the physicist's concept and indicate the parallel between physical (or natural) order and international order. The key to this is the concept of entropy.

Entropy is a measure of disorder. The point of measuring, or even giving attention to, disorder is to gauge just how improbable order is. Disorder is the far more likely state of affairs. Stable order is rare – and does not appear. It is constructed – but not by any grand design. It emerges empirically in a process. An understanding of this is essential to understanding the nature of order in international politics – and so of that which it is in American and Western interests to protect and preserve, given the degree to which they rest on the strongest strata of stability and depend on stability in the international system as a whole.

Entropy was taken as a concept referring to inaccessible energy, or even waste, by some political and social scientists in the 1960s.[26] These attempts reveal that linking concepts derived from the natural sciences to areas of social science can be risky. It is only too easy to take a half-grasped idea from the former as an image and turn it into a half-baked one in the latter. For example, the term was mistakenly attributed to the discipline of biology. In fact, as noted, it is from physics. In addition, the conceptualization itself was wrong.

It reflected nineteenth-century thinking on the topic when energy was thought of as fluid. It was believed that there were two categories of energy, accessible and inaccessible. The former is what could be used, for example, in steam engines, while the latter was what could not be used and was 'lost' in friction, or as steam, for example. Inaccessible energy was called entropy and was thought to be draining into a pool from which it could not be recovered. As the Second Law of Thermodynamics Clausius asserted this understanding: entropy is constantly increasing – that is, energy is gradually gathering in a pool from which it cannot be recovered for further use. Political and social scientists took this version of entropy as inaccessible energy as an image.

However, it is more helpful to stick to the understanding of entropy in physics, as its conceptualization of order and disorder provides not only an image that is useful in the study of international order, but also a mechanism by which to comprehend the construction of order. By reference to entropy as a measure of disorder, the improbability of order, and so an understanding of how order emerges in layers, where it emerges, it is possible to identify the same process operating empirically in international affairs. The pattern by which order emerges in international politics parallels that by which it emerges in the natural world, albeit with an increased role for human agency.

In modern, nuclear age physics, entropy is a measure of disorder, as conceived by Ludwig Boltzmann at the beginning of the twentieth century. The inaccessible energy identified as friction, or steam, or heat (and so forth) was not liquid flowing away. It was a random motion of atoms. Friction, or heat, represents the degrading of order – a process in which atoms assume an increasingly disorderly state. In this case, according to Boltzmann, entropy is the measure of that disorder. It is important in this context to understand that disorder is always more likely than order. Boltzmann was able to devise a theoretical equation for measuring disorder. The key to this was the probability that a particular state would be achieved – that is, from the number of different ways its atoms might be arranged. This confirmed that disorder was considerably more likely than order: almost any random association of atoms would be disorderly. There is, therefore, a tendency to disorder. Particular associations of atoms tend to break down.

But this is a tendency, not an absolute process. It is a matter of statistical probability. But, as Bronowski points out, 'statistics do not say "always"'. This means that order may be 'built up in some islands'.

The process of building these islands of order occurs in steps. Human beings do not appear suddenly as the product of a random association of atoms. Instead, they are the product of a building process in which, through evolution, one stable layer has been placed on another, from atoms to molecules to amino acids and so on. The same is true of matter: the instant appearance of iron or uranium, as Bronowski suggests, would be just as improbable through a random association of atoms as the creation of a human being. In reality, strata of stability are created, each waiting to fulfil its potential to create further layers of stability: 'a star builds hydrogen to helium; then at another stage in a different star helium is assembled to carbon, to oxygen, to heavy elements; and so step by step to the ninety-two elements in nature'.

Crucially, the shift from one layer to another is a matter of 'random encounter'. Each layer of stability contains the potential for a further stable form at a higher level, which has not yet appeared in reality. In nature, so long as the potential for greater stability exists, there is no other way for evolution to take its course: it is 'the climbing of a ladder from simple to complex by steps each of which is stable in itself'. It is this incremental tendency to order which creates a parallel with the international system. (However, it is worth registering that orders are not static; they need to be renewed if they are not to decay.)

The random disorderly nature of atoms can be equated with the 'anarchical' condition in which Hedley Bull famously argued that states existed.[27] But Bull was at the same time pointing out the first basic element of orderly relations between these basic components. Mutual recognition based on the principle of sovereignty, he argued, was the basis of an international society. But that society was in a state of anarchy because there was no overarching order, no superordinate supreme authority, or sovereign. In terms of the parallel with physics, the point of mutual recognition was the point at which new layers of potential order began; this was the point at which hydrogen became helium.

From the emergence of a basic element of order in the international system, as in the physical world, there has been the potential for increasing order. That potential has gradually been partially fulfilled. Strata of stability and potential stability have been established through the growth of bilateral and multilateral agreements between states, through the maturation of elements pertaining to international law, through the growth of regional and international organizations and through the normative content of each of these. The core of this process has been consolidation of the state in the international system.

In terms of the human world and particularly in terms of international order, it is a combination of potential, chance, human agency and necessity that provides the mechanism by which order empirically increases. The apparent disorder at the end of the Cold War is actually the measure of the degree to which layers of order have been established. However, those layers of order require stability. The disorder that comes into focus at the end of the Cold War does so not because such activity did not occur before. Indeed, there were always plenty of internal wars accompanied by human suffering and villains out to do no good in their neighbourhood. It occurs because for the first time the degree of order in the world is such that these activities become relevant as factors that one way or another can destabilize that order. Entropy, the measure of disorder, therefore becomes relevant as the lens through which this can most easily be perceived and understood. Without this way of seeing, the degree to which there is order cannot be fully registered and so the real focus on that which it is vital to preserve and protect cannot be established.

In the 1990s, the process of consolidating the state reached a level of stability at which the more or less random interaction of this layer of stability with a series of events catalysed the process by which new layers of stability were being put in place normatively and practically. Central to this was the decision of the Heads of State and Government of the United Nations Security Council at their Summit in January 1992 to reinterpret their understanding of what constituted a threat to international peace and security. In doing so, they moved matters of international peace and security to a new stratum, shifting the focus away from the state *qua* state, to the quality and condition of the state, as will be seen below. This represented a critical shift to a new plane of stratified stability in the international system.

# Layering Stability: The Evolution of the Sovereign State System

The international system evolved to the point where the major shifts occurred which enable the stratification of stability to be identified. I propose to review that evolution in order to understand two phenomena. The first is the way in which a new stratum of stability in international security develops. The second is that international order is built through the random interaction of layers of stability with events and human agency. The next section will identify some of the layers, which contributed to creating the conditions for the emergence of a major new stratum in the 1990s, as well as the nature of that new stratum itself. The present section will review the evolution of the state as the foundation stone of the international system – the atom of international order.

States are the necessary components of an international system and the principle by which they are ordered is that of sovereignty. The origin of the sovereignty system lies in the Peace of Westphalia of 1648. That agreement ended the Thirty Years War in Europe. It established peace, essentially, on the premise that the various parties would cease their efforts to create a universal Christian order in Europe, but, rather, would allow the sovereign (that is, the king) in each case to determine which variant of Christian doctrine prevailed in his realm (providing a charter for religious intolerance within kingdoms). The important aspect of Westphalia was its legal codification of sovereign statehood, for the first time providing a general and formal principle of law to govern relations between states and taking sovereignty into the inter-national sphere, giving it an external character – that of mutual recogni-tion by other sovereigns – in addition to its previous internal qualities. The treaties did not mean a rejection of the use of force, however, but merely removed doctrinal difference and intolerance as a *casus belli* and substituted for them reasons of state.

Whilst the principle of the Westphalian regime became the key to international relations, it did not fix the political-territorial dispensa-tion in Europe indefinitely. Indeed, geopolitical boundaries in Europe shifted during the eighteenth and nineteenth centuries, largely in response to the growth of modern nationalism. Crucially, however, in each phase of transition new entities confirmed the sovereignty system by seeking membership of it and agreeing to be governed by its key principle. Sovereignty is one of the concepts which falls into a cat-egory of ideas where a great part of their value is to be 'essentially contested'.[28]

In practical use, it has a number of purposes, as Alan James has pointed out.[29] The major ones are rhetoric, power, competences and status. It is because sovereignty carries with it a particular status that it is much played on and much sought after – it is the qualification, in conventional thought on international relations, for membership of the society of states. In practice, as Robert Jackson has argued with reference to the developing world, as others have argued generally and as will be discussed below with reference to post-communist states in Europe,[30] the quality of sovereignty associated with any particular state may vary. Thus the content of sovereignty will change from one state to another.

Essentially, this means that the state has decided for itself what to do. Sovereignty concerns the right of 'action without being bounded unto others'.[31] It is often taken to be a fundamentally legal concept.[32] For this reason many international lawyers, in particular Americans, assume sovereignty to be not only a legal concept, but to refer to a 'constitution'. This is because, in the United States, 'the Constitution' is held to be invested with sovereignty – although in reality domestic sovereignty is shared between the executive and legislative branches of government and the judiciary and, of course, the people. But sovereignty is, in reality, both legal and political. Indeed, it is ultimately a political concept because, as I shall emphasize below, the basic meaning of sovereignty is the political supremacy to make law (even though, in modern practice, the makers of law, themselves, are likely to be subject to legal restraint).

Whilst sovereignty may be susceptible of different interpretations, its general importance and formal content have remained constant: the key to the Westphalian system was mutual recognition between sovereigns. The content of sovereignty changed in one essential way as the system of which it was the guiding principle was extended. Whereas the Westphalian agreement had been made between sovereigns who were individuals (monarchs), this prescriptive mode of sovereignty had been generally supplanted by a popular one in Europe by the twentieth century – meaning that the exercise of sovereign rights was no longer the prerogative of a single personality, but that of the representatives of the state's governing institutions. Increasingly, if somewhat hypocritically, the degree to which power holders are seen to embody the interest of the people of a particular state through an 'act of national self-determination based on the will of the majority' has become a factor in their being accepted and granted recognition as representatives of the sovereign by others in international society.[33]

With the evolution of the international system based on states, various international arrangements including international organizations began to appear. Each of these in some way acted as a forum for states, but also in some way as a constraint on them. In the course of the twentieth century the position of the state became cemented through the two attempts to create a global organization to deal with matters of international peace and security, the League of Nations between the two world wars and the United Nations after the Second World War. The UN, in particular, through its codification of sovereignty and statehood as the fundamental elements to be protected in international society, created a framework in which a traditional mechanism for regulating relations between states in a condition of anarchy could be removed: wars of aggression or territorial expansion were not possible.

The understanding became embedded that it was not acceptable to attempt to change borders through a use of force. Of course, this by no means meant that the possibility of one state trying to do this had been completely eliminated. It did mean that in a number of cases around the world such attempts, even when couched in terms of self-defence, were not recognized: northern Cyprus, East Timor, territories occupied by Israel. The preservation of state boundaries became paramount other than in cases where the states in question agreed peacefully to change them (a mostly unimaginable occurrence).

A normative layer of stability had been created, underpinned by an organizational one. This was the notion, encoded in Article 2 (4) and (7), as well as Article 51, of the UN Charter that there was no ground for using armed force other than self-defence, or under the authority of the UN Security Council. While the Charter confirmed the legalist dimension to this arrangement, the embedding of the normative layer became toughened throughout the Cold War and beyond by both practice and further normative iteration in agreements. By the end of the Cold War, it was taken for granted in most international discourse that attacks on other countries and undue interference in internal affairs were simply unacceptable (although this did not, of course, mean an ideal world in which there was no interference whatsoever). When Saddam Hussein's Iraq invaded Kuwait in August 1990, this exception confirmed the rule.

The embedding of the non-aggression and non-interference norm was given further support in other ways. The principles of state sovereignty, mutual recognition by sovereigns and the inviolability of borders were reinforced by the decision of the post-colonial African states to affirm this understanding in the 1963 Charter of the Organization of African Unity (OAU). Although quite probably not a single border in Africa made sense, or, at a minimum, was beyond dispute, the new African states recognized that any other course of action would be a recipe for unending armed conflict across the continent. Although their decision did not remove the shadow of war from Africa, it restricted its scope and placed limits on those who resorted to violence: their scope was generally within borders rather than across them. The signing of the Helsinki Final Act in 1975, consolidating the Conference on Security and Co-operation in Europe (CSCE), also reinforced the increasingly unchallengeable norm of inviolable borders. Indeed, the CSCE was the spur to the inviolability of borders becoming a mantra for European security analysts. In part, this was because the Helsinki Final Act was the binding political agreement, which affirmed the borders established in Europe after the Second World War, including the division of Germany and the Soviet annexation of the Baltic states. The Western participants in the process added to an emerging normative layer of stability by inserting provisions for individual human and political rights within the Final Act as a quid pro quo. They were able to do so because of the Soviet desire to gain an agreement.

The Cold War itself was also a factor in all of this. In the manner of stable stratification, the threat of nuclear war meant that across much of the world there was a fear that to breach the norm might be to unleash annihilation. The nuclear-armed standoff between East and West meant that it had become too dangerous for the major military powers on either side of the European divide to risk war. This had implications in other parts of the world where Soviet–Western competition meant that each superpower was cautious, making as sure as possible that direct confrontation would not occur. Thus normative and pragmatic elements combined to create 'islands of stability'. Developments such as the UN and its Charter, the OAU and its Charter and the CSCE and its Final Act created a normative and organizational framework in which the inviolability of the state as the cornerstone of international life had been consolidated. The nuclear shadow of the Cold War had forced states to honour their normative agreements.

The importance of maintaining borders was also consolidated in the process of de-colonization and new state formation in the UN era. By 1996 the UN's membership had grown from the original 50 to 185 – and by the beginning of the new century it had become 192. These new states were formed in five categories, each of which was subject to the provision of *uti posseditis juris* in international law.[34] This meant that when the status of borders was transformed, the newly independent entity kept the territory legally in its possession. For post-colonial states around the world, as well as those states emerging from the collapsed communist federations in Yugoslavia, the Soviet Union and Czechoslovakia during the 1990s,[35] this meant that any violent attempts to change borders whose status (or quality) was changing would be contrary to international law and norms.

By the 1990s, legal, normative, organizational and pragmatic factors had consolidated the position of the state in international relations and the inviolability of state borders. This seemed to be reinforced as the unforeseen and sudden end to the Cold War left in place the basis for a degree of stability and co-operation in the international system as erstwhile opponents began a new era – George Bush's 'New World Order' in which things would not be perfect, but they would be better. Bush's 'New World Order' was based primarily on a conception of the old order working in the way intended at the formation of the UN. A stratum of stability had been created in the international system which meant that traditional warfare between states had become virtually unthinkable. Almost immediately after this layer had been consolidated, Saddam Hussein's Iraq proved that the unthinkable was not completely so by attempting to annex Kuwait in 1990, but by creating an absolute exception at an exceptional moment proved the rule.

Although it would take time to consolidate this and other new layers in the formation of international order, there was no going back. It had become clear that the situations receiving Security Council attention under Chapter VII could be far broader than had conventionally been the case. However, there was no indication of what the limits were to the expanding understanding of what could entail a threat to international peace and security. Nor was there any sense of what the implications and requirements might be for individual states, where the Security Council did not act and authorize action.

Even if the measures of the early 1990s were high tide marks which would take some time to reach again, or to establish as regular water levels, the fact that they had been made meant that it was certain that at some time in the future when another major tide-turn occurred in the international system, this would be a starting point. Or, to alter the image, in terms of stratified stability layers had begun to form, which were creating new elements of stability in international order, based on norms, treaties and organizations. Once that stratum of order was in place, the potential for greater order and stability was also created – and, critically, an international environment in which inter-linkage meant that any disruption of order could become a security challenge and require a response from those states whose security was threatened.

The evolution of order in international affairs was traditionally focused around the state and its protection from outside aggression. With this process achieving a fair degree of success and common currency by the beginning of the 1990s, as a result of the combined forces of time, norms, treaties and other agreements, organizations and real-politik, a layer of stability had been established within international society upon which the creation of new layers of stability could begin to be created. These new strata centred on the new definition given to questions of international peace and security by the UN Security Council and changing attitudes to the status of state sovereignty in this context. The new layers being created both suggested an emphasis on sustaining states weakened by conflict and placed new emphasis on normative components in international life.

These were crucial elements of the process of stratified stabilization through which international order incrementally evolves. That evolution involves the interaction of layers of stability with random events, which can generate the creation of new strata. Once one stable stratum exists, it inherently has the potential to be part of a further, higher level of order. In spite of the probability that there will always be a greater immediate tendency to disorder in international relations (as in physics), once the potential for greater order exists, there is only one way in which evolution can go.

The increasing interaction of non-state actors and communications networks incrementally creates islands of order, which need to be preserved and protected. That range of actors and networks includes transnational or multinational corporations and both electronic news and financial exchanges. It also involves states in a variety of ways – bilaterally and multilaterally, through treaties, agreements and normative standards, through organizations and, since the end of the Cold War, through the executive action of the UN Security Council. Occasionally, these layers encounter events which catalyse the creation of higher levels of order. This is what happened in the early 1990s as a system broadly stabilized regarding the protection of the state from outside aggression shifted to one in which the emphasis was on the consolidation of the state and the management of non-state-specific challenges to international peace and security. The critical element in this move to a new era and a new order was the approach taken by the UN Security Council. In the 1990s something changed. There was a critical move to a new level of stratified stability in international order.

## Stratifying Stability: Borders and Beyond

A series of events in the early 1990s, following the end of the Cold War, catalysed the process of revealing layers of stability in the international system and creating new ones. A series of random encounters between critical situations and a stabilized international environment generated rapid and radical change. These encounters ran from the Iraqi invasion of Kuwait and the subsequent Kurdish crisis in northern Iraq, through the international engagement in Bosnia, Somalia, Rwanda, Haiti and Angola, to the most radical changes regarding Libya, as well as the creation of the international criminal tribunals for former Yugoslavia and Rwanda. As a result of the interaction of order, events and agency, the world, led by the most developed islands of order in the West, stepped onto a newly forming layer of international peace and security. The newly forming stratum in the international order emphasized the need for stability – and in doing so confirmed the vulnerability of states with a vested interest in the system, above all, those of the West, to instability, disruption and disorder.

The radical shift involved crucial changes in the approach to sovereignty. The Security Council's altered approach to the way in which it defined international peace and security confirmed a move in attitudes towards state sovereignty. With the basic position of the state within the international system firmly secured, the reality of international security became the need to limit the disorder essentially within the boundaries of those states. What was seen as a growth in armed conflict and disorder by some was really only a shift in focus. With the question of direct action by one state against another being the cause of disruption in the international system more or less removed, emphasis was inevitably placed on other sources of instability. In quasi-entropic terms, the concentration on inter-communal and other manifestations of disorder within states but impacting on the international scene was a measure of the degree of order established in the state system.

The purpose of the sovereignty arrangement was always to limit war or, put another way, to protect the order on which the state system depended. It was not because there was a desire to protect the state as such. Rather, protection of the state from external action to alter its internal structure was the mechanism for reducing the incidence of war. While this did not prevent wars, it provided a significant framework for encouraging stability in the international system. Order would be maintained by non-intervention within the boundaries of another sovereign. This was the basic rule upon which international society came into being and, after 1945, was substantially codified. In the 1990s this began to change.

The Peace of Westphalia, as noted, was the starting point for developments within the international system that would increasingly circumscribe the grounds for going to war and generally seek to limit the problem of war and disorder. The culmination of this came in the United Nations era, with the provisions of the UN Charter for limiting the scope for the use of force. The UN Charter contractually reinforced this international system.

Although the UN's formal mission includes the aspirations to develop economic and social co-operation and to promote human rights, the chief purpose concerns international peace and security. The primary purpose of the UN was the maintenance of international peace and security, as identified in Article 1 of the Charter (this mission is both mentioned first and is framed as something achievable, whereas the other missions are desirable qualities to be encouraged). This meant creating a framework to protect states and international order as a whole from the external mischief of any state, or states, that did not observe the key concepts of non-interference and domestic jurisdiction. This codification of the sovereignty regime could be identified in Articles 2 and 51 of the UN Charter. The latter confirms the right to self-defence, but Article 2 is the reference point for the non-interference and domestic jurisdiction duality. Paragraph (4) of that article stipulates that states shall not use force or any other means 'inconsistent with the purposes of the United Nations' to act against the 'territorial integrity or political independence of any state'. This is reinforced by paragraph (7), which stresses the notion of domestic jurisdiction, even against the United Nations in normal circumstances (the exceptional circumstances are discussed below).

Within the system of collective security designed in the UN Charter, one body, the UN Security Council, is given primary responsibility for the maintenance of international peace and security. To ensure this, the UN Security Council is given special powers in Chapter VII of the Charter. These are the prerogative and responsibility to determine threats to international peace and security (Article 39) and, having done so, to authorize military and non-military responses to those threats (Articles 42 and 41, respectively). What is of greatest importance here is that the framers of the Charter gave the Security Council a position in which its Chapter VII enforcement measures became mandatory and binding in international law – superseding any other aspect of the law, including the rights of sovereignty. This last point is explicitly made in the final clause of Article 2 (7) – the very place where the principle of domestic jurisdiction is named. That final clause asserts that the principle of domestic jurisdiction does not prejudice the application of enforcement measures taken by the Security Council. In short, it is possible to override the prescriptions of non-interference and domestic jurisdiction in the interests of international peace and security.

This is a formal limitation on state sovereignty. Although generally unnoticed for forty years, UN Security Council enforcement authorization under Chapter VII means an exception to the core provisions of the state sovereignty system. However, by the 1990s state against state war had been effectively eliminated – even if the case of Iraq and Kuwait provided the exception that made a rule that states no longer tried to annex the territory of other states, and cases such as India–Pakistan and Eritrea–Ethiopia had conflicts over the legacy of partition. The reality appears to be that the central problem of war and order throughout history – armed conflict and competition between states – has been almost eradicated. In recognition of it, the Council adopted a new approach to peace and security.

The UN Security Council's altered definition of international peace and security confirmed the shift in attitudes towards ending the absolute protection provided by sovereignty. The old issue of international peace and security – inter-state war – was no longer the real threat. The real threats stemmed from a variety of other sources internal to and beyond the borders of states. Internal conflict and gross abuses of human rights fell into the first category, while environmental concerns might be placed in the latter – although even these had a point of accountability somewhere within a state responsible for action endangering the environment. In January 1992 this radical shift was confirmed and the UN Security Council Heads of Government and State issued a declaration formalizing the new approach:

> The absence of war and military conflict amongst States does not in itself ensure international peace and security. The non-military sources of instability in the economic, social, humanitarian and ecological fields have become threats to peace and security.[36]

Accordingly, the UN Security Council passed Chapter VII resolutions on a range of problems, approving a remarkably broad and innovative range of measures to deal with them. The Security Council resolutions on Bosnia and Hercegovina, Libya and Somalia were radical departures in terms of sovereignty in international relations: the extradition of suspected terrorists from Libya (Resolution 748, 1992); the restoration of peace and security within a country, Somalia (Resolution 733, 1992); with regard to arms supplies and involvement in war with reference to the former Yugoslavia (Resolutions 713, 1991; 757, 770, 781, all 1992; 816, 820, 836, all 1993). Further, with reference to Somalia, Libya, and then the creation of international tribunals for the former Yugoslavia and Rwanda, previously unthinkable definitions of a threat to international peace and security were given. However, although it became clear that the delineation of Chapter VII situations could be far broader than had conventionally been the case, the limits to the expanding understanding of what could entail a threat to international peace and security were not clear.[37]

These measures involved three areas – military-political intervention, justice and governance – which together altered the privileges associated with the rights of sovereignty. Military-political intervention changed enormously and was accompanied by judicial measures (*inter alia* to create *ad hoc* international criminal tribunals for the former Yugoslavia and Rwanda) and taking on full responsibility for governance in Kosovo and East Timor, in addition to partial responsibility in other places. This change ran throughout the 1990s. Although a number of critics have casually and erroneously judged that there was a great spurt of activity in the first part of the 1990s, which then fell away, the reality has been different. The scale and scope of interventions expanded throughout the period, while some of the most radical UN Security Council actions were taken in the second half of it. There were notable cases in the first half of the decade. Iraq, Somalia, Haiti, Libya, the former Yugoslavia, Rwanda and Liberia were among the most notable. Although often not noticed by scholars who judged there to be an end to such activity in or around 1995, radical resolutions continued into the second half of the 1990s. Those in the second half included the series of resolutions against Afghanistan between 1996 and 1999, Sudan in 1996 – perhaps the most radical of all Security Council determinations – Kosovo in 1998–9, East Timor in 1999, and the reiterated resolution over Bosnia and Hercegovina first made in 1995.[38] As the twenty-first century arrived with big bangs in New York and Virginia, the trend did not stop, with new resolutions (1368 and 1373) appearing to confirm an important shift regarding terrorism and self-defence, as well as non-state aggressors, at least implicitly. Security Council resolutions in these cases were essential departures in terms of sovereignty and, crucially, the management of international peace and security.

Even where the Security Council had not initially sanctioned collective action, it was able to add to an emerging arrangement where regional bodies took practical responsibility for crisis situations. In those cases, the UN role was limited to monitoring the activity of the regional force. In the cases of Bosnia, Georgia, Liberia and Kosovo, the Security Council authorized action, but regional arrangements began to work with the UN as an organization and then on their own, under a Security Council mandate (with some UN observers alongside). Regional activity was filling a gap between the needs of a situation, UN organizational capacity to act, and the UN Security Council's ability to authorize action.

The new use of Chapter VII powers, turning on the nexus of international security and international law, represented a new stage in efforts to protect states and international society. By redefining the notion of threat to international peace and security – and by definition, therefore, to the states that formed international society – the UN Security Council had revolutionized the governing principle that protected states and the order upon which they depended. The old notion, underpinned by sovereignty, had been to protect the state against interference within its domestic jurisdiction and to maintain order by taking measures to stop external action – most notably armed aggression – against states, which thereby disturbed the peace. Now, the needs have become diametrically opposed. The critical challenge to peace and security has come to be protecting the order upon which states mostly depend from the disorderly repercussions of events inside the borders of problem states. The priority was the need to tackle problems with an internal source. This meant preventing internal disturbance from infecting the international body and affecting the majority of states that depend on the order, where this was contingent overspill from internal conflicts disrupting order.[39] It also meant tackling regimes that posed questions for the international system. And it meant tackling more nebulous non-state threats, irrespective of the state boundaries from which they emanated. The scope and types of these threats to order and stability in general, and to Western interests in particular, is the subject of the following chapter.

# 4 THREATS

The shape of the world has changed. While it has always changed, in the twenty-first century it changes faster than ever before. In many respects, it has become smaller as modern communications shrink distance and time. In this shrunken world, an epidemic involving a previously unknown killer disease in China is immediately a matter of concern around the globe. A loss of financial confidence in Japan can undermine investment markets around the world. Famine in eastern Africa or mass murder and the gross abuse of human rights in Rwanda can challenge values and government in the more developed parts of the world. The highly visible use of commercial airliners to destroy prominent buildings in New York can tip airline companies into crisis and collapse – with adverse knock-on effects in terms of business, employment and economic activity. Challenges such as these would not have been the same in earlier periods. They would not have been physically connected, as they became in the last half of the twentieth century, or there would have been little or no knowledge of them – and as far as there was knowledge, it would come only after a significant delay. In a more closely connected world, it is the West that is most connected. It is the West, therefore, that is most vulnerable.

A range of problems – environmental, economic, technological, social, ethical and political – affect Western security in addition to more traditional military threats and their contemporary variants, most commonly termed 'international terrorism'.[1] (The term 'international terrorism' is problematic, but is used as a term of convenience, given its relatively prominent and extensive common usage.) The purpose of the present chapter is to outline the different aspects of the international strategic context and the range of potential threats to the West that lie in it at present and, as far as might be gauged, for at least the first half of the twenty-first century. While not all of these will necessarily involve the use of armed forces (or affect the use of the military), all have the potential to generate situations that might do so. The chapter is divided into two broad sections – physical threats and stability threats.

## Physical Threats

In a changing global strategic environment, several parts of the globe are in transition. It is possible that these regions in transition may present issues for Western strategic thinkers. This means that in some cases there is a direct overlap between stability threats and physical threats. The interconnected nature of the contemporary world and the broad reality that Western societies are multi-cultural has implications for defence. Transnational communities – those that are based in one country as citizens but have kin and communal relations in at least one other country – are increasingly common. This is a potential benefit to the world, where cosmopolitan communities interact, live side by side, and on various levels create value. However, one upshot of this might be a tendency on the part of members of some segments of a transnational community to express opinions for or against action using armed forces, but in either case against the prevailing opinion in government. This could be seen to some extent from the activism in Western countries of Serbs, Croats, Bosnians and so forth in those countries during the Yugoslav War, or significant portions of Muslims, irrespective of heritage, regarding US-led action over Afghanistan and Iraq in the 2000s. A far worse implication might be that situations of one kind or another around the world will place pressure on the social fabric, creating tension and instability. There is also a potential for disruption in the social fabric and a lack of community cohesion. This might play out in local inter-communal tensions, where groups, for whatever reason, are antagonistic. But it might even result in some individuals turning to political violence. Any situation that has the potential to generate inter-communal tension or trouble will also almost certainly present a threat to the essence of the Western way and Western values – and the challenge of how to handle that threat without losing those values.

## Ideological Islamism and international terrorism

A major factor linked to the issue of transnational communities, but conceptually discrete, is that of internationalized 'terrorism', particularly that governed by highly ideological Islamism and embodied in the al-Qa'ida network of Usama bin Ladin. Al-Qa'ida emerged in the 1990s as a phenomenon unlike any other, narrowly focused on the aim of forcing US forces from the Holy Land of Saudi Arabia, from Mecca. However, this movement was far more ambitious than this. Its mission was to destroy the modern Western state system and replace it with an Islamist pan-Islamic world, a world predicated on the vision of the seventh-century Middle East. This meant the overthrow of governments in Islamic-dominated countries. This was a worldview shared by the Taliban movement, which dominated Afghanistan until late 2001 and which harboured al-Qa'ida and its leader. Al-Qa'ida is unlike anything outside a James Bond movie. It has an organizational framework linking various local and regional groups into an international consortium promoting what for other Muslims is a perversion of the faith as the basis for destruction and suicide–mass murder. And it has a structure characterized by the flexibility and mitotic, self-reproducing and propagating qualities of a virus,[2] or the internet. It has been described as a virtual state.[3] There is something in this from a narrowly Clausewitzian trinitarian perspective.[4] In reality, it is an international amalgam of groups which, because of its bases in communities in over sixty states, also took on a transnational character – that is, one that crosses boundaries. In some senses, then, both its ideology and its composition, in their transnational nature, lie outside any traditional framework of international peace and security. This transnational character gives it a particular edge in terms of competition with modern states; outside a normal state framework, the support it builds can also be corrosive in the social fabric of the states it seeks to transform, or destroy.

There are two vital aspects to understand about al-Qa'ida. The first is that the movement is ideologically driven, promoting a narrow worldview that does not represent Islam (indeed, it excludes large parts of that faith and its adherents in the contemporary world, in many senses). Al-Qa'ida seeks to hijack Islam, as well as airliners. The second is that the ideology is inherently anti-modern and anti-Western – and those qualities make it inimical to the West and so a major threat. While a key part of that threat concerns the damage that its politically motivated violence might cause, perhaps even more important is the capacity it gains through such action and through its strong anti-Western position to add smaller, local groups to its network, or to win the support and commitment of individuals anywhere. It is this last aspect, coupled with the international profile of al-Qa'ida, that makes the link with transnational communities.

The problems associated with an outfit such as al-Qa'ida are contingently compounded by the challenges posed, on one side, by 'rogue' and, on the other, by 'weak', 'failing' or even 'failed' states (or a combination of the two). The latter constitute a problem *per se*, but this is augmented by the possibilities of their fostering, aiding and abetting al-Qa'ida or any similar group – whether for commercial gain, ideological commitment or the political convenience of an alliance of sorts with an enemy's enemy. This was clearly one of the principal concerns over Iraq in the early part of 2003, although there were always doubts in some well-informed quarters regarding the extent to which Baghdad and al-Qa'ida could work together. (See chapters 1 and 7.) Nonetheless, Iraq highlighted the logical dangers of a cocktail comprising anti-Western transnational terrorists, a weak or anti-Western 'rogue' state and nightmare weapons systems.

Statehood, or weak statehood, or the nature of statehood and governance, constitutes perhaps the single most pervasive, if not the largest, security challenge in the world over the first half of the century, at least. Instability in many regions derives from problems of statehood – whether these involve ineffective government and administration, or the quest for self-determination and changes to the map of relevant countries and the world. Equally, as Afghanistan showed above all, a weak state can provide the opportunity for those involved in international terrorism to operate. Any places where formal state control does not run can be the breeding ground for such a group – even where there is assistance of some kind from states, the latter might well be happier to offer that support in a grey zone rather than on territory they control, for which they might be subject to sanction. In an 'interconnected' world, the problems of instability and weak statehood in one place can easily disrupt the position of Western countries – dependent on open communications and free trade, as well as the maintenance of key values. To ensure economic and spiritual prosperity, the West needs a stable environment in which disruption of communications is minimized or non-existent. This requires some attention to situations of weak statehood that give rise to an impact of this kind. The armed forces, within the limits of availability, could be used proactively and preventively in state-strengthening capacities, as well as perhaps needing to be involved in more belligerent roles to address conflicts or other threats emerging from weak states.

## Weapons of mass destruction or impact, weak states, rogue states and countries of concern

Weapons of mass destruction or impact (WMD/I – the 'I' for 'impact' is because the destructive capability of these weapons is quite limited, especially regarding chemical and biological systems, but their impact is vast in other ways) are a major concern in and of themselves, whoever possesses them. But preventing their acquisition or use by anti-Western actors is paramount. The term WMD/I covers three separate types of weapon – chemical, biological and nuclear. Each of these weapon types has different characteristics and potential – and the issues they raise and how to deal with them can differ. However, that which unites them is their potential either literally to cause 'mass' destruction – an attribute of nuclear weapons – or to have an impact, not only physically, but, more importantly, psychologically and politically, because of the type of damage they can inflict. In each case, their peculiar status, and the reason they are generally considered together, despite the major differences between them, rests on their going beyond destruction to the capability to affect life mechanisms themselves so that their use is broadly regarded as unacceptable around the world.[5]

While it is the most advanced and modern states that have traditionally researched and developed the most dangerous weapons, it is also these states that have generated the concerns and controls to minimize the possibilities of their use, based on an understanding of what they might achieve. The major concern for such states has come to be the possibility that failing states, weak states and what might be called 'rogue' states, or states of concern, might be the source of WMD/I weapons transfers or development, to confront the West with these types of weapon. There are two problems with failing or weak states in this regard. The first is that controls over whatever might exist regarding such weapons do not operate, allowing weapons transfers either from the state's own capabilities, or simply taking place on its territories because the state is not in a position to exercise control. The second problem concerns 'rogue' states (which might also be weak ones). The term 'rogue' is potentially problematic, reflecting initial prejudices and certainly creating a 'labelling' effect that limits possibilities for positive change – and states of concern (to the West) might be a more appropriate term, although it is both more general and less immediate.[6] Importantly, the term 'rogue' denotes an actor that does not observe the rules and conventions of international society and might be regarded as actively seeking to challenge and disrupt that order and the stability and possibilities for communication and openness that it offers to others in that society, above all those at its Western political and economic core. 'Rogue' states are a decisive threat if they are developing and possessing these weapons and can use them to disrupt order and to confront Western power.

Weak statehood and access to WMD/I became a continuing concern with the collapse of the Soviet Union in 1991 and its succession by fifteen states, each of which had some challenges to the quality and strength of statehood and all of which had previously been caught in the net of Soviet defence capabilities. There are two major concerns from a Western perspective. The first is that instability and state breakdown, already an issue in some of the former Soviet states, might create disruption in terms of population movements or damage communications, particularly concerning mineral fuel resources. At the mild end of this scale, British Petroleum lost out heavily when its US$0.5 bn investment was lost in the desert of chaos and collapse.[7] This was simply a matter of economic collapse, given the degree to which internal cohesion was lacking. However, it is not impossible that situations in a country such as Georgia might have significant physical impact if further conflict were to affect it, or an already weak state were to collapse completely. (This was already a question before the deployment of US troops there in 2002 to assist the authorities in dealing with forces in the country linked to al-Qa'ida.) The more important concern, however, is the possible seepage of WMD/I weapons, or related material and know-how – and how to stem their proliferation.

Whether nuclear or chemical and biological, counter-proliferation issues are considerable. There are several areas where proliferation might be a concern, such as Asia, the Middle East, or even around the Mediterranean. Chemical weapons may be a particular interest. Reluctance in North Africa, as well as parts of the Middle East, to sign the Chemical Weapons Convention in January 1993, against a background of knowledge and well-founded suspicion about capabilities, cannot be ignored as a factor shaping the strategic environment. To some extent the same problem may apply regarding nuclear weapons. Underpinning the development of chemical and possibly nuclear capabilities in North Africa and the Middle East are two other factors. These are the political evolution of the region and the development of Tactical Ballistic Missile delivery systems.[8] The latter include the Libyan *al-Fatah* and Egypt's *Badr 2000*. Both of these systems would be capable of striking continental European targets. The existence of delivery systems, in itself, is a particular strategic concern for Europe. The uncertainty about their potential warheads adds to this. However, these concerns are both framed by the political character of the region. The possible strength of Islamists, suggested *inter alia* by the electoral performance in Algeria of the Front Islamique du Salut at the end of 1991, is a factor that makes these weapons an issue that Europeans cannot afford to ignore, because their immediate and significant impact could only be on European countries.

While failing states present the most serious challenges in terms of disorder and environments in which other threats can develop, a range of weak states, sometimes also falling into the rogue category, present serious challenges with a more traditional aspect. North Korea certainly fits the weak or failing traditional pattern. While it has hovered on the verge of internal collapse for many years, it has also maintained a conventional military threat to its southern neighbour and it has developed a nuclear weapons capability. That weapons capability plus a hostile anti-Western outlook would make it a threat. The compound of internal weakness and potential collapse makes it especially troublesome. The risks include the possibility that either for money or simply through inability to maintain control, nuclear or other weapons of mass impact capabilities might pass into the control of other actors who might be more proactively hostile to Western interests.

This may well be why US forces intercepted a North Korean vessel carrying ballistic missiles on the high seas in 2002.[9] The boat was headed for Yemen, but as it turned out on a legitimate contract with the Yemen government. However, the fear must have been that the weapons were destined for al-Qa'ida, given its strong presence in that country. Even the degree to which the Yemen authorities had begun to co-operate with the US to combat that organization's presence rather than face attack by the US might still only have tempered concern as the country had previously indulged Usama bin Ladin's network.

North Korea and Iraq were accompanied by Iran in President George W. Bush's 'Axis of Evil'. The reason to link the three was WMD/I, particularly the quest for, or possession of, a nuclear capability, accompanied by anti-US, anti-Western tendencies. While Iran's reformist leadership under President Khatami had been seeking to move the country away from the Islamist revolution of the 1970s and towards a form of democracy, this was not the whole picture. In some senses, there were two Irans – that of the President and many of the young people, and that of remnants of the revolutionary old guard, both mullahs in the mosques, preaching narrow political-religious doctrine, and in the intelligence and security services, still developing nuclear and other weapons capabilities, assisting international terrorists and generally oriented against the West. While Iran under Khatami has moved towards democracy and has taken on its form and institutions, the underlying reality in the first years of the twenty-first century was murder and imprisonment of dissidents after 1998. This indicated an authoritarian system, with power structures still dominated by Islamist ideology in many respects – and in crucial ways, aiding and abetting others, whether local terrorist groups in the Middle East, or those with more international horizons. Until there was real political change, and while ever Iran continued its pursuit of WMD/I, especially nuclear weapons, it constituted a considerable threat to the West. Iran's quest for a nuclear capability could not really be disguised, as protestations that its programmes (aided *inter alia* by the Russian Federation) were purely for civilian purposes did not really add up, given that the country is so overwhelmingly rich in other sources of energy that nuclear energy could not be necessary. Moderate impulses to agree to extensive and intrusive inspections of nuclear programmes, following the US-led action against Iraq in 2003, were welcome and signs of common sense. But these also put pressure on the political moderates, adding to the potential for internal turmoil. That prospect of internal violent conflict, with WMD/I available, has to be a concern for the West: the Islamist mullahs may have largely lost the young people in Iran – the majority of the population is under nineteen years of age – and many of them might have followed the line of the mullahs who since 2000 have had the courage to denounce their Islamist colleagues (on any reasonable understanding of Islam, correctly) as being un-Islamic for sponsoring terror, torture, murder and maiming; but there remain strong and powerful Islamist elements, who could wreak havoc in an internal conflict, even if they did not prevail. The West could not ignore such a conflict and it could not assume that an Islamist Iran would be benign.

The problem with proliferation of WMD/I was most clearly posed in June 2002 in South Asia, where India and Pakistan went to the brink of nuclear war. Both countries had covertly acquired a nuclear weapons capability, while refusing to sign the Nuclear Non-Proliferation Treaty and eventually revealing their capabilities with highly publicized tests. With long-term pressures between the countries focused on Kashmir, a province formally in India but with a largely Muslim population and political activists seeking transfer of the province to Pakistan, an ambition held since the 1948 Partition that created Pakistan by the authorities in Islamabad, the capital. Divided by a Line of Control (LoC) following the 1971 war over the province between the two countries, the Pakistani Inter Service Intelligence agency sponsored and organized an insurgent terrorist campaign against Indian forces on New Delhi's side of the LoC. Following attacks on the Indian parliament in December 2001, a period of tension grew, with India mobilizing around 1 million troops and moving them towards the LoC and the Pakistani border. While India presumably calculated that an attack would not meet with a nuclear response – and that if it did, then India, consistent with its no-first-use policy, would be in a position to respond, the reality was quite likely otherwise. To outsiders, it appeared that neither side had adequate command and control arrangements and policy communities that understood both this and their own capabilities, let alone that of the other side. The result appeared to be that, to complement India's apparent judgements regarding the prospects for using nuclear weapons, Pakistan might well have assumed that it could use its nuclear capability to neutralize India's largely airborne nuclear arsenal before it could be used – and Pakistan's use might well have been without political safeguards on the decision to fire. While Pakistan might well have had the better overall understanding, it was still limited in understanding its own position. And for both sides and for the world, there was the prospect of a war that would go nuclear – probably at an early stage. The June 2001 confrontation was stopped a week before it started through international diplomacy, particularly by promises to India from the US on behalf of Pakistan, regarding control of the insurgents, that the Americans could not be sure to deliver. Thus the prospect of a new cycle of confrontation remained – and the prospect of a threat to international peace and security that the West could not afford to ignore, whether seeking to prevent it, or, should it occur, to take action to protect Western security.

WMD/I have also been a concern regarding the former Soviet Union. To some extent, while the complete collapse of Russia, the major former Soviet state, was not very likely, it was certainly a risk factor concerning the potential problems of weak state control and adverse social and economic impact, as well as the scare of WMD/I falling into the wrong hands. In some regards, this aspect was of greater concern than any potential threat emanating from Russia's military inheritance from the Soviet Union. Despite considerable co-operation since the end of the Cold War, Moscow has remained a chief concern in terms of Western defence for two reasons: its general prominence – size, leading-edge research and development in some areas of technology (in all probability, given its record), and military capability (although significantly diminished from the past) mean that it cannot be ignored in defence planning; and the possibility that despite co-operation at some levels – notably political and economic – Moscow still regards itself as being in strategic competition with the West. While each of these is inevitably tempered to a considerable degree by Russia's essential reliance on the West for financial, economic and know-how assistance, meaning that for some time ahead there will be nothing resembling the Soviet threat, it does not mean that Russia can be ruled out when considering defence of the West.

Presently in a period of convalescence and transformation, Russia might emerge as a strong European partner. Equally, it could re-emerge in a different light. There are those in Moscow who would see Russia's present position as being akin to that of Germany in the late 1920s: it is waiting to reconstitute its power and regain that of which it has been stripped. For present purposes, the likelihood of this view coming to dominate thinking in the political elite is of limited relevance. What is crucial is the physical reality that Russia, whatever its problems, has the largest armed force of any country between the Atlantic and the Urals and that while ever this is the case and the country is not solidly locked in an alliance, the hypothetical worst-case scenario of revanchist views dominating policy must be addressed by Western security policies, even though Russia seems a waning military power.

The Russian question is, in reality, a limited one. In Western strategic terms, it is an issue for nuclear strategists, especially those who need to work out the reason for French and British nuclear capabilities in a European context.[10] Are these formally and jointly to be at the behest of the EU as a whole? Are they to be available to European partners in an 'existential'[11] sense? Are they to remain independent national capabilities, which might or might not be applied to other Europeans? Whatever the rationale for a continuing European military nuclear capability, it seems clear that in nuclear and conventional force terms, if Russia is a problem then it will be the kind of problem which will also merit US attention (although the degree of attention may vary, as will be discussed below).

## China

China is perhaps one of the biggest concerns for Western security, looking several decades into the twenty-first century. A more traditional and common-sense judgement regarding China would note that the country is insular and historically has not been expansionist. However, the questions facing China might conceivably mean that it presents a different kind of problem in the future. The point that

China has not historically been expansionist also needs to be taken with care. Historically, China has never had the demographic and economic requirements that it has now developed and will have further developed in thirty years' time. That kind of development can break the historical pattern. Certainly, if, as is the case, defence-planning considerations mean that security policy on Russia allows for an unlikely worst-case scenario, similar scepticism should be applied to China.

China presents a bigger potential problem than appears to be accepted by many. In terms of its interest in aircraft carriers during the 1990s, Beijing gave some sign of being interested in a projection capability. Bearing in mind that for the Chinese the equivalent of the six-months view that constitutes 'long-term' for most Western policy makers could well be five or twenty-five years, the prospects for 2030 need to be considered judiciously. China already has enormous demographic problems and potential. As it develops economically and industrially, against the backdrop of its demographic position, it certainly cannot be excluded – and might well be very likely – that China will seek access to resources, especially in the Pacific. It is possible that this may be done through business, but there is some possibility that armed forces may be a relevant instrument in this context.

Threats over Taiwan may not be the limit of Chinese coercion two or three decades hence – indeed action against Taiwan may be the first step in any programme to secure China's future. As noted in the UK Ministry of Defence's *Strategic Context Paper* in 2000,[12] resource issues in the Asia-Pacific region can be anticipated. It should also be anticipated that China would be implicated in such questions. Any developments involving Chinese military power and projection would require US attention. At a minimum, a consequence of this would be reduced US attention to Europe, including the UK, balanced by the possibility of a need for as much European partnership with the US (inevitably including a number of countries, such as the UK). A gloomier (and, of course, extreme) scenario could see the US severely weakened by internal problems, including relations between Chinese kin-communities and other groups, undermining domestic US strength. Bogged-down and drained in a complex struggle with China, the UK and Europe would be left in a strategic environment where the US notionally remained a member of NATO, but would already be diminished as an influence over the intervening period. The weight in European security, on this scenario, would have shifted to European states – possibly with stronger and more positive links developing to Russia, in light of any US–Chinese conflict.

This is an extreme scenario and one that may remain quite unlikely – especially if preventive action is taken to ensure that it does not emerge. However, as a worst-case scenario for planning, it may well be more likely than, say, the resurgence of a Russian threat, given that China is waxing, where Russia continues to wane, and that China will inevitably have to confront and find solutions for a number of major problems, including its population and its economic development, as well as its enormous and increasingly enhanced military capability. It might be noted that an alternative, equally extreme scenario cannot be excluded – and would equally pose a major headache for Western policy makers in 2030, or beyond. A Chinese puzzle of this kind might well lead to an implosion under the strain of change and growth that would see something akin to Yugoslavia writ large. With communist rule and military command established on a provincial basis, there is a superficial similarity to the Yugoslav situation. This is compounded by similar kinds of social, economic and political disparity to those which characterized the Yugoslav federation in the 1980s, with the wealthier, modernizing, coastal areas apparently content for the time being to have wealth re-distributed to the poorer northern internal regions. The discrepancies between Shanghai, at one extreme, and Xiang province, at the other (and with the latter also affected by elements of inter-communal unrest and local terrorism, possibly with links to the international network that is al-Qa'ida), are such that it is hard not to imagine a point where, one way or another, the pressures create more widespread difficulties and force a divorce that will implicate all provinces. In such a case, just as the break-up of the Yugoslav federation and the fall-out from the war that went with it posed immense challenges for the wider international community, it would be impossible to avoid Western involvement, politically or militarily, in the Chinese fission.

While developments regarding China are too complex to foresee accurately, neither of the polar extremes considered above can be excluded. Defence of the West must be predicated on the capacity to deal with either possibility, or any other that might emerge. At one extreme, the outcome might be a major power, acting in its interests and expanding its regional and international influence (entirely understandable and acceptable, from its own perspective – but a challenge to the West). At the other extreme, there could be a massive internal collapse under the pressure of transition. Or there could be challenging developments at any of the points on the scale in between. Most of all, following the logic of partnership advocated in chapter 6, there might even be co-operation in the defence sphere, as an economically booming and politically adjusted, democratic China worked with the West. Whatever the outcome, China will be a major concern for Western security.

# Stability Threats

While physical threats offer a more obvious, immediate and, in most cases, more traditional version of that from which the West needs to defend itself, physical threats and attacks are linked to the less obvious, but often more sensible, threat domain, stability threats. Attacks by opponents of international order perhaps achieve far more than physical destruction if they are successful. They also have a big impact on perception and order, and so stability – disrupting the order, already, explained in chapter 2 on which Western countries rely. It is as much defence against instability, whether caused by the factors in question, or by competition or resentment focused around them, that has to be the primary concern of the West. The present section explicates some of the relevant issues that can be regarded as stability threats.

## Energy and the environment

Environmental issues may not themselves constitute threats, but their potential social impact and politicization certainly might. There has been some degree of global warming in recent years and projections for the twenty-first century suggest a possible increase in average temperatures of up to 3.5°C. While it might be premature in the context of the earth's physical history to presume that this will not change at some point (the capacity of nature to be self-regulating over time should not be excluded), there can be no doubt that for as long as the phenomenon is present, it will be a source of problems. Implications may include changes to plant life, affecting agriculture in different parts of the world, rising water levels in some parts of the world as a result of melting ice caps or shortages in other parts of the world because of excessive heat. In each case, there is the potential for socio-political tensions to be exacerbated, possibly giving rise to armed conflicts.

In terms of freshwater shortage and the consequent impact on local food production, the salience has been present in the Middle East and in parts of Africa for a long time – water rights was among the key obstacles to Palestinian agreement to the Camp David peace terms in late 2000. Given the essential importance of water, there can be no doubt that one political actor or another might have reason at some point to use armed force in an attempt to secure a supply for itself. It might well be that another political actor's approach to control and distribution of water, in the context, could constitute a threat.

Equally, in terms of rising water levels, it might well be that one political actor's behaviour could be judged as contributing to the potential for rising water levels and actual or potential flooding – with consequences for property, human life and, among other things, food production. That too might be deemed to be a threat and to require a response involving the use of armed force. And in an interconnected world, wherever there might be an issue that can be, or be seen as, a threat to one or more political actors and possibly requiring armed action, there is a problem for those with an interest in international stability as a whole.

What applies to water also applies to hydrocarbon fuels. The developed world depends to a considerable degree on oil and gas supplies, even though there is also considerable potential regarding recycled and renewable forms of energy. The key issue in terms of Western security is openness and stability in the countries and regions that produce and export these resources. In terms of gas production, by mid-century the main sources are likely to be Russia and parts of Central Asia, Iran and North Africa – notably Algeria – and possibly China. Western Europe could be almost entirely reliant on these sources and their supplies. At once, this can create a strategic vulnerability. In part this vulnerability concerns hostile action by any one of the governments in question, which might simply terminate supplies – generally unlikely given mutual economic and business concerns, but not impossible. In part it concerns the potential for supplies to be impeded by political instability and armed conflict. *In extremis*, as with water, this might involve armed hostilities over those resources themselves – particularly where offshore fields are concerned, as well as where exploitation still has considerable scope for development, notably in the Asian Pacific.

There is a similar situation, though perhaps even more aggravated, when it comes to oil. Again, the main issues are stability and openness (not control and price, as so many seem to believe).[13] While the number of countries and regions involved on the supply side is perhaps more diverse, it remains fairly limited – and, as with gas supplies, the shadow of political change and instability hangs over the decades ahead. Turning to alternative sources, at least in the short term, might well circumvent trouble in any particular case. This assumes a diversity of suppliers and the possibility of maintaining good relations with all, or at least a majority, of them. In part, this can mean encouraging new alternatives – so Brazil, Mexico, Russia and Central Asian countries, as well as some African countries, might be some kind of alternative to traditional dependency on the Middle East for oil. However, the reality is and is likely to remain that the bulk of oil reserves will be in that region.

While good diplomacy and political relations could go some way towards safeguarding Western needs in general, and diversity is essential to avoid dependency on particular sources, there can be no doubt that situations might emerge which will require the use of armed forces to protect Western interests. This might be because of openly hostile political action, or it might be contingent on political fractiousness and armed conflict over those resources or surrounding them. The major hypothetical example is probably Saudi Arabia, if it were to turn against the West under the influence of anti-Western ideologies supported by many in the country, or if there were political violence, a revolution, or armed conflict involving supporters of such ideologies, hostile to the al-Saud dynasty and the regime itself. In either hypothetical case, as well as seeking supplies and good relations elsewhere, action to restore regional stability and security might well be necessary. In situations short of this – and in the interest of avoiding such situations – the maintenance and development of good relations and partnerships that can foster stability and change is of great importance.

## Bio-politics, populations and disease

Demographic development has the potential to augment any of the other environmental issues. Western populations are generally ageing but otherwise stagnating (the US, however, provides a significant exception to this, with a more youthful and expanding population), while continuation of significant population growth in the less developed world can be anticipated. This poses a number of questions concerning the capacities of political communities to absorb growing numbers of people under thirty. One likely consequence of failure to ensure that their needs are met could be disaffection – and, with it, the potential to turn to radical agendas and political violence. Another possible consequence is that governments faced with large population growth will need additional resources, which will increase pressure on and competition for sometimes scarce resources – possibly leading them to resort to armed force.

Against these risks that emerge from demographic projections for the global population, there is also a need to take into account the potential impact of disease, particularly of AIDS – probably at different levels of projection for impact. The implications of AIDS include the impact on available personnel for Western armed forces, especially in those countries most obviously affected by the condition at present. Recruitment and retention difficulties could be exacerbated if the return to growing AIDS/HIV levels in Western countries at the beginning of the century continues. They also involve the likely questions, including conflict and the need for humanitarian assistance, that might emerge and require armed action. There may well be situations in which Western countries might need to use armed force to address threats based in fatal communicable diseases, in order to preserve public health and social stability.

## Economy and technology

Economics underpins any society – and the Western market system has been particularly successful in providing for social development and growth. As the twentieth century progressed, Western economies became ever more interdependent and reliant on openness and free trade. Historically, this applied to development within the borders of a state. This remains true and in some cases such development continues to be protected. However, to a large extent trade and finance have become internationalized and transnational (the former means that they occur between two or more countries, while the latter means that they involve actors and activities crossing boundaries).

The phenomenon of economic interconnectedness is often dubbed globalization, although much of the time the developments in question are more appropriately described as international. Globalization exists in a narrow range of economic (and related) activities, mostly depending on rapid means of communication. The principal example of this is the electronic linkage between different financial markets around the world, while the development of the internet more generally has created a global space with few breaks in the chain. However, even the internationalization of economic activity means that most Western countries – including the US – are vulnerable in some respects (and the details might differ) to international pressures and change. This can mean business losses, job losses, inflationary pressures, or currency depreciation. It can mean a single business that conducts its operations across the borders of different states deciding to shift investment, employment and profits from one place to another. And it can mean networks of communication, information and benefit that are at once an asset and a strategic vulnerability to hostile action – if damaged in some way, the overall impact might be deeply wounding. Moreover, in an increasingly interconnected world, enormous disparities are likely to remain between those who benefit most and those who apparently lose out. Closer links can mean a sharper sense of differences – and so the potential for resentment that can be mobilized to support anti-Western political violence. Seeking to address these disparities proactively will be important, but being prepared to deal with any threats that emerge is vital. Connections count. The answer to the question 'Why does X problem in Y country affect me? Why should I care if we do something about it, or not?' is often not immediately apparent, but can emerge contingently through a handful of links. Maintaining international economic stability is a priority for Western governments and cannot be excluded from the defence equation.

Economic strength and vulnerability are linked to the development of technical means and technological development. (It is important to note that there is a distinction between the existence of technical means – the physical apparatus – and technology, which concerns the uses and applications of those technical means as a social phenomenon.) The technical superiority of the US is unmatched, even generally, by other Western countries. So too is its technological accomplishment, tending to be open to the best developments outside the US and having the means and the commitment to import them. However, while preserving a position of such superiority is important for the West as a whole through commitment of resources, it can even be a source of resentment by other Western countries – in this sense, the potential of the European Union to exceed the possibilities available to any of its Member States has not been exploited. The competition from other parts of the world, which lag even further behind the US than the EU, Japan, or a small number of additional countries, has greater potential than might be immediately obvious from this situation. This is because a remarkable change occurred towards the end of the twentieth century in terms of investment in research and development – private investment, for purposes of private commercial innovation and gain, outstripped that of governments for defence purposes for the first time. This was mainly because of the importance of electronics and computers, and the potential for commercial gain at the cutting edge of innovation.

With this change came two significant implications for defence and security. The first is vulnerability to the commercial companies involved in research, development and production themselves – in a sense, a modified version of that already described above regarding dependency on particular countries for particular resources. A politically hostile company, especially in a world of transnational activity and ownership, might conceivably seek to hold Western governments hostage, or even to undermine them, in some way, by taking advantage of defence dependency on the most advanced technical means. While this is unlikely, given the often symbiotic relationship that exists between such companies and governments, it cannot be excluded. The second implication for defence is therefore the greater – that civilian, commercial development and exploitation means that these means are far more likely to be available to any potential adversaries, whether through open commercial transactions, or on the black market. It is equally likely, in this context, that whoever might have information, or technical, electronic or communications means of this kind available might also develop their own technological approach and adapt the means in unforeseeable ways, which might include preying on Western vulnerabilities.

While information, technology, electronics and communications (ITEC) products may become widely available, the degree to which potential adversaries could exploit these to breach secure features of the type currently produced by the US National Scientific Agency is limited. To some extent, continuing US predominance might be assumed, in which case there would be little chance that the lead possessed by the US (and 'shareable' with close allies) will be significantly dented – indeed, this lead could be extended. Against this, however, worst-case concerns and their implications cannot be ignored. Indeed, as September 11 showed, those with a will to damage the West will be innovative in acquiring the means to do so and in using them. In the domain of ITEC, where capabilities are commercially available, care is needed. Even larger problems ought not to be excluded, either – for example, in worst-case scenarios there could be implications in this regard for the relations between the US and China that could decisively alter the picture. Apart from a scenario such as this, the West would surely retain an advantage in the field of technology, given its wealth of such means, whereas any adversary might be expected only to have a limited range of them. But the West could still be vulnerable to threats posed in this way.

There is a wide range of risks, challenges and threats to the West. These concern not only actors who might physically oppose the Western way, but also conditions and processes that can undermine that way. The list of threats includes the possible emergence of powerful and antagonistic states and the activity of international, transnational and sub-national actors using political violence; human and physical resource issues and their impact on Western needs and societies; threats arising from communicable disease; and, finally, technical and technological threats, including weapons of mass destruction. Having comprehended how some of these factors can threaten the West directly and the international system that it had created and on which it depends, it is necessary to turn to the question of how to respond to those threats. This is the subject of the remaining chapters. The last two will deal with the concepts of partnership and pre-emptive self-defence. The next one will address adaptation in both the international organizational arrangements and strategy needed to meet the needs of protecting the West and defending it against both physical attack and instability.

# 5 ALLIANCE

On 4 April 1999 the North Atlantic Treaty became fifty. A few weeks later, the members of NATO gathered for a birthday party in Washington, DC. The party was intended to celebrate this milestone, but events were more subdued, as the shadow of conflict in Kosovo meant that the planned party became a working summit on war in progress. At the planned party, one of the biggest candles on the cake was to have been the unveiling of a 'New Strategic Concept' for the Alliance. This was needed to match the changes both in the Alliance and in the world at large that emerged in the course of the 1990s. The concept had to address the needs of NATO's members – which had come to number nineteen by the time of the summit – as well as the relationship of the Alliance to non-members. The challenge in defining a concept for NATO's work had to serve the essential purpose of embracing the sometimes differing perspectives of its members, while binding them together. In the end, clear definition of NATO's path to the future came not from the fine words of those engaged in conceptualization, but from the real-world experience of engagement over Kosovo. Kosovo was the manifestation of the new concept and gave the broad-brush definition to it.

While the elements that would contribute to NATO's new mission had gradually begun to emerge, the shape of the concept itself still required definition. If the needs of NATO as the unique military-political organization created by the US and its Allies were to be met, then NATO had to find a strategic mission that upheld international order, yet set limits on that mission. As the previous chapters have shown, it was necessary to meet the needs of Alliance members and partners for defence against both physical threats and stability threats to the international order on which they depended. Defence against instability, or attacks, was needed, whether in face of local conflict in some regions, or of the international threat of 'rogue states' and the terrorist campaigns of both state-sponsored and non-state actors. The need to respond to the threats posed and to protect stability meant that the organizational framework for Western security would need to adapt to match circumstances. This meant NATO, for sure. But it also meant new developments, such as the nascent formal and organizational defence arrangements, such as tri-lateral initiatives involving the US, Canada and Mexico, or the naval co-operation agreement among the member states of the Organization of American States in January 2003. And it included emerging trends of coalition and co-operation that saw new patterns emerging in Asia, with Japan's joining a coalition operating in Iraq during 2003; Australia deepening and extending its close co-operation with the US, while the latter was changing the scope and pattern of its troop deployments; but, most of all, the need to adapt to new conditions and emerging circumstances meant the EU. And it meant something between America and the Union, at the Euroatlantic core of the West, which, while not comprehensive, was essential. Thus, evolution in the international system during the 1990s and Alliance engagement over the Yugoslav lands effectively determined the parameters of NATO's future.

This evolution might be dubbed 'postmodern'. The present chapter seeks to complement the philosophical and more metaphysical erudition associated with interpretations of that kind by focusing on the practicalities and the 'real-world' manifestation of what Christopher Coker has termed NATO's transcending its origins.[1] The place of the Alliance in the twenty-first century could not be other than as part of a Western core to a broader concern for international peace and security. It is the necessity of and attachment to 'working practices' – in conjunction with the EU – that require attention in order to foster stability in the world, as I argue below. Thus the evolution in line with the new international environment and engagement over Yugoslavia certainly constitute a manifestation of the continuing ability of the Alliance to adapt and survive, and, in doing so, to preserve the Euroatlantic relationship. Part and parcel of this has to be evolution at the European end of the equation, with developments in the EU and European Security and Defence, as well as the European 'pillar' in NATO. The improvement of European military capability will be discussed later in the chapter. The starting point for the present analysis is the evolutionary character of the Alliance. As with other aspects of international politics, the evolution of NATO and the EU, at the geographical and strategic-historical core of the West in the second half of the twentieth century, exemplified Constructivist Realism. Neither the creation of the Alliance, nor any part of its evolution, was the result of an ideal type or an architect's template. As will be seen, the creation and adaptation of NATO and the EU were the product of agency and necessity – change came only when circumstances needed it, but also only because those in positions of responsibility took decisions and carried out actions that responded to necessity.

## The Evolutionary Alliance

On 12 March 1999 three new members, the Czech Republic, Hungary and Poland, joined the sixteen members already in NATO, opening the way for others to join later – at NATO's Prague Summit, in October 2002, seven further countries were invited to join the Alliance: Bulgaria, Estonia, Latvia, Lithuania, Romania, Slovakia and Slovenia. The three acceded to the Washington Treaty just a few weeks before it became fifty years old, in time to be members at the summit in Washington, DC, to mark that anniversary. However, those three new members were not the only countries in town to commemorate the foundation of the Alliance. Numerous other countries in the previous decade had become associated with NATO through developments such as the Partnership for Peace (PfP) programme and the Euroatlantic Partnership Council (EAPC). Indeed, there were ways in which the three newcomers to the Alliance (and others who would join later) could be seen to have served an apprenticeship through those programmes. This did not mean that all countries involved in partnership with NATO would become full members. But it did colour the range of questions to be asked about the future of the Alliance.[2]

NATO's fiftieth birthday and the changes the Alliance had undergone during the 1990s prompted questions about lifecycles, ageing and maturing. Confirming the saying that 'life begins at forty', the Alliance began ten years of radical change just after its fortieth birthday. Initiated by the speech by the Soviet leader Mikhail Gorbachev at the United Nations in 1987, the Cold War began to draw to a close. This was confirmed by the success of Solidarity in Poland in pluralist elections there, which elections were echoed elsewhere in Central and Eastern Europe as Soviet force was withdrawn. These developments were part of a series of events that led to the fall of the Berlin Wall and the ending of Soviet control throughout Central and Eastern

Europe in the last quarter of 1989, culminating with the reunification of Germany and co-operation over Iraq in 1990. The Cold War had been necessary to the signing of the North Atlantic Treaty and to the subsequent formation of the most integrated international military-political organization in history – with the most deeply developed set of assets ever. Within two years, military-political bodies on the other side of the Cold War divide had dissolved – the Warsaw Pact was no more and the Soviet Union itself was in the throes of breaking up.

To a large extent, this appeared to many to have removed NATO's *raison d'être*. Established to confront a foe, it was expected and argued by some that the Alliance would go the way of all alliances in history: it would break down once the purpose for its creation ceased to exist. Instead of going to an early grave, however, the forty-year-old embarked on a new lease of life. The subsequent ten years saw mostly unimaginable developments at a diplomatically heady pace.[3]

These developments did not stop questions about the longevity of the Alliance. Was the fifty-year-old for which life began at forty due to set its sights on retirement? Would it take early retirement at fifty-five? Would it draw its pension at sixty? Or, would it take the British route to the third age, and withdraw from active employment at sixty-five? This last date was not inconsistent with the UK's Strategic Defence Review during 1997–8, which imagined the world until 2015, at which point the Alliance would be sixty-five. However, rather than an end to the Alliance, it was inherent in that British process, and in the approach taken by other members, that NATO would remain the centrepiece of security policy.

NATO had proved itself capable of great adaptation and would continue to evolve. When life began at forty, NATO found new *raisons d'être*. This was consistent with the pattern of evolution developed in the Alliance over the previous fifty years. Evolution in the Alliance always came in spurts, not evenly. These spurts were always spurred by reaction to circumstances, not by grand designs. The preceding ten years confirmed, again, that all those discussing 'the New European Security Architecture' in 1989 and 1990 were reading the wrong discipline. Perhaps in reacting to, managing and cultivating environmental conditions, they should have been concerned with organic evolution of 'the New European Security Agriculture' instead.

The Transatlantic Alliance was destined to continue its evolution. In this sense, its future lay in its past. Therefore it is appropriate to consider NATO's evolution during the 1990s, before moving to outline some of the issues and events, including Kosovo, which would shape the Alliance and the character of its continuing evolution. This involved building on the three main strands of transformation after the end of the Cold War – enlargement, partnership and support for strategic peace support operations. These heralded an era of more productive partnerships, fostering international peace and stability and contributing constructively to missions for which the purposes could be summarized as supporting and enhancing international order.

## The Alliance Transformed

NATO was formed as a defensive alliance, in the early days of the Cold War. Although Article 5 of the Washington Treaty was not as tightly defined in terms of military commitment as the Brussels Treaty signed between European countries less than a year before, it did entail a significant commitment to collective defence. While the latter bound all states party to the treaty to offer military support in the event of one of their number being attacked, the former offered no more than a promise to consider what could be done. While the commitment made concerned any situation theoretically, in practice it was the determination of a threat from the Soviet Union which drove the countries involved to form these collective defence pacts. It was probably only that threat, especially put into operation in a massive way on the Central Front in Europe, which would have seen them respond.

That response was made considerably more likely as the North Atlantic Alliance developed from treaty to agreement to organized and established political and, particularly, military arrangements. It was one thing to have an agreement. It was something completely different to have a military-political organization engaged in planning and preparation for potential war against a known enemy.

In particular, the military preparations involved meant that valuable time would already have been gained if war seemed in prospect. As was seen on numerous occasions in the 1990s, from Iraq in 1990 to Kosovo in 1998–9, without political and operational commitment in place at the outset, it took many months before major collective groupings of troops could be deployed. NATO, for all its relative failings, was able to develop an established and integrated military-political construct unlike any other in history. At the end of the Cold War, even without the necessity of countering the Soviet Union, this was a precious and expensive set of assets which none of the allies wanted to lose, whatever the desires for a 'peace dividend' in 1989.

This collective body might be expensive and the obvious need for it might not be there any more, but it was inconceivable that it could ever be re-created if it were disestablished.

Of course, these assets were not part of the picture in 1949. They were only developed as the Alliance set out on the evolutionary path by adding 'Organization' to 'North Atlantic Treaty' after North Korean troops had crossed the 38th parallel in 1950. The 'O' in NATO did not exist to begin with. Its appearance was the first in a set of evolutionary steps throughout the Cold War period, which included enlargement, in 1952, 1955 and 1986, as well as strategic change. However, it was not until after the end of the Cold War that the pace of evolution increased markedly.

With the end of the Cold War, NATO was perceived by many to have lost its *raison d'être*. The removal of the Soviet military threat to Western Europe removed NATO's apparent strategic rationale and main purpose. NATO had been created to deter or defend against a Soviet military threat. The removal of that threat, according to simple reasoning, meant redundancy for the Alliance. The reality that NATO had at least two other major purposes in the eyes of most of its members did little to counter this reasoning. Neither NATO's role in assuring US engagement in European security matters, nor the part it played in the otherwise potentially sensitive area of integrating German military capability, could be perceived (or presented) as over-riding reasons for the maintenance of the Alliance. In addition, the prospect of regenerated Moscow military power seemed too dim and distant a prospect in an era of near horizons and short-term needs to justify NATO's existence. The Alliance needed to evolve in new ways.

That evolution in the 1990s was marked in three particular ways: by strategic enlargement, by the development of arrangements for partnership and co-operation with non-members, and by support for operations to maintain international peace and security. Each of these gave the Alliance a new role in contributing to peace and stability, well beyond the old role of collective defence for the members alone, against a particular threat. Usually without knowing it, all members were also indebted to the Canadians who had insisted on including a commitment to fostering peaceful and stable international relations in Article 2 of the Treaty, especially those Americans whose fore-bears had done much to prevent such a role. This permitted the Allies to step out of the Cold War mode and to reach out to other parts of Europe, thereby removing the opportunities for many parrots to repeat the early 1990s' notion regarding NATO: 'out of area, or out of business'. Both NATO's area and its business changed.

NATO enlargement, partnership programmes and support for operations to maintain peace and security cannot be properly understood without reference to the Balkans. The Alliance's evolution was partly forged in the region and its satisfactory accomplishment would be determined by NATO's continuing role in it. Enlargement, partnership and peace support involvement in South-Eastern Europe were essential to NATO's future. Just as all of these emerged as strategic imperatives for the Alliance as it sought a new *raison d'être*, all continued to be the focus for NATO's existence. If it could not continue to meet these strategic imperatives, the relative success story of NATO in the 1990s would be brought into question and with it, possibly, the longer-term effectiveness of the Alliance.

In the end, the military elements of international involvement regarding the Yugoslav War provided one of the contexts in which enlargement and partnership could be forged, as well as offering a chance to practise support for the maintenance of international peace and security. Instant enlargement was not possible, but *de facto* co-operation in Bosnia was. It was difficult immediately to move to enlargement for three main reasons.

First, the implications for the Alliance and its existing members would have to be worked out. Secondly, the potential candidate countries themselves would have to have come far enough in the process of post-communist transition to be able comfortably to be incorporated as members. Finally, the overarching political question of the West's relationship with Russia would have to be settled. Aside from earlier developments (discussed below), it was NATO-led peace implementation in Bosnia which created the situation in which each of those issues could, partly, be worked out.

In the meantime, to create time and space for any evaluation of the changed strategic environment, as well as to give consideration to possibilities for enlargement, NATO adopted other approaches. Following the initial step of creating the North Atlantic Co-operation Council (NACC), under which arrangement all non-Alliance states had equal standing, the Alliance devised a variable programme with individual countries under the label Partnership for Peace. The NACC had been an arrangement where that which the Alliance did with one of the countries involved, it would have to do with all of them. Under PfP individual co-operation programmes could be designed, allowing both the partner countries and the Alliance to work out a specific relationship. Complementing PfP exercises and activities, the countries of Central and Eastern Europe looking to join NATO could demonstrate something of their mettle by working with the Alliance in Bosnia and Hercegovina.

Implementation of the Dayton–Paris peace agreement regarding Bosnia and Hercegovina was a major consideration for the Alliance and those working with it, first with an Implementation Force (IFOR) for the first year of the peace, involving 53,000, then with SFOR, the Stabilization Force, with around 33,000 troops. A crucial feature of the NATO-led deployment was precisely that it was NATO-led. It was not purely a NATO operation (as would also be the case with the force deployed to Kosovo during 1999). While the Alliance provided three-quarters of the force, it was important that, parallel with PfP, Alliance members were working with units and groups from partnership countries. The joint operations in Bosnia and Hercegovina were a model for the development of the complementary military organizational concept of Combined Joint Task Forces (CJTF). This complemented the notion of partnership and began to give meaning to the slogan of 'separable, but not separate' forces for use in a purely European context. This met the evolutionary needs to create a European Security and Defence Identity (or Capability, or Force – all marginally different aspects of the same issue), linked to the European Union, but formed around a European pillar in NATO (discussed below).

Peace implementation was an opportunity for two things to occur. First, a number of countries seeking Alliance membership could prove their worth and their sense of commitment to playing a responsible role on the international scene, in conjunction with NATO. Thus Poland and the Czech Republic committed troops to Bosnia and Hercegovina with half an eye on Alliance membership – there could be no better way to approach the Alliance than through enthusiastic, *de facto* engagement. In a different way, the same could be said of Hungary, which to a large extent became the first *de facto* new member of the Alliance through its role as a forward base for NATO operations in Bosnia and Hercegovina.

The second way in which peace implementation in Bosnia and Hercegovina contributed to enlargement concerned the palliation of Russian disquiet. The deployment of 5,000 Russian troops alongside US counterparts under a special arrangement was a practical demonstration of the ways in which engagement could generate transparency and build confidence. One of the most astonishing features of the deployment was the way in which, at first, Russian troops could not believe that information they were being given was genuine, as it was clearly of a confidential nature. As a result of necessary steps of this kind, as well as day-to-day collaboration and wider diplomatic moves, it was possible for the Alliance to move towards the signing of the Founding Act with the Russian Federation at the end of May 1997.

The place of partnership in Alliance evolution and experiment could not continue in the way initially established. In that context, direct partnership activity was worked out on a 16 to 1 basis, with no real scope for directly including other partners in planned activity (although, in practice, arrangements were made and collective exercises took place). Yet, when considering operations such as that in Bosnia and Hercegovina, it was the well-established assets of NATO which planned and prepared for operations and then invited others willing to join in to do so on a take-it-or-leave-it basis. Partners had no role in planning. This had to change.

To accommodate the desires and concerns of partners, at its Madrid Summit in 1997, as well as inviting the three Central and East European countries named to open talks on accession, the Alliance also announced the EAPC. This would enable allies and partners, in whatever groupings, for whatever purposes, to join together and both plan and execute military operations. The *ad hoc* character of arrangements under the Partnership Council offered flexibility, whether the issue was training and management, operations to support the maintenance of international order or, should the circumstance arise, non-NATO collective defence. (On this last point, it should be noted that Partnership, or EAPC, engagement and activity probably offered more in terms of real and practical defence to countries involved than did the formal protection offered to full members by Article 5 of the Treaty; it was not possible to walk away from a practical joint commitment, whereas it might always be possible to 'consider', in terms of Article 5, that a finely worded message of support would be the most appropriate action to take when an ally faced attack.)

The experience of Bosnia and Hercegovina, PfP and the development of the Partnership Council, as well as pressures relating to EU developments, all demonstrated that the Alliance had been transformed. On the operational side, NATO minus some of its members, with or without one or more partners, could put together combined forces. While it retained its narrow collective defence role for its members, it had, in effect, become a club with assets that some or all of the members, in conjunction with one or more others, might use for particular purposes – providing that there was not an unlikely veto from one of the members. It is this club with valuable assets at the disposal of its members that would confront the future. The nature of the club at the beginning of the twenty-first century is such that key strategic assets – heavy lift, air strike and technical strategic intelligence-gathering capabilities – rest with the US. Therefore, one version of the 'club' formula, if there were US involvement, could be to rely on the traditions and practices of the club *ad hoc* without formally involving the club as a whole. The extent to which this might happen – as it did, in some senses, over Afghanistan and Iraq – would depend on the overall balance in European developments, especially of relevant capabilities and of perspectives.

# The European Dimension: Illusion, Invention and the Indispensable

The development of European defence capabilities is a matter of necessity both for the successful evolution of the Alliance and for the development of the EU itself and to meet the collective needs of its Member States.[4] There is a need both to provide a complement to US capabilities within the Alliance in order to free the US in certain regards and to provide the means to buttress European policy in those areas where the EU Member States seek to act. The remainder of the present chapter considers developments at the end of the 1990s and into the first years of the twenty-first century, as well as the underlying forces impelling the development of a significant European capability and indicating the limits of that development.

The issue of harmonization between NATO and the EU is vital. Developments such as CJTFs and the EAPC spawned by NATO, and the European Security and Defence Identity, the subsequent European Security and Defence Policy (ESD), and the appointment of a High Representative for security matters, on the part of the EU, were all instrumental in creating new weaves and reinforcing the existing tissue in the fabric of European security. The appointment as the first High Representative of former NATO Secretary-General Javier Solana, a European with a grasp of EU, NATO and US needs, was important in fostering these developments. Solana's appointment was reinforced by the appointment of Lord Robertson as his successor at NATO. Like his Spanish predecessor, the Briton understood the needs of all involved and had their confidence. The important aspect of this harmonization was the emergence, with a little design, of *de facto* arrangements, rather than grand schemes with little credibility. The same was true, by extension, of the role played by both bodies regarding enlargement to the east: it was the practical steps offering co-operation and prospects of possible eventual membership that made the biggest difference.

It is the assets, as much as the politics involved, that define this position. The assets, for the moment at least, rest with NATO. But it is conceivable – even likely – that in fifteen or fifty years' time, the EAPC will be the key body, with NATO reduced to a relic from the genesis of the EAPC, still in existence, but no longer the same key part of European security that it was in its first fifty years. By that time, a variant of the Partnership Council could have become the main element in the management of peace and security in Europe and a pillar for the US and the Europeans to play a role in preserving global stability. This would be an extension of the organic development permitted by the EAPC. The Alliance could not avoid continuing to evolve as a club with assets that some of its members might use in conjunction with partners and in which, whether within NATO itself, or under the Partnership Council, all would understand the benefits of inter-operability.

Evolution in NATO and in the EU is vital not only for the preservation of security in Europe itself, but also for the European relationship with the United States and the security of the West as a whole. Only if the Europeans prove themselves able to develop in this direction are the Americans likely to be kept on board for the long term. It is necessary for all concerned to understand that this is a vital issue for Europe as it approaches EU enlargement. It is also vital to questions of security that whatever happens should be geared to maintaining a friendly, harmonized relationship with the US. Yet this should also free the EU to act without the Americans where it might be appropriate to do so.

The key to the success of ESD is likely to be the pivotal role played by the UK. Analytically, ESD can only be realistically developed with the UK playing a significant role in Europe on defence and security matters, while offering some reassurance to Americans, worried about what they perceive to be European irresponsibility, that European action would not pose risks to America or be designed to undermine American interests, while the implications and impact of the fall-out between the US and some of its European allies would have to be absorbed. It is quite probably the destiny of the UK, as the pivot between the US and the EU, to lead ESD – and that of Europe, hard as it may be to accept – if a viable EU-linked defence force is to emerge; and if it does not do so, disaffection with a lack of European capability could shake the transatlantic bond in NATO. It must be the place of the British to provide the bridge between Europe and the US, if there is to be one – and so between EU and NATO use of the assets. (This should not be construed as a political judgement, or preference – or one that is pro-British, simply because I happen to be a British citizen; rather, it is the outcome of reflection and analysis of the political and strategic conditions for evolution towards greater European military capability and the maintenance of the Alliance.) Yet a cardinal UK role would inevitably be problematic politically. In terms of the perceptions and attitudes of others, France, particularly, as a comparable military power and as the arch-proponent of a European defence capability over several decades, might wish to lay claim to such a role. And, while the British might remain reluctant to take it, the reality is that only the UK has the political and operational profile to take on this role and to make the effective sharing with the EU of assets held by the Alliance work out. This kind of analysis, backed by political responsibility and a desire to work with France, underpinned the UK approach to the St Malo initiative at the end of 1998 which has since given rise to remarkable progress in the EU defence sphere and is vital to the prospective use of EU Security and Defence development, alongside that of the EAPC.

Within NATO, the full development of the British-led Allied Command Europe Rapid Reaction Corps (ARRC) meant that for the first time there was effectively a European force that could be deployed, albeit reliant on US and NATO strategic support. It was this force, wholly composed of units from European countries, which provided the framework for NATO deployment of troops to implement the Kosovo peace agreement. While the particular demands of former Yugoslavia required an American presence on the ground for military-political credibility in the eyes of the parties to the conflict, it was now conceivable that, at some stage, a purely European force might be deployed, with US acquiescence on the use of NATO military assets.

This context led to the Helsinki decision to prepare for European Defence Autonomy at the end of 1999. Recognizing the *de facto* emergence of such a European capability meant that EU leaders could envisage the formal appearance of a European defence force within two years, which, on paper at least, was accomplished. The questions in achieving such a force would be organizational and political. Within that timeframe, a fledgling planning capability would have to be adapted to the new requirements. Politically, the obstacles to engineering a viable force would have to be overcome between the European members of the Alliance, while European–US links would have to be managed. This was because some Europeans held grand ideas of creating a force that was beyond European means, but those dreams made the US uncomfortable; meanwhile some in the US were not always ready to accept the degree of autonomy these arrangements would allow, fearing that the US would ultimately be dragged into whatever the Europeans did – a summation of what happened over Bosnia, in some eyes. And there were equivalent concerns the other way round over Afghanistan and Iraq.

This was a sensitive situation. European forces could only carry out limited missions – and, given European inadequacy in strategic intelligence and command and control, as well as heavy lift, would even need to benefit greatly from the Defence Capabilities Initiative (DCI) announced at the NATO Washington Summit in 1999 before operations at the higher end of that limited spectrum of peace enforcement and humanitarian operations were to be feasible. Thus, for the project to prosper, American goodwill would be needed and, in theory, could be expected. First, the DCI was Washington's idea to help assure that a greater and less dependent European contribution would be possible in the future – Kosovo had demonstrated Europe's potentially fatal deficits in a number of areas. Secondly, it was in America's interest to be relieved of responsibility in certain areas. Should Washington choose to be involved, this would not be in question. However, the ESD arrangements allowed for the possibility that the US would not be involved and that the Europeans would be able to act in an effective manner on their own.

Reaching a stage where an independent ESD initiative might emerge remained many years away, but by 2003 a limited European capability was in place and quite significant deployments in South-Eastern Europe were all set to commence. Developing initial agreements on NATO–EU mutual arrangements originally established in Berlin in 1996, on 17 March 2003 NATO and the EU cemented agreements and practical preparations through further agreements, labelled 'Berlin Plus', which included arrangements for sharing defence and security information. The somewhat arcane and technical Berlin Plus arrangements permitted the EU formally to launch Operation Concordia in Macedonia on 1 April 2003, which took over from the NATO-led operation that had been there previously. The EU was also preparing to take over NATO responsibilities in Bosnia.[5] Europe was beginning to come to a point where it would eventually have matured enough politically to be capable of strategic decision-making. Until then, there would be a need continually to review and develop the nature of European Security and Defence and its needs. Bearing in mind the imperatives of strategy set out by Clausewitz, any European military potential would not be soundly based if it did not recognize that successful use of armed forces, *inter alia*, depends on a form of legitimization – harmonization of the trinity of armed forces, state and people.[6] The development or use of armed forces without coherent policy and not organically connected to a political community would be folly.

Several messages emerge from the continuing involvement in former Yugoslavia. One example is the strong possibility of potential need regarding common political action and a military capability to underpin it. Another is that the strategic parameters set around European security in the decades after the Second World War have shifted: the nature of the US commitment has changed. It is clear that the US remains a crucial factor in European security. But the commitment has become variegated. The European countries can no longer rely on the US to be there in all cases – and, more contentiously, to be wholly reliable when its presence is felt. And, of course, *pace* the US-led engagement in Iraq, vice versa. It is essential to conceive of any strategic rationale for a European military as being based on the need for common perceptions and on incremental and empirical evolution of European (meaning EU-related) capabilities – political and military. Approaching the issue this way suggests that, in reality, if there is to be one at all, there will be a two-tier strategic rationale for European armed forces, based on the missions of 'partnership and periphery'.

It is not clear at what stage European armed forces will unquestionably be in a position to operate on this basis. Developments regarding Macedonia and Bosnia were positive signals. However, for some time to come, there can be no expectation of a single European military organization, especially given the critical lack of strategic air strike, heavy lift and technical intelligence-gathering capabilities. Rather, there will continue to be a set of national capabilities, which may be capable of operating jointly at certain levels and within particular frameworks or structures – NATO, CJTF, ESD, Eurocorps, bilateral capabilities, or *ad hoc* arrangements. No European action at the strategic level will be possible without coherent forces being available – indeed, no strategic rationale will be rational unless it takes account of the material which will be available to those making critical military-political decisions involving the possible use of armed forces. The salience of these points is confirmed by NATO's experience after the end of the Cold War.

# The Euroatlantic Order

Two matters combining policy and practice ensured NATO's relevance. One was the growing relationship with non-NATO members, particularly in Central and Eastern Europe, which gained a formal character with the creation of the Partnership for Peace programme, PfP, apart from opening channels for co-operation through which the prospect of NATO enlargement could begin to be worked out. This broadened NATO's role from defence of its members to promotion of peace and stability across Europe. Alongside this, NATO took on an increasing role, under the same rubric of promoting peace and stability, regarding the territories of former Yugoslavia, primarily Bosnia. This was, above all, a role sought by many in the NATO bureaucracies in Brussels which were conscious, first, that unless NATO found a role, its position would be undermined, and then, that its position would be damaged by a failure to be seen to be effective.

The NATO engagements regarding Bosnia and Kosovo were complicated by strains in the transatlantic relationship, as were the US-led operations over Afghanistan and Iraq, although, in late 2003, Afghanistan became a NATO mission – perhaps prefiguring other engagements later in the Middle East. These strains also served to reveal the relative vanity of trying to cite US engagement in Europe as a reason for NATO's existence: Washington's background stance on many issues and its arguments with some of its European allies did not suggest that this, in the gaze of the short term, was compelling. Eventually, however, it was the sense of the way US–European differences were affecting the Alliance and transatlantic relations that focused NATO minds and gave substance to involvement in Bosnia.[7] If the inherent value attributed to the Alliance by its members was to be preserved, then action was required. Former Yugoslavia, along with PfP and the stabilization of transitional Europe, had become a *raison d'être* for NATO. But the new strategic rationale had only emerged because there was a straightforward link to reality and practice. This was the case even if the other reasons for its members to keep the Alliance intact – the possibility of Russian resurgence, American involvement in Europe and German military integration – were still at least as relevant in truth, if not perception.

NATO's role in former Yugoslavia resulted from a concatenation of actions, which saw deepening external involvement. NATO involvement in organizing IFOR, SFOR and KFOR, the peace implementation and stabilization forces for Bosnia and Kosovo, was a direct product of its overt and growing role initially in support of UN peace forces in Bosnia. Such overt activity grew from its implicit role underpinning the UN force in Bosnia. That role in the shadows came because the ministerial council of the Western European Union (as the putative defence arm of the emerging European Union) decided to commit troops to Bosnia – which troops then came under a UN umbrella. The countries involved were also NATO members, used NATO structures and turned to the UN because the Western European

Union (WEU) was not capable of planning, organizing or managing the force. The WEU and the UN, separately, had become involved consequent to EU diplomatic investment in the second half of 1991.

Each further step taken on this trail of engagement confirmed the interconnectedness of the states and organizations involved, as well as the nature of their security and security policy links. It also suggested the inadequacy of European structures *vis à vis* their members' compound needs. Rather like perceptions of the need for US involvement in Europe regarding NATO, there was no simple sense of European interests or needs in the security sphere. *Ex post facto*, it became possible to see how the external involvement in former Yugoslavia was a matter of common security policy interest. The difficulty was that this emerged dimly, often challenged by critics charging that there was and should be no security policy concern in the area.

In retrospect, it is possible to identify the security policy issues which generated the European and international military involvement in former Yugoslavia. Although 'humanitarian action' was cited as the altruistic motivation for the external military involvement in the region (and was undoubtedly an important reason), it was by no means the only factor. Had it been the only issue, it seems almost impossible to conceive of generally reluctant states being prepared to devote human, physical and financial resources on the scale they did. Humanitarianism was a factor and was important in marketing terms as a policy rationale – it was a simple, positive idea, which was comprehensible and met with popular support.

Other possible reasons of security policy were less straightforwardly communicable and comprehensible. These included containment of the conflict to prevent the possibility of wider war, which could have implications for EU and NATO members. They also included stemming the refugee tide created by the Serbian campaign of ethnic cleansing and a limited commitment to resisting the Serbian (and later Croatian) attempt to draw new borders, or to confirm old ones, using the same strategy of ethnic cleansing.[8]

Above all, there was a security policy imperative to address challenges to credibility in both domestic and external arenas. Once the EU, hubristically seeking to act in the spirit of the coming Common Foreign and Security Policy, had dispatched the troika to mediate on the second day of fighting in Slovenia in June 1991, a stake had been placed. With each effort to protect the stake placed, the stake grew. With the ever-incremental stake, those involved were increasingly confronted with the realities of their situation. Crucially, for some EU Member States, this meant that what seemed initially to be unimportant and distant questions concerning others were in reality a concern for all.

That concern stemmed from the fundamental that those states in the EU (and indeed in NATO and active in the UN and other forums) were members because they had reached the limits of what they could achieve individually. Key players in the fields of military and security policy, such as France and the UK (whatever the contrasting perspectives of those two), had long ago reached the point where it was recognized that the exercise of security policy had to be through collective arrangements for practical reasons, or, in the case of the US, for reasons of political legitimacy. The reality of a state's seeking to exercise its security policy through the EU, NATO or some other body is that the concerns of others are its concerns: if security is to be assured through the relevant collective body, the health of that body must be maintained. In essence, this means that a question for one is a question for all, however complex or dimly perceived this might be, because failure to deal with one question impairs credibility. That undermines the value of the body as an instrument of security policy and so the security of one and all.

# US Leadership, European Capability and Responsible Action

As with the Yugoslav War, Europeans may be required to act at some stage in the future. This means that there must be a European military capability to act. The evolution of Western involvement in former Yugoslavia is instructive for understanding the context in which any use of European military capability might be foreseen. Throughout the Cold War, there was an evident European dependency on the US – which dependency was confirmed in the course of the Yugoslav War. Neither politically, nor militarily, were the Europeans able to act decisively.

For the most part, differences between the US and its European partners were driven by Washington's overwhelming reluctance to place its troops on the ground. Put simply, the US could not be relied upon to be there in certain situations (as some in Europe had feared would be the case even in the Cold War). Worse, from a European perspective, Washington could not be relied on to support European action. Instead, in French and British eyes, at least, the Americans undermined the substantial military commitments being made in

Bosnia through public assertion of the 'lift and strike' option, imprac-
tical though that was and in spite of the US priority being to keep
British and French troops on the ground.

What the Americans probably wanted out of this in reality was a
proxy force. In effect, this is what they achieved by the end of the war
in Bosnia. The Croatian and Bosnian government armies, along with
some elements of the UN Protection Force for Bosnia (UNPROFOR),
were effectively acting as the ground forces for operations covered
by American air power. Ideally, from Washington's perspective, the
key European components in UNPROFOR would have been the
ground force component of a co-ordinated forceful campaign. This
framework is likely to be important for European states in the
future as they seek (and are obliged) to work more closely together
– operating either with US air power, or even with purely limited
European air power.

Considering the US perspective and Washington's needs of the
Europeans, the iconic impact of the twin towers collapsing on
September 11 and the US mobilizing in response made its leader's
position unassailable over Afghanistan.[9] Yet the narrow approach
to leadership opened the way for problems of legitimacy when the
security policy agenda returned to Iraq, twelve years after Saddam
Hussein's forces had invaded Kuwait. It became clear to major
Western governments in spring 2002 that a variety of international
pressures, mostly under the authority of the UN Security Council,
such as a crumbling regime of economic and political sanctions, had
not contained Baghdad sufficiently when two developments rang alarm
bells. The first was information that Iraq was advancing in attempts
to develop a nuclear weapons capability and was determinedly active
internationally to secure what it needed to complete the programme –
primarily weapons grade plutonium. The second was the presence of
senior al-Qa'ida figures in Baghdad and Iraqi support for al-Qa'ida
training camps in the Kurdish north-eastern parts of the country.
However, while Western capitals were apprised of these developments,
issues over how to approach the threats involved differed sharply.

Washington sought to treat Iraq as a follow-on to the still incomplete mission in Afghanistan, taking exactly the same narrow and
assumptive approach to leadership, based on a self-image that almost
seemed oblivious initially to the views of others; but those others
had different perspectives. While Sydney was closely in line with
Washington, London, the next-closest ally, immediately sought to
broaden the US Administration's horizons and to overcome the immediately evident problems of legitimacy, while remaining unconvinced

that the nightmare scenario was yet in place – that Saddam's macho-attachment to WMD/I would come together with al-Qa'ida's irreconcilables. As London noted that Saddam's efforts were worrying enough in themselves, Paris and other capitals shared that concern, but considered other approaches to be more viable, preferring to reinforce the existing containment policy, particularly by using American pressure to secure the return of UN weapons inspectors, some destruction of WMD/I capabilities, and the creation of conditions in which Saddam's rush towards the nuclear finishing line could be impeded. While these different views reflected assessments of the threats and the most appropriate responses to them, they also reflected attitudes towards Washington and resentments arising from the manner in which Afghanistan had been handled to the exclusion of others in decision-making and the virtual exclusion of others in execution.

As had been the case with Bosnia during the first two years of the Clinton Administration, so with Iraq, the Bush Jr White House had fixed on a policy that sought legitimacy on a somewhat arrogant presumption of self-importance and offered no space initially for friends and allies, many of whom judged the US approach to be inappropriate or, at best, in need of refinement. As a result, while Washington realized the advantages – including domestic legitimacy – of seeking backing through the UN Security Council, that process provided a key forum in which legitimacy fractures were exposed and would have to be remedied. The decisively militarized US response to Iraq brought a new dimension of 'irresponsibility' into attributes of would-be leadership. Where Bosnia had shown a smoke-but-don't-inhale, strong on prescription but weak action facet to assumed leadership, Iraq appeared to have produced a new variant, where desperate guzzling of hard substances and anti-social action undermined by seemingly weak reflection caused greater damage to the legitimacy of US leadership than anything perhaps since the Second World War. It had become clear that, after the considerable dismissal of allies and partners over Afghanistan, following the frictions that had peppered the Kosovo intervention, the leader's standing had become negative in many eyes.

This left the US in a similar position to that in the early period regarding Bosnia – but there was also a notable contrast. Whereas that Bosnian period had required preparedness to assume responsibility and to take action to restore the image, over Iraq the problem was to demonstrate responsibility by complementing a commitment to action, perceived by some as overwrought, with necessary moderation in its staunchness on using armed force if necessary and paying attention to others. By changing its initial course and following the path of UN Security Council authority, Washington managed to temper sharply negative criticism and, albeit with many blots on it, established sufficient legitimacy to permit potentially not only military operational but also strategic success.

Despite some murmuring concerning the demise of NATO after the Iraq operations, the reality was other – as the launching of NATO's mission to Afghanistan confirmed, even while operations in Iraq continued. As with NATO's past, its future would be determined by evolution and reaction to circumstance. Evolution during the 1990s was radical with reference to enlargement, partnership and the maintenance of international peace and security. Above all, this was the case regarding Bosnia and Hercegovina and Kosovo. Further development of this kind was logical. Politically and organizationally, the Alliance had to shift towards Europe, as a result of enlargement and any deepening of the European Security and Defence Identity, Combined Joint Task Forces and the Euro-Atlantic Partnership Council. But these shifts depended on the firmness of an alliance with the United States, as well as on keeping NATO's unique, valuable assets in good repair. At the same time, the US had to facilitate its global role by use of NATO and its unique military-political arrangements. Without the NATO context, US action would be seen as lacking legitimacy, not only in the eyes of the world, but crucially in the eyes of its own people. No Administration in Washington, DC, could afford this. The US needed a multilateral framework for its global role.[10]

The strategic challenge in terms of major armed forces activity that will primarily concern the EU comprises the promotion of stability and the establishing of security around the boundaries of the EU itself, with possible partnership and stabilization roles developing further afield.[11] For the most part, regarding other major questions which would engage the US – those such as the Middle East, or Russia – the EU is likely to be working in partnership with others – above all the US, most likely through NATO. European thinking on the organization of the asset structure within NATO has to lead in that direction. There will be European activity either in partnership with Washington, or possibly some way down the line, say, Moscow, over the major strategic issues, or alone, somewhere closer to the European periphery where US strategic involvement is not required. The EU will have to be capable of dealing with security problems of a certain kind on its own – and in addition to have the capability to play a significant role as a partner, at other times.

The Washington Summit in April 1999 and its aftermath created the conditions in which the possibility of European Security and Defence arrangements could be made a reality. This would both satisfy the aspirations of those in Europe who sought a European force and permit the European NATO countries to take responsibility for tending stability in the areas of immediate concern to them. In turn, it would finally open the way for practical burden-sharing of the kind long wished for by Washington (over 80 per cent of the aerial power used was American for Kosovo). In return, the US could benefit from NATO in carrying out its global responsibilities. The later decision in October 2002 further to enlarge the Alliance confirmed the trend already set. NATO would be less focused than ever on collective self-defence. It would be more fluid and flexible than ever, with similar qualities required in the nascent European Security and Defence capacity. And using these flexible frameworks, along with other partners around the world, a dynamic, flexible, variable and multi-level, multi-tempo approach to defence and the promotion of peace and security would emerge – and, in practice, began to do so. In terms of Constructivist Realism, necessity would evoke appropriate agency. Whatever the temporary pressures and different perceptions that could lead to assessments of a Euroatlantic dividing of the ways, the reality was that necessity would require actors on both sides of the Atlantic to adapt and adjust and join forces. Both the Europeans and the US, through the EU, NATO and also *ad hoc* arrangements, would need to confront the realities of twenty-first-century international security, acting collectively to enforce and promote international peace and security, both through active self-defence, discussed in the final chapter, and through partnership – the theme of the next chapter.

# 6 PARTNERSHIP

The consolidation of organizational and structural change in the Alliance, accompanied by political and security developments outside it, had the potential to create more or less permanent arrangements *de facto* out of *ad hoc* partnership activity. That change had been prompted by necessity. The same requirement for self-interest also dictated that one of the purposes of structural adaptation was to meet the demand for partnership. It was no longer an ideal position to make commitments to partnership. This was not altruism. The constructed realist history of post-1945 Western Europe had already demonstrated the benefits, in face of a real and present threat, of forming not merely temporary alliance, but genuine partnership, requiring responsibility and commitment. The need to preserve order and stability in the international system as the twentieth century passed into the twenty-first meant new engagements. Even where these required the use of destructive force, as involvement in former Yugoslavia, then Afghanistan and Iraq demonstrated all too clearly, they also required partnership to secure situations and strengthen the quality of statehood and governance, beginning with the security sector, once major armed conflict was over. However, the security imperative was not only to use partnership to stabilize post-conflict zones, but also to secure, foster, or create stability by engaging in a web of partnerships. There was a need to deal with situations before it became too late. In some cases, as is argued in the following chapter, this would require pre-emptive use of force, following which continuing engagement through partnership would be necessary. However, in others, perhaps the majority, the relevant action to take before matters got out of hand would be a commitment to assistance and partnership. If stability were to be maintained, order preserved and interests protected, there had to be a widespread commitment to engagement and partnership around the world – for all those with a vested interest in Western security, although above all for the US.

Developments within the Alliance, such as European Security and Defence, coupled to those with partners under the Partnership Council, might well organically create a situation in which European countries would face the question of membership simply because it made functional sense. If a country's partners in the EU were making use of NATO assets and said country were engaged with those partners and in effect using those assets, it could make sense to that country to join. If a country were *de facto* co-operating in partnership in such a variety of ways that it had become *de facto* involved in membership and even in a *de facto* commitment to defence, although it had no legal or formal alliance, it might be reasonable to pose the question rhetorically, 'Why not join?' (Of course, the same *de facto* position might be reasoned in the opposite direction: given the *de facto* position, why bother to make it *de jure*?)

In this case, there could be serious questions for a country such as Sweden where many people in the security policy establishment favoured joining NATO during the 1990s, but politically could see Sweden doing so only if Article 5 of the Washington Treaty were to be changed – a change that was out of the question. Yet a Euroatlantic Partnership Council, European Security and Defence Force, or some other *ad hoc* arrangement could place Sweden in a position where it would have at least an equal obligation, in practice, to that which it would have had, in principle, as a member of the Alliance. It was in this way that the agricultural evolution of NATO structures was an issue determining the future of the organization.

The potential blurring of lines between membership and non-membership and the issue of Article 5 commitment were related to the definition of 'defence'. The redefinition of defence was central to the formation of a new strategic concept by the Alliance. The concept was to have been a major item on the agenda of the Washington Summit. The thrust of the new concept turned on a re-orientation of purpose and a redefinition of defence. The nature of that redefinition and the purposes of the Alliance had to bind the allies and harmonize relations between the two sides of the Atlantic. It also had to go beyond traditional notions of collective defence to embrace a wider role in maintaining international stability. Stabilization required partnership and pre-emption. And while the former, discussed in this chapter, might seem more obviously associated with the Clinton era and the latter, covered in the final chapter, a product of the Bush Administration, there is, as Robert Kagan has noted, considerable continuity.[1]

# Productive Partnership and Constructive Engagement

NATO's transformation in the 1990s demonstrated that concerns with stability would dominate its future – whether or not the pace of change remained so great as it had been. The Alliance had marked its fiftieth birthday by transformation from a collective defence arrangement to a military-political club with assets and partners. Aside from engagement in South-Eastern Europe, its evolution was being shaped by factors such as functional and organizational adaptation, the nature and concept of defence, and the various relationships involved, between the allies, old and new, and various partners, as evolution continued and NATO enlarged. It was the way in which these issues developed which would then shape the longer-term future of the Alliance.[2]

The key task for those working to conceptualize NATO's strategic future was to maintain Alliance cohesion and coherence. There was a need to incorporate the needs and interests of each member. But new strategic approaches also had to encompass the vital interest of each member in sustaining the Alliance itself. This included preserving its credibility as an instrument of deterrence and, by definition, as an actor on the international stage. If it could not, or would not, act when necessary, NATO's status as market leader in security affairs would be corroded and its deterrent power would be doomed.

In terms of the major member of the Alliance, the understanding of the purposes and ways in which defence should be understood was clear from statements by US Secretary of State Madeleine Albright in *Foreign Affairs* and again in the US State Department's *Dispatch* regarding the need for 'productive partnerships' and 'constructive ends'.[3] This understanding followed the logic of the line taken by the UK Strategic Defence Review during 1997–8.[4] It was extended and explicitly matched with 'principle' as the most important strand of US security strategy by Secretary of State Colin Powell.[5] In line with changes in the world, this effectively meant new definitions of defence. While the British and American views noted here could not be regarded as definitive for the Alliance as a whole, they provided an outline of the elements that needed to be part of such a redefinition and found support in capitals such as Madrid and Rome.

The approach adopted in the Strategic Defence Review took as its starting point the removal of any direct threat of attack on the UK with the end of the Cold War and the need to remove the straightjacket that the Cold War had imposed on strategic thinking. It then went on effectively to define the threat to the UK, as to all similar countries in a modern, interdependent world, as instability: national security and prosperity were said to depend on 'stability, freedom and economic development'.

This understanding reflected the change resulting from a series of events in the early 1990s, following the end of the Cold War. These catalysed a process of creating new layers of stability in the international system, thereby demonstrating the nature of international order built through overlapping layers and interdependent actors. A series of random encounters between critical situations and an international environment locked together by strata of order and depending on stability generated rapid and radical change. (See chapter 2.) From the Iraqi invasion of Kuwait and the subsequent Kurdish crisis in northern Iraq, through the international engagement in Bosnia, Somalia, Rwanda, Haiti and Angola, to the most radical changes regarding Libya, as well as the creation of the international criminal tribunals for former Yugoslavia and Rwanda, the September 11 attacks and beyond, the world, particularly the Western Allies, recognized the reality of interdependent order and formed new layers of international peace and security.

With the basic position of the state within the international system firmly secured, the reality of international security became the need to limit the disorder essentially within the boundaries of those states. What some saw as a growth in armed conflict and disorder was really only a shift in focus. With direct action by one state against another unlikely to cause disruption in the international system, emphasis was inevitably placed on other sources of instability.

It was vital for the Western democracies to preserve the stability upon which their interdependent physical, political, economic and normative well-being relied. While the need for stability characterized the international system broadly, regarding the protection of the state from outside aggression, it was undoubtedly the case that order in some parts of the world, or aspects of life, would be more important for the preservation of stability than others. Thus disorder in the Euroatlantic region and on its periphery was more likely to oblige Western countries to take action to maintain order than, as it turned out, disruption in Central Africa. This did not mean, however, that order in Africa did not matter and could not have impact. And it certainly did not mean that security in the Middle East or Asia would not matter. It was important that there was emphasis on consolidation of the state and the management of non-state-specific challenges to international peace and security.

The role of defence was to assist in the management of stability. Defence was defence against instability. Thus it was the risks to stability which required attention: the break-up and the break-down of states and concomitant conflict, both inter-communal and across borders, terrorism, international crime, human rights abuses, the spread of Weapons of Mass Destruction and the behaviour of so-called 'rogue states', among other things. The risks, challenges and threats in all of these lay in the fact that the consequences of them 'may spread dramatically in an ever more interdependent world'.[6] In short, the experience of Western countries demonstrates that there may be apparently low priority questions, which, in reality, strike at the heart of security policy needs. The fulfilment of any one state's security policy requirement is a function of the credible and efficient operation of a collective body as a whole.

Defence was no longer solely, or primarily, a question of homeland protection from massive physical threat, whether a conventional invasion, or nuclear attack. It was a matter of responsible contributions to the maintenance of international peace and security, which would also serve to limit the growing inevitability of physical attacks of an occasional, unconventional and terrorist type. Above all, for NATO, this meant in Europe and on its periphery. But, in line with US needs, NATO's role did not have to be exclusive to Europe and its periphery – indeed, given the internationalized character of security challenges facing the West, it probably could not be. Moreover, in addition to dealing with those who posed physical threats to peace and stability, it was vital that countries such as the US, the UK and their allies should uphold the ethics and values upon which their societies were based. Not to do so would be to concede democracy's high ground to those who would undermine it and to risk internal corrosion. The allies had to be true to themselves.

The vision offered by US Secretary of State Albright and by the UK Strategic Defence Review was one in which the links between stronger countries were reinforced, while transitional and weak ones were assisted, in effect, because their instability could contaminate the broader economic and political stability on which the prosperity and security of the stronger countries depended. And it meant dealing with states and non-state actors that disrupted order. In Secretary Albright's words, the US was 'seeking, through relentless diplomacy

and tough law enforcement, to create a multi-layered web of agreements, laws, inspectors, police and military power to deny weapons
and operating room to terrorists, criminals and aggressors'.[7] This was
perhaps a more pronounced definition of the *de facto* defence requirement than the British version, but conceptually it was very close. At
the same time, the concept embraced the needs of Germany and other
Alliance members in Central and Eastern Europe, as well as those of
France, Spain and Italy in Southern Europe.

Defence has proved to be a far more evenly achievable way of
fostering democracy than across the broad economic-democratic
spectrum in countries in transition. At the beginning of the 1990s,
all talk was of the former communist countries joining the EU, and
there was no question of their joining the Alliance. That question was
turned on its head by the NATO decision announced in Madrid,
on 10 July 1997, to invite three countries to begin accession talks –
Hungary, Poland and the Czech Republic. It had come to be understood that the EU required extensive progress across a whole range
of socio-economic issues, whereas defence constituted one narrow
aspect of public life. However, precisely because it is a narrow aspect,
it can be used to catalyse progress in other areas: encouraging democratic control of defence policy has been a spur to democratization in
other fields.

The emphasis on democratization of defence and the role of
co-operation in providing security also made a contribution to
the conceptualization of security and defence. Thought was already
directed to this question in NATO before the Washington Summit of
April 1999. This was largely stifled because of events over Kosovo.
But this did not remove the issue. A strategic concept for NATO had
to be one that was appropriate for the EU and vice versa. In terms of
the understanding of security and the meaning of defence, there had
to be further change in both quarters. The UK Strategic Defence
Review of 1997–8 had already indicated the importance of international stability and order for countries such as the UK. What was
true for London was true for all members of the EU and NATO, as
well as for their partners and associates across Europe. Productive partnerships, working towards constructive ends, constituted the essence
of security, not just using armed forces to bomb those who had been
disruptive of order and stability. A key purpose of armed forces, in
conjunction with other means, was to foster security and stability. In
this context, there was a range of security questions beyond armed
conflict, including terrorism, organized crime, borders and boundaries, to address.

In the near and medium term, the assets of the Alliance were destined to continue to be used to foster peace and stability in Europe, both through co-operation and exercises and, where necessary, through the mounting of operations, involving those members and partners willing to engage responsibly in the maintenance of international peace and security in evolutionary ways, including in a global context. Bosnia and Hercegovina and, especially, Kosovo were the long-term focus for this. Yet, whatever the near- and medium-term prospects for NATO, it was also necessary to recognize that, fifty years before the Washington Summit of 1999 and the Kosovo conflict, nobody could have imagined where NATO would be at that point – in terms of membership, scope or roles. Imagining NATO in another fifty years was probably beyond the capacities of anyone, as was the ability to forecast the circumstances which would require further evolution. However, it was certainly possible to shape NATO's continuing evolution as a vehicle for partnership and constructive action in European and international security. This would facilitate political and military evolution in the Alliance, accommodating present and future needs for both sides of the transatlantic relationship. This was the material of productive partnerships for creative ends.

## Partnership, Engagement and Stability

The West cannot defend itself with walls. It is generally not feasible to create the type of border that Spain has with Morocco at Ceuta and Melilla, with big walls and barbed wire, fortification and a large no-man's land, and to expect to achieve security. A border of this kind is not possible because security lies ultimately through inclusion, co-operation and trade – through aspects of partnership and holding out the hands of friendship. Security policy requirements are broader than narrow homeland defence and territorial integrity, vital though these are. They also involve formal and *de facto* commitments, as well as the promotion and protection of interests, values and influence. Thus commitment to partners, allies and the forums for common policy forms a second level for security policy and the promotion and protection of interests, values and influence constitutes a third level (including the vital question of the merit of the partnerships and alliances themselves, as well as the organizational forms they take – over Bosnia, for example, it seemed that unless NATO acted decisively, its own 'value' would be diminished). At this level the use and projection of armed forces may be to secure influence on an issue. The evidence of the 1990s indicates that harmonization of commitment to partners, allies and bodies is necessary because there is every chance that there will be questions and challenges which will require attention.

Partnership and engagement developed successfully to stabilize the European continent during the 1990s. The big test was South-Eastern Europe, where both NATO and the EU made a substantial commitment to seeking an end to the Yugoslav War. This has created such an enormous strategic stake for both the Brussels-based organizations that success is vital – and for both, one major measure of that success will be the degree to which these countries emerging from conflict are brought into the fold as partners and quite probably, eventually, as members. There remain issues to be resolved, even if there is not a major return to armed hostilities. The prospect of partnership with the EU and that of eventual accession, as well as co-operation and partnership and eventual membership of NATO, is vital to carrying forward that process. The strategic claim that has been placed on that region is such that there can be no acceptance of failure. But neither can there be any expectation of overnight or early success for NATO or the EU. Yet if they cannot pull it off, then it will eventually corrupt both of those groups, undermining the essence of each of them. Failure would be a sign of their limitations and weaknesses, which would in turn presage a falling away of attachment to the ideas that bind them together in Union and Alliance. That means making a full and proper commitment to creating polities and societies which are fit for co-operation with, and possible membership of, NATO and the EU. There is no real alternative here. The only question is over how long they will take to do it, bearing in mind that the Brussels bodies could afford to take a very long time (and indeed have no alternative, as there are no quick fixes), yet they cannot afford to extend the process indefinitely if any sense of credibility is to be retained. This mission involves the war-affected lands of what was the Socialist Federative Republic of Yugoslavia, including Macedonia, and also Albania, which was not part of the Yugoslav federation, but is implicated in that situation.

Partnership is central also to NATO's achieving success in its major peace implementation operations in South-Eastern Europe. The measure of NATO's success will not be withdrawal. NATO is not going to withdraw; it could not afford to do so and nor could the EU. The point will come when the commitment is transformed from being one of peace implementation, prepared to act against parties obstructing the peace process or stepping out of line, to one of partnership. This is exactly in line with the whole thrust of NATO since the early 1990s.

It would be a general benefit if the key mission of the EU were to bring in the war-affected countries of South-Eastern Europe and to make them partners, worthy collaborators, rather than recalcitrant, awkward, challenging recidivists.

In Kosovo, as in Bosnia and Hercegovina, this meant a fifteen-year programme that would come to include partnership activities with NATO and its members aimed at strengthening relations with the Alliance. Thus, Alliance engagement in Bosnia and Hercegovina and in Kosovo had to include the prospect of co-operation through Partnership for Peace, the Euroatlantic Partnership Council, and even potential membership. To facilitate this activity, moreover, a commitment was needed to create the conditions for prosperity and the possibility of a normal life for the people of South-Eastern Europe. This activity would be central to the development of the Alliance over the first decade and a half of the twenty-first century. It would be a manifestation of NATO's future. And it was likely to be replicated in other parts of the world – Afghanistan, where a commitment was made in 2003 and, at later stages, quite likely the Middle East.

NATO's mission to create peace in South-Eastern Europe has had two significant aspects about which it is important to have a clear and correct understanding. First, engagement in South-Eastern Europe has not been NATO's only mission since the end of the Cold War; no one should underestimate the importance of PfP in terms of security and stability in Europe, as it developed through the 1990s and was then enhanced by EAPC. Without PfP there could have been other Croatias and Bosnias in other parts of Europe – for example, it might well be that it was PfP, in conjunction with other aspects of international action, that saved, say, Estonia and Latvia, with many comparable conditions, from a similar fate in the mid-1990s. The role played in this context by PfP should not be underestimated, because it brought NATO and EU armed forces – and with them a political-security connection – into a relationship with those countries that had a stabilizing effect. This, as well as complementary activities of the Organisation on Security and Co-operation in Europe (OSCE) and especially the EU at the time, all helped to foster stability in what was an uncertain situation.

Having identified the Baltic states as a special case and a test in terms of relations with Russia, and with the Baltic states pressing for membership, it was necessary to address the Baltic question in some way. Yet immediate accession would not be popular with many allies, given the position regarding Russia. In principle, there could be no reason not to include the Baltic states. After all, if Russia had ill intention towards them, it would be the right thing to do. Yet, if Russia were well disposed towards Tallin, Riga and Vilnius, it could not, in the end, do any harm or make any difference if they were to join the Alliance. Of course, the reality was that Russia objected and that many of the existing members remained reluctant to adopt a measure which might be taken as deeply provocative in Moscow. In terms of defence, this made little real difference, as NATO engagement in the Baltic states through partner initiatives made the prospect of direct Russian intervention unrealistic, although it provoked Russian counter-engagement and, in the longer term, might be a source of tension for the Alliance. Despite its relative weakness in 1999, Russia remained a major military power and a potential threat. Partnership possibly offered more in the way of actual defensive capability than being a signatory to a treaty.

If the Baltics were a 'special case', Ukraine is a particular challenge for partnership. It is the one country regarded as being large and important, requiring attention, but for which no defined approach has been found. Ukraine's relationship to Russia cannot be ignored, but that relationship should not dominate understanding and interpretation of Ukraine and its position. It is a big country, one that really ought to be like France or Germany, in terms of its size, human resources, communications, and both agricultural and industrial capacity (albeit with a need to modernize). It is one of the greatest failures of the post-Cold War era that neither the Ukrainians themselves nor outsiders have been – or appear likely to be – able to turn the country round and nurture its potential. There is reason to treat Ukraine in a special way. This is something Ukraine recognizes in its demands, but does little to justify, causing considerable frustration amongst EU and NATO representatives. It may well be that only an explicit promise of eventual membership of the EU or NATO, if Ukraine fulfils the appropriate criteria, will be enough to spur Kiev on to achieve objectives that are more or less agreed across the political spectrum. While there are 'Soviet' sympathies in segments of the population and while the integrated Soviet legacy in some respects (notably economic) cannot be overlooked, and while Moscow sometimes casts the possessive shadow of a jilted lover (making Kiev uncomfortable), these elements cannot be taken to define Ukraine. Ukraine's underlying orientation is towards the West and towards Europe, even where some legacies of the Soviet era remain and some elements politically and socially still turn more to Russia. It is clear that eastward enlargement of EU and NATO Europe will find a frontier with Ukraine that cannot become a barrier. Thus there will be no alternative to embracing Kiev and seeking to assure its future as an 'insider-outsider'. Perhaps just as NATO established a special relationship with Ukraine, the EU might arrange a particular partnership arrangement, rather than just whatever kind of Partnership and Cooperation Agreement there might be already.[8] It is likely that more than existing arrangements would be required to accommodate Ukraine's singular status, even though senior figures in Kiev may be reconciled to the realities of this in-between status.

The NATO–Russia Council provides a significant forum for the type of co-operation that might be required. However, over the medium and long term, to have any real significance, the problems that dogged its predecessor – the Permanent Joint Council, established in 1997 (ironically, not so permanent) – and most other aspects of Western co-operation with Moscow on security affairs would need to be overcome. These were a lack of Russian engagement and distrust – with the latter no doubt causing the former to some extent. With many in the Moscow security sector still affected by Cold War attitudes, even gaining negative responses to Western initiatives was often impossible. Sceptical Soviet-hangover attitudes also affected the Permanent Joint Council, as well as a Russian sense of betrayal over matters such as Iraq or Kosovo. Those attitudes were vital in determining Moscow's approach, which saw NATO as no more than a mirror of the old Warsaw Pact and read relations both in and with the Alliance accordingly: only Washington, DC, counted, as the other allies were mere puppets (a view tempered only by the acknowledgement of a separate German agenda regarding economic matters, whether independently or in the context of the EU).[9] Once there was distrust of the US – which, *inter alia*, was cemented the moment Moscow realized that the Permanent Joint Council would not give it a real say in what NATO did – this body, as well as broad co-operation on security, evaporated.

In that context, there was significant space for the EU to develop relations with Russia, especially from Moscow's side, based on the notion that Germany had a separate economic agenda, to be exercised through the EU. However, whatever small progress could be made in that regard was transformed by September 11. The Islamist attacks on New York and Virginia provided an immediate and somewhat revolutionary catalyst, not only in US perceptions of the world, but crucially in the relationship with Moscow. Primarily in the intelligence sphere, there was a breakthrough in contacts and sharing of information between Moscow and Washington. This put the focus back more than ever on the US–Russia relationship, with NATO a notable context for that relationship and having some significance in terms of the NATO–Russia Council (but even that was seen by Moscow, in a sense, as a bilateral relationship, not as 19 plus 1). As a consequence – especially in the absence of any particular, meaningful or coherent EU policy towards Russia – Brussels became relatively unimportant for Russia, leaving a major strategic hole for the EU and perhaps also for Moscow. Yet, if the EU were to deepen and develop its security policy, a strategic partnership with Russia, or at least a strategic initiative towards it, would be needed – and something of this kind would be required simply to deal with relationships across new EU–Russia borders established by enlargement.

EU engagement in the Caucasus complemented any US or NATO military initiatives there and, to a lesser extent, Central Asia. Georgia was, perhaps, the largely unnoticed signifier for both NATO and EU security policy into the future, especially in terms of relations with Russia. At the time of writing, there has been implicit competition between some Western countries (whether EU or NATO) and the Russian Federation – and possibly other actors in Georgia. This is an issue relevant to future energy and resource questions for all involved. Until the US commitment to train Georgian troops to hunt groups linked to al-Qa'ida, said to be in the country, associated with Chechen armed groups already pursued in violation of Georgia's sovereignty by Russian forces, former Soviet states of this kind were regarded as within Russia's sphere of influence and hegemony. This was punctured by the arrival of US troops.

The arrival of 290 US military personnel in Georgia at the end of February 2002 to provide training and assistance was a significant marker regarding the boundaries of European and international security. It broke a taboo – troops from a NATO country were trespassing on the ghost of the Soviet Union and the shadow of its Russian successor. Breaking this taboo was an outrage to many in Russia, with ideas of Moscow's near abroad infringed – although President Vladimir Putin showed greater cool and diplomacy than others in Moscow by welcoming the initiative to temper international Islamist terrorism – thus giving the signal to others over what the party line should be. There was little prospect of disengagement by the US – rather, this was the initial step of a likely increase in NATO and EU involvement in Georgia, given that a Western presence would continue and that, to continue, it would inevitably need to grow in order to support itself.

This involves a fairly simple strategic logic: if co-operation between US and Russian forces emerged in Georgia, then engagement would need to continue and be enhanced, including through involvement of other allies and partners, as well as complementary measures by the EU, to ensure that a positive relationship was cemented; and if there were to be competition, then equally there would be an imperative to remain engaged, not to concede the Western interest in Georgian security and return to the *status quo ante*, which would be regarded as a victory for forces in Moscow hostile to good relations with the West. The mission against international terrorism was also, it must be recognized, part of the underlying competition between Moscow and Western capitals over the fate, status and ultimately security and stability of countries lying beyond the boundaries of the Western organizational sphere. That sphere, defined primarily by NATO and the EU, even after enlargement in the first decade of the twenty-first century, would not necessarily stretch so far as Tbilisi, the Georgian capital. However, there would ultimately have to be limits of some kind to Euroatlantic enlargement; but when those limits were clear, there would still be a need to foster conditions of peace, security and stability beyond them.

Georgia might appear to be that little bit too far beyond the borders of EU and NATO enlargement to be an immediate focus for frontier and stability issues – even with an understanding that frontiers will inevitably be fuzzy, in some way. Yet there is a need to think several steps ahead, to whichever one it is that embraces Georgia and its neighbours. The logic of Western security needs, which has driven the record of partnership and enlargement, confirms that there is no alternative to moving in the direction of further investment, engagement, partnership and even, eventually, enlargement. This plays into a range of issues concerning the nature of security and stability across the whole of the European sphere. The limits of that sphere – that is, the boundaries of the West – are not, as noted elsewhere, constituted by any geographical points, but are focused around the spread of values and almost certainly the emergence of a security community must be based on those values.

This logic extends beyond the boundaries of NATO and the EU. In North Africa, of course, despite the pressures on it, attempting to maintain a hard border of this kind is easier (although it is not welcome to say so) because of the European–Arab divide and implicit racism. Even so, there must be doubts over how sustainable such a border is in the long term. There must even be a question, in the very long term, over whether the logic of the EU is for parts, or even the whole, of North Africa to join, one day. Indeed Morocco, reflecting the logic of the situation regarding the Spanish sovereign territories, as well as its generally pro-Western pro-European position, has raised this possibility, but has received no encouragement, as yet, from the EU. If the initial rationale for the creation of the EU and for its subsequent enlargement, in terms of inclusion and security, is followed, there is an underlying strategic logic that suggests Moroccan accession and possibly that of other North African countries at some point. The presence of Spain's sovereign territories on the North African coast lends the central dynamic here, although, as the inclusion of Cyprus and Malta in 2004, as well as the existing membership of the United Kingdom and the Republic of Ireland, in the EU indicates, the presence of a sea does not disturb the logic of enlargement.

The strategic and security rationales that underpin both the EU and its enlargement indicate that the EU might have to devise its own equivalent to NATO's PfP, while that programme itself may have to be extended beyond the OSCE region.[10] This would need to be an 'in-between' arrangement which fostered stability by creating a framework for outsiders who wish to have a closer relationship and for whom the partnership arrangement will make them feel that little bit nearer to being insiders. The essence is to create a partnership arrangement that serves to turn the EU inside out, by bringing the outside at least part of the way in. And what applies in Europe, for the countries and organizations there, might equally apply in other parts of the world – in Asia, for example, for Australia, New Zealand, Japan and other Western-oriented countries with a vested interest in promoting stability through partnership.

# Strategic Flexibility: Operational and Political

Questions remained, despite the common benefit of this vision of security, about the scope of NATO's role. This served to emphasize the differences between allies and to beget arguments. These arguments could be broadly defined as the US versus the others, with the possible exception of the UK, as Iraq exemplified. However, it was in the interests of both the US and the Europeans to accommodate mutual needs. This meant accepting political and operational compromises to permit use of NATO assets by some members of the club, but not to require all of them to participate. For the US this approach meant the use of political assets, above all. For the Europeans, over time, it would primarily mean use of strategic military assets.

There were a number of issues, in this context, aside from future enlargement, which contributed to the spread of stability. These included the following: nuclear doctrine, NATO's responsibility beyond the European theatre for dealing with the proliferation of Weapons of Mass Destruction and the challenges posed by 'rogues', as well as the role of nuclear weapons. The threat of the spread of WMD/I was not a purely European question, it was a global one, as was that of 'rogues', whether state actors, or non-state actors, disrupting the order essential to modern international life. All of this required attention.

The US, as a global power, cannot avoid these questions, while some Europeans want to focus on more parochial European issues. However, the global problems that Washington could not avoid were ones that it preferred to tackle in partnership, rather than alone. This was true whether the issue was disciplining rogue states such as Saddam Hussein's Iraq, or Slobodan Milošević's Serbia, managing Weapons of Mass Destruction and proliferation issues, or dealing with non-state terrorist actors, or nuclear doctrine.

In terms of the role of nuclear weapons in the Alliance, while reductions were made by all three nuclear states (the US, the UK and France), there were still pressures from other countries to change nuclear doctrine in the Alliance, given that the end of the Cold War effectively removed the old requirement for deterrence. Canada strongly promoted the adoption of a non-first-use policy. Given the potential flaws in such a policy, there was no chance that any of the existing nuclear countries in the Alliance would accept it.

A commitment to non-first use would at best be an ambiguous contribution to stability. The credibility of any threat to use such weapons in relation to proliferators, where there might be a case for deterrence, would be compromised, while there would always be uncertainty and distrust as to whether the commitment would be honoured. This could only reduce stability. At the same time, in the event of a situation of rising tension, a return to the possibility of first use might be needed, but the escalatory impact would be enormous. In the interests of maintaining the significant layer of equilibrium that emerged over fifty years of nuclear deterrence and management, it was better to maintain an arrangement that would maximize security.

While the nuclear part of the strategic concept for the most part depended on the possessor states, other dimensions were equally important, but required more harmonization. The US wanted to bring its allies on board, as well as its partners, in dealing with problems such as proliferation and counter-terrorism – in part to share the burden, in part because US leaders knew that it could be a strategic weakness to act without support at home and that support at home generally approved of action on a multilateral basis, rather than action that was unilateral. Specialized research revealed that the US public had no problem supporting use of the country's armed forces, including the deployment of ground forces, when three specific conditions applied: that the public had a clear sense that there was a point to the action; that the US was not acting alone; and that, ideally, the US should contribute around one-quarter of any force being sent into action.

While the last of these factors was less important than the others, it was a clear indication of Washington's need to ensure that it had partners when it took the responsibility to use armed force to foster stability. This was crucial in light of the need for political and popular support. It was striking that the US public was wary of engaging the country's armed forces where there was not support from other countries. Evidence in particular regarding US participation in Bosnia and Hercegovina showed that the greater the public perception that the US was acting with others, the far greater the degree of support for that action. The same research showed that the optimal contribution the American public thought the country should make was around one-quarter: an overwhelming 78 per cent of respondents supported 25 per cent participation in the NATO-led SFOR operation in Bosnia and Hercegovina (as it happens, the actual level of the US contribution). The same research found that the mean level among the US public was marginally below this, yet closely in line, at 23 per cent. Similarly, the research found that support for US action would be at least 10 percentage points higher where the US was not acting alone. A further finding was that the perception of success was also a significant factor.[11] Thus for the US to have political legitimacy in its actions domestically, it had to be seen by the American public to have political legitimacy internationally through the support and partnership of others. It is noteworthy, in this context, that in the spate of predominantly US attacks against Iraq at the beginning of 1999, President William J. Clinton repeatedly mentioned UK Prime Minister Tony Blair and the UK role in joint action – even waiting until Blair, in London, had made the initial announcement of attacks, before lending the voice and might of the US in support. Similarly, President George W. Bush was keen to be pictured in the White House Rose Garden, surrounded by the flags of seventeen countries operating in the US-led coalition in Afghanistan, as well as representatives from those countries. This was visual evidence that the US was not alone. And over Iraq, US Secretary of State Colin Powell was keen to emphasize that twenty-nine countries were involved in coalition operations – even though the overwhelming bulk of the force came from the US and the UK and only two other countries registered at all sizeable contributions (Australia and Poland – and President Bush was keen to mention those countries, too).

For the US, NATO's strategic approach had to support Washington's necessary military engagement in the world. In doing so, it would invoke the support of some members in the NATO club, politically and operationally, to use the strategic assets where appropriate, for operations beyond the traditional Euroatlantic region. If the US was to meet its global responsibilities, then it needed allies and partners in order to be legitimate in the eyes of its own people. To be able to act to protect its interests and values, the US needed NATO. One of those interests was Washington's maintenance of NATO as its vital channel of influence in Europe, the most important region in the world for US strategic and economic interests. For the Europeans, conversely, the American presence continued to be a vital stabilizing and enabling factor in the fabric of international security, even if some of them seemed temporarily unaware of this, at certain moments.

Over time, a continuing commitment to collective defence of territory supplemented by a more important commitment to a wider notion of defence focused on the maintenance of international stability would enable harmonization of US and European positions, giving the US more scope in its membership of NATO and the Europeans more capability to underpin the long-term project of inevitable integration. For the US, such an approach was the best way to facilitate its global role and spread the weight of responsibility. For the Europeans, as the UK had realized in its commitment at the end of 1998 to being at the heart of developing the European Security and Defence Initiative, a NATO based on balanced relations and a strategic concept that addressed the needs of stability offered the best way of maintaining the Euroatlantic link and preparing the Alliance for the future.

Much in the twenty-first century would depend on the outcome of discussions on new approaches to defence and the roles that flowed from them in connection with the new strategic approach. This entailed a broader role for the Alliance, commensurate with its organizational evolution, to make those productive partnerships formed in and around NATO have the constructive ends of making Europe, its periphery and the world as a whole more secure, more stable and, as far as possible, more peaceful. Where there were regions of stability, such as North America, Europe and Japan, these had to be preserved and enhanced. Where there was instability, this had to be addressed. The more it affected international life in those regions of stability, the more this was the case. Where there were actors disrupting order, they would have to be contained and combatted. The safety and the stability of Western countries depended on the strength of NATO to respond actively to challenges to stability that, inevitably, undermined the security and prosperity of free and open societies and economies.

Equally, its members needed the Alliance to engage through enlargement and co-operation in promoting peace and strength in the fabric of Western and, more generally, international society. The need was for an organizing principle that allowed for flexible use of Alliance assets by some members, possibly with partners, but without necessarily including every NATO member. There was a need to empower the West and its partners to be discriminating in their treatment of problems of instability and threats to the peace.

There was no doubt that the same issues of stability and security that impelled enlargement of the EU and NATO and partnership arrangements would be present wherever, exactly, the borders of the West fell at any particular moment. The sense of 'inside' and 'outside', already strong for countries engaged in accession talks with the EU and the Alliance, would be reinforced as the boundary of 'the West' as a geographical, political and security space was explored. That exploration was to be made against the backdrop of the need for those inside both to preserve their internal strength by not spreading themselves too thinly, but also to protect themselves on the outside by promoting democratic transition: economic and social stability, as well as security. This was the hub of a Constructivist and of a Realist approach – whether in Europe, the Middle East, Asia, Africa, the Americas, or the Pacific, the only way to seek to preserve peace and security was engagement through partnership, above all in the sphere of defence.

There could be no simple and direct approach to this issue. But the security rationale and strategic logic that underpinned both the origins of the EU and its repeated enlargements indicate that political values and security, rather than geography, define the scope and limits of Western security. Organizational evolution in NATO and the EU, particularly the development of PfP, the EAPC and a European defence capability, reflected the need to foster stability by creating a framework for 'outsiders' who wish it to have a closer relationship and to feel that little nearer to being 'insiders' – that is, part of the Western security realm. Whichever dimension of Western security is involved, there is a logic that means there is no necessary point at which partnership and enlargement stop, or at least there is a very big question about identifying the point at which they can stop. In the twenty-first-century world, threats come from all corners and strata of international order, and only partnership and engagement wherever necessary can limit or even prevent threats. Partnership will promote stability and serve the interests of the West and its individual countries and peoples. However, this partnership, engagement and enlargement may not be enough. Some problems require a different approach – the hostile use of armed force in defence of those same peoples and their ways of life. This means a shift to pre-emption – the theme of the final chapter.

# 7 PRE-EMPTION

Approaches to defence by Western states have evolved to meet contemporary needs. The emphasis is on proaction and engagement to foster peace and stability. Partnership and co-operation, as well as various military commitments short of war, marked a significant shift in strategic concepts, in the post-Cold War period. The degree of stable stratification in the Western world, involving considerable co-operation and an apparent de-emphasis on borders, has to be protected. The optimal way to achieve this concurs with the approach taken by the major Western countries, starting (albeit sometimes unenthusiastically) with America, and the major Western security organizations, NATO and the EU, as they adapted to export stability to Central and Eastern Europe through partnership and enlargement. At the same time, they explored new forms of partnership between the two organizations and their various members, with increasing responsibility in some areas for the European side in the Euroatlantic security relationship – although there was awkwardness, suspicion and resentment at times. Nonetheless, this approach was adopted and began to be expanded beyond the European theatre into the Middle East and Asia. However, there has been considerably greater reluctance to accept a similar, but equally appropriate, necessary – and indeed, complementary – transformation of the approach to self-defence. The re-conceptualization of defence that took place did not address that part of the equation where states, individually or collectively, might find themselves needing to use hostile force to protect themselves, in circumstances where there was no action by the UN Security Council – that is, the notion of self-defence.

The impact of the September 11 attacks indicated even more clearly than was previously the case that there was a vested interest in order and stability, which could easily be disrupted by such action. Earlier understanding of this had prompted the new approach taken to 'threats to international peace and security' in the 1990s, when the first ever summit meeting of the Heads of State and Government of the UN Security Council formally reinterpreted the meaning of that term. The term 'threat to international peace and security' is the gateway to formal, binding decisions and resolutions in international law when invoked by the Security Council, as discussed in chapter 3. That radic-ally altered approach reflected the need to align the concept with the realities of the world, not those of the preceding 300 years, for which it had been developed. However, the authority of the UN Security Council to address 'threats to international peace and security' was only one pillar regarding the use of armed force in the international system. The other was self-defence, which fell to the states in the system themselves. When the Security Council redefined the meaning of the first of these pillars, enlarging the scope both of what it covered and of the responses that might be made to that wider range of threats, a conceptual gap, or lag, was created regarding this second pillar.[1] If the nature of the threats posed required a new definition of threats to international peace and security and the possibilities for using force, then commensurate change in the scope of the right to self-defence was a logical corollary. The scope of the right to self-defence had to change conceptually, but this was not addressed. At the time of writing, it has still barely received the attention required – and as much as there has been attention, this came only after the September 11 attacks and the responses to them, and subsequent developments gave empirical indicators of that conceptual gap.

This is the theme of the final chapter of this book, in which I argue that, following the logic of the redefinition of threats to international peace and security by the UN during the 1990s and the US response to the September 11 attacks and beyond, the West and the world must radically reinterpret the concept of self-defence. And it is important to be clear that this is about defence, not humanitarian intervention, nor some more nebulous 'duty to prevent' – although the latter, adapted from the 'duty to protect' concept developed in the UN's Brahimi Report, at least acknowledges the issues of threat and order, and de-fending against instability.[2] To use humanitarian intervention or even a duty to prevent to cover those things that threaten Western security would be to discredit and devalue the emergent value of the former and the potential of the latter. The issue is not a responsibility to do good deeds. It is to defend. This is an approach that many will find controversial, uncomfortable and hard to accept.[3] But the traditional conceptualization of self-defence – response to an armed attack by a state on a state – appears to be out of date. The present chapter argues that pre-emption is required. It is both necessary and inevitable at some stage, but a move in this direction is not without problems. The chapter considers the Iraq events of 2003, where the shadow of pre-emption was present, though not pre-emption itself. It then outlines and explores the imperatives for a change to pre-emptive self-defence, which make a move in that direction both necessary and inevitable. However, such a move is not without significant problems, in terms of the traditional notions of immediacy, necessity and proportionality, as well as in terms of intelligence and evidence issues, and issues of legitimacy. These areas are considered in the following section, which also offers initial suggestions regarding how appropriate parameters might be set to ensure a suitable legal-political framework for pre-emption.

to p 125

## Iraq 2003: The Basis for Action and the Shadow of Pre-emption

With Afghanistan still unfinished business – if nothing else, the fate of Usama bin Ladin (UBL) remained to be settled – Washington's sights moved on to target Iraq. Those sights passed over Somalia, where al-Qa'ida bases remained, but were dormant. They also passed over Yemen, where al-Qa'ida remained active and strong, but where the previously less accommodating government had decided to serve its narrow self-preserving self-interest and co-operate with the US against the UBL network operating widely within the country. With US engagement in Georgia and the Philippines, and with Syria, Iran, North Korea and other places emerging as issues, there was a growing movement to set the world 'right' in order to protect and preserve the West, above all, the US.[4] Initially, this received fairly comprehensive international support after September 11 (or at least acquiescence). However, by 2003, any chance of holding onto any kind of consensus ran into the troubled waters of sceptical debate over Iraq. Many voices, within the West and outside it, questioned the need and, above all, the propriety of taking armed action against Baghdad. Although not technically a question of self-defence *per se* (as is discussed below), the action against Iraq had serious implications for any serious discussion of pre-emption.

The failure to gain political agreement among the Permanent Members in the first months of 2003 on an additional Security Council resolution has been interpreted to mean no legal authority for the action over Iraq,[5] or at best a challenging situation.[6] However, it is hard not to acknowledge the combined effects of UN Security Council Resolutions 678, 687 and 1441, in particular. The first of these, 678, was the important early resolution on Iraq in 1990, which authorized the use of all necessary measures to restore international peace and security in the region. It was under the auspices of this resolution that the UN-authorized coalition acted to evict Iraq from Kuwait in 1991. The second of the key resolutions, 687, was explicitly linked to 678. This obliged Iraq to disarm in certain categories of weapons systems and to end development of such weapons systems, to which Iraq agreed by signing a binding document, in return for which action under 678 would be suspended, but its authority not terminated. Thus, if 687 and the agreement signed by Iraq to disarm and co-operate in inspections were not observed, 678 would come back into full effect, its suspension over. Finally, Resolution 1441, which referred to the previous resolutions, confirmed their currency and noted that Iraq was in material breach of its own agreement and the terms of 687. It thereby signalled non-compliance, in which circumstances the continuing authority and reanimation of 678 became relevant.[7] The quest of the UK government, in particular, to seek an additional Security Council resolution prior to any action against Iraq was a matter of socio-political legitimacy, both domestically and internationally. Thus, in terms of authority and law, UN Security Council resolutions provided the relevant legal authority (as France, which was one of the more problematic countries in terms of getting a further Security Council resolution, made clear, when representatives asked why the UK and US were seeking this extra cover, when 1441 provided it anyway[8]). Iraq was not, then, as such about pre-emptive self-defence, even though it could have been, in principle, had UN authority not been available (and the possibility of a self-defence argument was inserted in President Bush's statement on the justice of launching military operations in March 2003, where he cited the UN resolutions, but also America's sovereign rights[9]).

The disbelievers questioned the justice of military action against Saddam Hussein's Iraq, doubting it in terms of necessity, ethics, international politics (and consequent domestic repercussions), as well as international law and norms. Such doubters even came from within the ranks of US President George W. Bush's Republican Party – prompting the President to say that he would listen, engage in dialogue, but in the end 'act according to the latest intelligence'.[10] This, in principle, pitched the dilemma exactly: there could be a situation clearly requiring action, but one where the scope for action was constrained or undermined by the perceived legitimacy of it – whether US domestic political opinion, or international public opinion. There is a need to bring the understanding of acceptable use of force into line with the responsible need to use force. Action over Iraq was neither a breach of international law, nor the end of the United Nations.[11] It was an important incident in the continuing evolution of international affairs, and particularly with regard to the laws of armed conflict. The point is that the law has begun to change, has to change and will change. The better approach is to embrace this and establish the parameters of change, rather than to insist on an anachronistic interpretation of the law. In the international security context of the early twenty-first century, there was no place for ostriches with their heads buried in the sand – this was a recipe for those particular ostriches to become extinct. Politics makes law and in the international realm this is true with bells on, shaped in customary fashion by action, precedent or interpretation. This is a process that holds dangers, which might also have concerned those sceptical of change. Despite general objections to the notion of breaking the law, action forging new law might also be seen to breach previously understood legal arrangements, particularly if objections to it are not strongly and formally raised, as the precedent gains credibility. While such action might be positive, any perception of breaching rules can equally have a negative impact, possibly encouraging the less scrupulous to break other rules that bind them in the international system. Thus prudence and judgement are important elements in any such radical action.

On the one hand, the doubting Thomases are right. There is some responsibility on the US, UK and whomever else might be engaged in such action to establish the need for action as far as this can be done in public terms. And they are right that traditional interpretations of international politics and international law would not permit such action. Only UN Security Council authorization or self-defence are recognized as normally justifying the use of force. To this, exceptional humanitarian cases requiring the use of force should be added, as was argued, for example, regarding Kosovo in 1999.[12]

However, the head-in-the-sand critics of and resisters to change sponsor a limited and almost irrelevant discussion. The argument had already moved on. In reality, the US-led response to the September 11 attacks on New York and Virginia had already significantly enlarged the scope of 'self-defence' – going some way towards filling a conceptual gap that had emerged during the 1990s. But those sceptical of action over Iraq had not noticed this happening, as they mostly supported the campaign in Afghanistan. Not having noticed this, they have been even less aware of the continuing need to explore and quite possibly further to extend the scope of self-defence. Self-defence has to embrace questions such as that posed by Iraq, or, indeed, a range of other questions that might arise, if America – and all states with a vested interest in international order and stability (if they are not considered as, or do not consider themselves to be, part of the West) – are to be able to ensure their defence. Washington and other governments, to paraphrase Jean Anouilh's Thomas à Becket, will have to be able to do what is necessary, when it is necessary, to protect themselves.[13] It is not that the action envisaged is so much outside the law, as that existing law and norms were developed to address different problems in a different era. It is time to act – and part of any action has to be reinterpretation of the law.

The need, therefore, is to explore and define new interpretations of international political norms and international law that will accommodate the very real and urgent imperatives of contemporary security challenges and threats. The rules have already been changed by and for some states, and will change more to meet the needs of security. Because of the concerns that this provokes, it is better to understand the major changes taking place and their context. And this should also involve some sense of where the reasonable limits of radical change might lie. The latter are considered in the penultimate section of this chapter, along with other issues of legitimacy and pragmatics. Before that, however, it is necessary to focus on the imperatives and arguments for redefining self-defence in the international strategic context at the beginning of the twenty-first century.

# New Bearings in Self-Defence for the Twenty-first Century: The Need for Pre-emption

A redefinition of defence is necessary to accommodate the altered structure of international order and to keep pace with changes in the interpretation of international peace and security. This is important to all states in international society, and, especially, to Western countries. In the discussion on a new NATO strategic concept (essentially fudged at the April 1999 Washington Summit because of the Kosovo campaign), there was an implicit move in this direction. Emphasis was placed on the need to use war-fighting capabilities to contribute to the maintenance of international peace and security and defend against instability.

Immediately after September 11, the conceptual lag that had emerged during the 1990s began to be filled in practice. The concept of self-defence was almost immediately modified *de facto*, without any formal acknowledgement. This began to bring it into line with the realities of the early twenty-first century. However, the process remained incomplete. And, as circumstances suggested new areas very likely to require action, the lack of clarity in the concept became apparent. In the contemporary world, the preservation of stability might mean acting forcibly to stop harm being done, rather than responding to it. Protecting self and stability are intertwined. It is necessary, therefore, not only to understand the need to adjust the concept of self-defence so that it addresses real needs, but also to ensure that anticipatory or pre-emptive action has an appropriate place.

It is not true that anticipatory self-defence has long been accepted, contrary to the assertion made in the US National Security Doctrine.[14] At best, the issue is disputed, with some radical international lawyers arguing for a limited right, but a conservative majority rejecting any notion of pre-emption whatsoever.[15] This division was also reflected post-September 11, where some suggested that there was nothing new really, while others noted a radical shift.[16] In terms of the real international actors, the US had consistently strongly and firmly resisted any suggestion of anticipatory self-defence,[17] including Israel's claim to an anticipatory right regarding both the 1967 'Six Day War' and the 1981 air strike on Iraq's Osirak nuclear reactor, believed to be linked to a weapons programme. But now Washington was showing itself ready to change.

The events of 11 September 2001 provided an abrupt short-cut to years of academic and policy-linked debate. Overnight, as noted above, the scope of self-defence broadened radically. The empirical needs of that situation provoked a conceptual great leap – literally overnight – to address an evident conceptual lag. For around a decade, there had already been a clear logic requiring a radical shift in the concept of self-defence to bring one pillar governing the use of force into line with the other: Security Council scope for action and that of the states themselves.

The provisions for the maintenance of international peace and security in the UN system and the right to self-defence were conceived as serving the same purpose at the time the UN Charter was drafted.

But a new, more flexible definition of defence was logically implicit in the UN Security Council's 1992 conceptual shift: if the meaning of threat to international peace and security has had to be expanded, then it follows that definition of threat to a country needs commensurate expansion. A situation that can be identified as a threat to international security also constitutes a threat to the individual and common security of states. Defence of the state has to embrace the range of new risks. As much as states might have needed the right to self-defence against external armed attack in the past, in the twenty-first century they may need it to protect themselves from disorder and disruption emerging from within some other states, in the absence of action by the UN Security Council.

If this extrapolation is followed, then an expanded reinterpretation of the right to self-defence entailed in Article 51 may be required to parallel that made by the Security Council regarding peace and security. That article, appearing in Chapter VII, declares that 'Nothing in the present Charter shall impair the inherent right of individual or collective self-defence if an armed attack occurs against a Member of the United Nations, until the Security Council has taken measures necessary to maintain international peace and security.' While the last clause of this sentence opens the way for the right itself to be overtaken by Security Council action (this is a complement to the clause permitting the overriding of domestic jurisdiction provisions offered in Article 2 (7)), it is clear that in the absence of any such action, self-defence governs the right to use armed force in the face of an attack. However, if the chief threat to international peace and security is no longer armed attack by one state on another, then the need for defence must change accordingly.

States will rarely, if at all, need to defend themselves against aggressive conventional attacks by other states. It may be more relevant to modernize the understanding of defence to meet the real threats that states are likely to face. If conflicts such as Kosovo are a threat to international peace and security, then they are threats to the security of existing states – and in future might be subject, in part, to legal acts of self-defence, under Article 51. Crucially, if action beyond the traditional protection offered by the quality of sovereignty is permissible to restore peace and security, then defence, it may be reasoned, has to be possible on the same basis. It might well be that a state, or group of states, is threatened by a situation arising within the boundaries of another state. In such a case, the latter, because of abuse, or dereliction, regarding the exercise of sovereign rights, might be judged to have lost the respect of others demanded by the sovereignty system.

In the absence of action by the UN Security Council to deal with such a threat, it may well be that action by states in self-defence might be appropriate.

It could be argued, in this sense, that the Kosovo campaign of 1999 could have been interpreted as an act of self-defence, although the Alliance obviously did not claim it to be that.[18] However, NATO's strategic position and credibility were on the line, its status and future as a unique military-political arrangement were at stake, and the values that it was formed to embody and to protect were gravely challenged. Defence of these and maintenance of the Alliance were vital to the security interest of each member state. Given this, an argument of self-defence, based on protection of vital interests, could have been made, hypothetically. It would, however, have been quite radical – and, while intellectually convincing, would have encountered the problems of political persuasiveness that in reality bedevilled discussion of the Kosovo operations, as well as later ones concerning Afghanistan and Iraq.

While such a position may be subject to challenge on the grounds that Article 51 gives authority for self-defence in the event of an 'armed attack', there are two reasons to consider that such a challenge is inapt. First, there are precedents for an extended concept of self-defence, including cases where there was no direct armed or physical threat. The case of the US invasion of Panama falls into this category, while the concepts of extended and pre-emptive self-defence were cited by the US and Israel in other cases. The list of such cases includes the US invasion in Grenada in 1983, US air strikes against Libya in 1986, US air strikes against Afghanistan and Sudan in 1999, and Israel's air strike against Iraq's nuclear reactor in 1981. However, each of these was deeply contested by most states and was not generally accepted. Secondly, an extension of reasoning is relevant: if the understanding of the term 'threat' related to international peace and security has been cosmically expanded in its scope, it is hard to see why the same extension should not be invoked for the concept of self-defence. Beyond this, it might also be noted that self-defence is a *jus cogens* principle – one that cannot be definitively superseded by any treaty or written legal provision. This could mean that the definition of self-defence in a document (even in the UN Charter) does not necessarily exceed that established by state practice. However, although not necessary, it is clearly better and preferable, in terms of order and legitimacy, if the UN Charter is taken as the core of all relevant law and an international constitution.[19]

The traditional concept of self-defence in international law, derived from the *Caroline* case, dating back to 1837, assumed an armed attack by a state actor (as did the UN Charter implicitly), and that any response would be absolutely necessary, proportionate and immediate. The *Caroline* case involved an eponymous private steamship, which was carrying arms across the Niagara River to assist anti-British rebels in Canada. British forces attacked and captured the boat, then set it ablaze and pushed it over the Niagara Falls. This was an act of self-defence for the British. However, this was not accepted by the US side, and in the subsequent diplomatic exchanges US Secretary of State Daniel Webster laid out what have since been taken to be the classical terms of the right to self-defence: immediacy, necessity and proportionality. In Webster's formula, iterated in a letter in 1841, which was accepted by the British, the test was 'necessity of self-defence, instant and overwhelming, leaving no choice of means, and no moment for deliberation'.[20] Traditionally states and international lawyers have read this as meaning an equivalent to the domestic self-defence provisions in which, say, the aggressor's hands would have to be around the victim's throat before forceful self-defence would be permissible.[21] However, given the time involved in mobilizing armed forces to respond to an armed attack in the international system, as well as the complexities of taking decisions and making judgements, this does not mean that all non-forceful action must have been taken prior to a use of force. Armed force is the 'last resort' not only in a sequential and chronological sense, where other alternatives have been tried in practice, but it is also relevant where other means would be futile.[22] This, in itself, meant that the analogy with the domestic context could not hold entirely. David Rodin notes what he calls a 'disanalogy'.[23] This can be explained as follows. The domestic right to self-defence applies for the duration of the assault, meaning that, once the assault has been stopped, any right to use force ceases. However, the international version of the right applies only to the commencement of an act of self-defence, meaning that, once force has started to be used defensively, it is then permissible to continue its use beyond immediate defence, translating it potentially (at some point) into offence. Thus, once the decision to act forcefully in self-defence has been taken, stopping an attack is not the limit of the right. Rather, a state is entitled to make war on the aggressor state, even to the point of unconditional surrender (as did the allies in the Second World War), to ensure that a repeat attack is not possible.

The difference between the domestic and the international contexts lies in the time and complexity that a response to an attack might take, which can include gathering intelligence and undertaking necessary diplomacy to build support. Thus, although conceptually the terms of immediacy imply a clear and simple formula – too soon, unaccept-able anticipatory action, too late, unacceptable reprisal – the relevance of context makes this impossible to render quite so sharply or straight-forwardly. However, in terms of any conventional interpretation, there could be no justification for reprisals after the event, nor excessive use of force, nor, crucially, anticipatory action. The September 11 attacks, revealing trends already recognized regarding threats to peace and security, did not easily fit this bill. Al-Qa'ida was a transnational, non-state actor. The attacks were launched from the territory of the US itself. The weapons were civilian commercial aircraft. And the re-sponse required an extensive action initially focused on Afghanistan, but needing to address the transnational and international character of the aggressor, and its links to allies. This constituted radical, over-night change in the conceptualization of self-defence.

The shift was supported by America's NATO allies and by the majority of states around the world. But those rushing to give back-ing did not generally grasp the degree to which it represented change. With a group like al-Qa'ida involved, very few governments, in the context, were thinking through what they were doing. They were meet-ing the needs of the moment. As perhaps unconscious Constructivist Realists, they were doing what was necessary legally and conceptu-ally to confront the problem with which they were faced. Alongside this, the UN Security Council, still (formally at least) unaware of the perpetrators of the attacks on New York and Virginia, appeared to confirm the relevance and currency of the right to self-defence in Resolutions 1368 and 1373, at least absent further Security Council action. Such further action would have to include identification of any aggressor against whom action might be authorized. Further Security Council action is relevant to the reservations of comment-ators suggesting that Security Council Resolution 1373 did not confer or confirm the right to self-defence because the references to that right were contained only in the preamble to the Resolution.[24] However, as Müllerson correctly observes, when Resolution 1368 was passed on 12 September 2001, the Security Council was not in a position to use more specific language, at the same time as it explicitly recognized a case for self-defence in a resolution entirely concerned with terrorist acts.[25] This resolution was later confirmed in Resolution 1373 on 28 September, although no greater definition was apparently thought necessary at that stage. In terms of international law and custom the support of NATO and others for American-led action over Afghanistan in response to the September 11 attacks clearly constituted a widening of the right to self-defence.[26]

This transformation does not have clearly delineated boundaries. More important, it is not enough. It does not address the real needs of the twenty-first-century environment, which might well require preemptive action. This imperative can be explained hypothetically. I shall do so in three steps. The first step is taken by reference to the September 11 attacks. The second is taken by reference to Iraq as though it had been a case for pre-emption. And the final stage concerns an understanding of the pressures, including those of accountability and responsibility, on Western leaders in a democratic system with essentially hostile news media standing ready to damn them at any point.

The September 11 attacks were not foreseen. But they might have been. This is true, on one level possibly, because in retrospect there might, in fact, have been enough pieces of evidence available to get a closer idea of what would happen. But, on another level, it is theoretically conceivable that the CIA, or the SIS, or some other government agency could have discovered the plot to hijack the airliners and fly them into their targets in New York and Virginia.[27] Certainly, Western governments were aware, at various levels, that some action by al-Qa'ida was in preparation. There was awareness for up to four months beforehand and heightened awareness in the six weeks prior to the attack. It was clear that something big would happen soon. But there was no clear indication of what would happen exactly, where exactly, or when exactly – or who exactly would perpetrate whatever it was. It could have been otherwise, however. Precise details might have been known. In practice, in that particular case, knowing the plot fully would probably not have entailed a use of force. Nonetheless, for the sake of making the argument here explicit, I want to assume that preventing September 11 might hypothetically have required armed action against targets, say, in Afghanistan or Yemen. In that situation, it would seem unreasonable, in and of itself, to suppose that the US Administration, or others, should not have used force to protect its territorial integrity, its people and its property, but instead should have waited and allowed the attacks to take place. It would also be unthinkable politically that a president, apprised of an imminent attack, would not seek to prevent it. And the same would be true for any leader of any country, especially a democracy.

Iraq also provides a useful case – albeit one with uncertainties in some regards. While Iraq was not a case of pre-emption, it could well have been. As noted already, the *US National Security Strategy* published in September 2002 had raised the prospect of pre-emptive action already. Around the same time, the UK government had produced a dossier on Iraq's WMD capability, which, perhaps above all else, was paving the way for a legal case that might be made in terms of the right to self-defence. That case was not made in the end, but it is clear that in identifying Iraq's weapons and couching their existence as a threat to the UK and its interests, it offered some material for an argument of self-defence at a later stage – one that would inevitably have had to be pre-emptive. While later doubt has emerged on the scale of Iraq's weapons holdings, capabilities and programmes (see below), from early 2002 onwards, the US, the UK and all their major partners and allies had been convinced that Iraq possessed and was developing a range of dangerous capabilities that represented a grave threat. In that situation, had there not been legal authority claimed by Washington and London in the Security Council interlinking and cross-reading of Security Council resolutions, then it is hard to imagine that the legal case for action would have not been made in terms of a right to anticipatory self-defence. With or without the possible operational link to al-Qa'ida – about which the British and others were sceptical, but some in America appeared to have strong convictions – there was no way that the West could afford, say, to let a persistent and active anti-Western force acquire, let alone use, its capability against it. A judgement had to be made to use force, given the information available to it and the full confidence in that information on which it was basing its action. The interpretation of information, in this hypothetical case (closely related to the actual Iraq case), would be shaped in Western capitals by awareness that Iraq had consistently played the role of 'rogue' for well over a decade. Faced with continuing non-compliance, obstruction and possibly, let us say hypothetically, an intention to use WMD/I one way or another against neighbouring countries, or even, one way or another, further afield, necessity would dictate taking forceful action.

Building on these hypothetical cases, created using material that relates in some way to real and known cases, which demonstrate the need for a right to pre-emptive self-defence, there is a third point of reasoning that identifies the necessity of action. This concerns the responsibilities and pressures for accountability on political leaders, which could be applied contingently to the two hypothetical cases based around real events dealt with above. This is that no democratic leader in a position like this could be expected realistically not to take action. No responsible democratic leader, let alone one with an interest in their future reputation and possibly re-election, could afford not to take action, if they had credible information regarding a threat and were in a position to take such action. Any leader who failed to take action knowing, say, that a 9/11 kind of attack was going to take place would be irresponsible and foolish in every sense. For sure, there would be no come-back later if and when an attack had taken place. Political opinion, public opinion and above all the news media would not allow space for any political leader who appeared to know something and failed to take action to stop it. The bottom line is that if that action is judged to require the use of armed force, then the leader will have to resort to the use of armed force. If international diplomatic circumstances or the urgency of the issue do not permit recourse to the UN Security Council to authorize the necessary action, then action will still need to be taken. The only possibility then for such action would be to invoke the right to self-defence. Yet the traditional interpretation of the right to self-defence would not permit such anticipatory action. This is why the scope for the right to self-defence has to change.

If America and its allies are to tackle the kind of movement with which there is not much, or absolutely no, scope to seek compromise, this means that there can only be self-defence. With an emerging need to combat threats more widely, there has been more hesitancy and confusion – for example, concerning September 11- or Iraq-like circumstances – over taking action that might require pre-emption. That it will happen where necessary, if a threat requiring action is identified, is a political certainty, as well as a theoretical one, in terms of the approach taken throughout the present volume. As it develops, or even before it is really developed, the implications of whatever change takes place for the rules will have to be acknowledged – in particular, regarding definition of key principles of immediacy, necessity and proportionality. This must be part of a new framework on the international scene, one that has already begun to be sketched. The issue is not whether or not there should be acknowledgement of a right to self-defence, but, as soon as possible, to create an accepted and acceptable broadening of the scope of self-defence, including some understanding of how the old principles fit the new circumstances. These principles feature in discussion of some of the difficulties surrounding a shift to pre-emptive self-defence in the following section, having established that such a shift is necessary and therefore ineluctable.

# Intelligence, Legitimacy and the Boundaries of the Self-Defence Revolution

Pre-emptive self-defence is necessary and inevitable. Informed by theory, logic and a sense of reality, it is impossible to avoid pre-emption. The question is not to accept it or reject it. The challenge is to work out the best possible terms for its emergence and satisfactory adoption. But it is a deeply contentious development, with potential dangers attached to it, some of which cannot be foreseen, it must be presumed. Because of the sensitivity and the possibility of unintended nightmares that might lie beyond its introduction, it is imperative to initiate – and if possible settle at the earliest possible instant – discussion on the conditions for legitimate pre-emption. The purpose of the penultimate section of this book is to identify some of the problems of legitimacy inherent in the pre-emption puzzle, and to offer at least some initial suggestions for the conditions that will attend its introduction and use.

I have already indicated that, although Iraq 2003 was not a case of pre-emption, there was a strong possibility that it could have been treated as such. Indeed, although it was not a case of pre-emption, as Adam Roberts has noted, many of its opponents appeared to think that it was and to cast it in those terms.[28] Because of the association with ideas of pre-emption and the sensitivities of the case, Iraq points to one of the key problems that any decision to invoke pre-emptive self-defence would face – legitimacy, meaning international and national socio-political support and acceptance, rather than legality. However, it must be noted that legality was – and could be expected to be – one of the key focal points for discussion of the legitimacy of actions. This is why it is necessary, above all, not only to recognize the need for a possibility of pre-emptive self-defence, but also to work on establishing terms that would make it a more broadly acceptable advance in the international legal-political framework.

The question of legitimacy can be focused in hypothetical discussion of both the debate over Iraq and what could have been done if the US, or others, had known something detailed about the September attack beforehand, and had wanted to do something to prevent it that would have required action in, for example, Afghanistan. What would at least half (and probably a far greater proportion than this) of any population group have said? Given the reaction in some quarters to the US-led response, even after the September attacks, or to public discussion regarding possible action over Iraq, it seems quite likely that most people would have been sceptical and that there would have been even more reports of US 'imperialism' or 'aggression' or 'bullying' or something similar, at the political level. It is hard to believe that many people would have accepted that an act of self-defence was required, however many times Donald Rumsfeld, or Geoff Hoon, or Tony Blair, or George W. Bush, warned that an attack was coming and that it was necessary. Rather, an energetic Doubting Thomas and Know-All society of journalists, intellectual and cultural commentators, political activists and academics would have questioned and rejected whatever the governments said. At best, some might have moderated their challenge to the limited demand to produce evidence.

However, so often the evidence, by its nature, would not be suitable for public transmission. It would not be believed. Disbelief would be even greater than that which sometimes met official statements over Afghanistan. There, some seemed to question the very existence of UBL, while many more could not bring themselves to accept the face-value evidence of the home movie video discovered, in which UBL discusses the success of the attack on New York, especially. In each of these cases, it was possible to find people who said that either the man himself, or the video, was a creation of the CIA, which was really responsible for the attacks, in order to have a pretext to spread US power around the world. What this makes clear is that it would be hard for a government easily to justify such action to its people in a manner that would be widely accepted, as was (and continues to be) the case regarding Iraq. However, that people generally might not perceive a problem does not mean that it might not be perceptible to some.[29]

The fallout from the Iraq campaign in 2003 has complicated this picture considerably. The British MP Gisela Stuart, a former government minister at the Foreign and Commonwealth Office and a member of the House of Commons Select Committee on Foreign Affairs, concluded that pre-emption had been killed off by events in the wake of the Iraq operations.[30] This was wrong – as already established, there would be circumstances in which pre-emption would be necessary and political leaders would be placed in a position where not to take action would be impossible. Pre-emption had not itself been inadvertently pre-empted. But discussion of it and eventual application of it had indeed been made more difficult by the events that Stuart had in mind, given the contentious and complex issues that already enclosed pre-emptive self-defence.

Those events were the suicide of the UK chemical and biological weapons scientific expert Dr David Kelly, the subsequent report into the circumstances of his death by Lord Hutton, and the resignation of David Kay in the US as head of the Iraq Survey Group (ISG), at the same time as Hutton was reporting. All three put a focus on the importance and sensitivity of intelligence regarding Iraq – or in any situation requiring pre-emption. Kelly had become publicly known because a BBC news report in the UK in May 2003 had alleged that the UK government had knowingly and falsely embellished a dossier produced in September 2002 assessing Iraq's WMD/I potential.[31] That document was described as being produced by the government's Joint Intelligence Committee, and was widely taken as making the case for action against Iraq, although it was not formally presented as such. The impact of the story was to question the claim that the dossier was based entirely on intelligence and to question the nature of the intelligence. After his death, Kelly turned out to be the source for the reporter, Andrew Gilligan, who had gone beyond anything that Kelly had told him in making the key allegations in the report. Kelly committed suicide, after finding himself under pressure in public and realizing that, while Gilligan had exceeded that which he had been told, in making statements to his Ministry of Defence employers and to the Foreign Affairs Committee he had lied and was being exposed. However, his emergence in public and his death had highlighted the importance and sensitivity of intelligence, especially secret intelligence, in this and similar cases.

The subsequent Hutton inquiry into Dr Kelly's death continued this focus. Although Hutton set the parameters for his report to exclude making judgements on questions relating to WMD/I and government intelligence, in doing so, he quite extensively discussed that issue so as to raise a series of questions somewhere on the boundary between implicitly and explicitly that might be for others to answer. As he was doing this, David Kay resigned as head of the ISG, the 1,400-strong body that had been charged with investigating and identifying Iraq's WMD/I capabilities and programmes. The underlying factor in Kay's resignation was surely frustration that his requests to give the ISG greater resources and more time had been denied. However, the prominent public reason was his judgement that his team was not now going to find WMD/I capabilities and programmes on the scale he and others had believed. If the weapons and programmes had existed on the scale previously believed, the ISG would have to have found appropriate evidence by that stage. Kay maintained a belief that the chemical weapons were elusive, rather than illusive (that is, were escaping discovery, rather than imaginary), but that they could not have existed on the scale that officials previously assessed. This, he pointed out to the US Senate Select Committee on Intelligence, meant that 'we almost all got it wrong'.[32] More than this, he estimated, this outcome would mean a generational loss of confidence around the world, and in the US, and possibly even in the intelligence agencies themselves, in US intelligence-gathering, analysis and assessment capabilities, as well as those of its allies and partners.[33] While this was possibly overstated, given that around the same time Western intelligence agencies had discovered and intercepted other capabilities, notably Libyan (and the role of Pakistani actors in that case revealed broader past Pakistani activity), it nonetheless posed a vital question in terms of potential pre-emption.

The problems that had surrounded discussion of Iraq prior to and after the major combat operations in spring 2003 about the nature and extent of any Iraqi threat were significant. The public discourse around the world, including divisions between and within governments, challenged the legitimacy of the action. The doubts at that stage and the impact of the failure to discover chemical weapons had a big implication for the future. (Chemical weapons were the category of WMD/I about which those involved had no doubt – and continued to have no doubt, even when empirical examples were not produced in the first nine months of occupation, following the ending of major combat operations at the end of April 2003.) It must be assumed that any pre-emptive action must, in part, be based on secret intelligence. Yet, given the doubts that were evident over Iraq, accentuated by the absence of any image of chemical weapons to assay the accuracy of the earlier assessments, it seems reasonable to assume that assertions of evidence that could not be placed in the public domain would only result in doubt and dissonance. These kinds of doubt were reflected when the directors of the major US intelligence agencies appeared before the Senate Select Committee on Intelligence.[34] As one report noted, '[h]anging over the hearing was the track record of all US intelligence, given the track record in Iraq.'[35] It was also reflected in some of the questions posed to the intelligence directors by Senators Diane Feinstein and Richard Durbin. 'When we send out our military and then find nothing, and then Dr Kay goes over and finds nothing, it's a pretty bitter pill to swallow with regard to the value of intelligence,' said the former. 'How can we fight a war against terrorism, or have a policy of pre-emption, based on what we have just lived through in Iraq?', challenged the latter.[36] Although in all probability not correct, it would also not be unreasonable for a critic to reject any government intelligence claims by pointing out that 'all we were told about Iraq turned out to be absolutely wrong – this new situation must be the same'.

Trust and legitimacy are critical. Where decisions are taken and action follows based on secret information, public trust is needed – both in the governments making the decisions and in the news media which report, discuss and interpret them. Fragile legitimacy makes it harder to make the necessary decisions and to undertake the necessary action. Because the news media constitute the crux of the legitimization process, framing discourse about the just character and rightfulness of both cause and conduct of whatever action is taken, it is vital that governments are as transparent as possible, demonstrate integrity as far as possible, and do not alienate news organizations or make them unduly sceptical. And it is even more vital that journalists, while doing their jobs, are responsible and, within reason, recognize that governments may well need leeway on certain issues. Both government and press would be serving the public interest.

Trust and legitimacy are vital qualities for any decision to use force and for the conduct of armed hostilities. This is not only true in terms of international socio-political legitimacy. It is acutely true in each domestic context where a decision of that kind is taken and armed forces are committed. In terms of the Clausewitzian trinity of government, armed forces and people, harmony between the three elements is an essential condition of success.[37] However, a loss of confidence, trust and legitimacy in government (and other social institutions, contingently) makes the decision to use armed force and the subsequent application of force that much harder, risking the success of any operations. With legitimacy such a vital aspect of any decision to use armed force and such a sensitive facet of any pre-emptive action, the problems of legitimacy regarding intelligence and government authority only give added emphasis to the imperative of seeking to establish the appropriate framework of rules covering pre-emptive self-defence.

The importance of not only legal authority but international–national socio-political legitimization of any action is only one of the difficult issues surrounding the development of a revised understanding of self-defence. Among key issues driving sceptics is an entirely reasonable concern to avoid possible abuse of power and authority. One of the key reasons for the evolution of self-defence in traditional terms was concern not only to limit the phenomenon of armed hostilities, but also to limit the potential for abuse by the powerful. Furthermore, concern over abuse by the powerful cannot be limited to anti-Western or anti-US doubters. A key issue with any change in scope of the right to self-defence is to limit the potential for abuse. Within two or three months of the *de facto* Western-led change in the concept of self-defence that followed the September 11 attacks, action by both India and Israel invoking the right to self-defence raised questions regarding possible abuse of the concept.

In the wake of the September 11 attacks and the response to them under the rubric of self-defence and the 'War on Terrorism' label, both countries were faced with terrorist attacks and both responded with action that appeared excessive. America and some Western allies were necessarily enlarging the scope of self-defence; in other parts of the world the dangers of untrammelled redefinition of self-defence were evident. India took a bullish stance against Pakistan and in doing so took the world to the brink of nuclear war, highlighting the very real worries about abuse of the concept that might occur. Such concerns about abuse of power affected discussion over further Western action. Israel served its underlying, longer-term political and security interests ill (and did its image in the world little good) by occupying Palestinian territory, bulldozing villages and towns along the way, and laying siege to the Palestinian Authority Headquarters and the Church of the Nativity in Bethlehem. In both cases, there was a considerable degree of 'right' on their side. The Kashmiri militant attacks on India had Islamabad's sponsorship. Jerusalem reasonably judged that Yasir Arafat's Authority had sanctioned the Palestinian strategy of suicide bombings. Yet in each case the scale of the response appeared to be out of all proportion with the initial attacks, leaving the impression that the notion of self-defence in response to small attacks was being used as a pretext to exert strong – many judged excessive (and inappropriate) – coercive force. And while India and Israel had some justice in their cases, even if their approach was dubious, there was the potential for other cases to emerge where actors invoked the notion of self-defence on entirely spurious grounds as a pretext for action – especially of an allegedly pre-emptive kind. For example, it is not hard to imagine, other things being equal, Saddam Hussein's Iraq alleging a threat from Kuwait and invoking its right to self-defence to justify action such as it took in August 1990. This highlights a potential danger of undefined and untrammelled scope for pre-emption. It also suggests that prudence must play an important role in judgements on pre-emption, both in practice and in terms of defining the acceptable scope for the concept.

Arising from this is a second issue: the absence of any formal arrangement for deciding and authorizing action of this kind. The question is 'Who is to say if self-defence is justified?' The situation is very different from any analogous domestic situation, in that no authority exists to approve an action in advance and issue a warrant, or to render judgment in court afterwards. The closest to this is the UN Security Council, and where its authority is available there can be no doubt that it should be used, nor that all concerned would find its use desirable. However, as Kosovo and (to a limited extent) Iraq in 2003 showed, there may well be cases in which that option is simply not available, but those who have an understanding of a particular situation deem action necessary. In practice, the only restraints would be self-limitation and the interaction of domestic and international public opinion. This might act as a constraint on action at a given moment, or it might serve as a 'court' to which the action might be justified *ex post facto*. In the absence of initial self-limitation, or given an over-riding need for action, it is highly unlikely that either domestic or international opinion would prevent action. So there could be little restraint on abusive action by 'rogues', while there could be a contentious atmosphere surrounding necessary action by 'the good'. Thus enhancing the issue of self-defence was not only a political and practical issue for the West, it was a problem of international diplomacy and ethics, which required close attention and, as far as possible, agreement on the boundaries of the expanded concept.

In the interim, those boundaries are absent, given the hurried manner in which the scope of self-defence began to be changed *de facto*. The reality is that self-defence needs to be changed still further, but the fact is also that all of this has occurred, of necessity, without appropriate political and ethical reflection, discussion and, where possible, agreement. As an initial attempt to set broad boundaries, I would make three suggestions. First: it should always be preferable that matters are handled under the authority of the UN Security Council and where possible they should be raised there; however, a failure for any good reason to secure authority there cannot mean no possibility of action – and any action, and the grounds for it, must be reported to the Security Council. Secondly: any action taken must be carried out with maximum discretion and restraint – something that has already characterized the unusual missions over Kosovo and Iraq. Thirdly: any commitment to action under a broadened concept of self-defence should be accompanied by the responsibility and commitment to transform defence into partnership at the earliest stage possible, preferably under the authority of the UN Security Council. In the end, action of this kind needs to be justified not only by the certainty of a need to act, but also by a mature and conscientious follow-up – indeed, this is not just a philosophical requirement, it is also one of interest in ensuring peace and security. On this last point, the relative failures of subsequent transitional administration in both Kosovo and Iraq do not invalidate the action taken. Rather, they highlight the great importance of making sure that there is a clear political follow-through to the military campaign that is well developed. Among other things, this might include a clear mission to establish governance, to remain responsibly engaged until those conditions have successfully been achieved, rather than a limited change in the situation, and, perhaps most importantly, one that treats temporary responsibility for another territory as though it were permanent responsibility for one's own. This would be fully taking responsibility for one's actions, something that ethically ought to be a condition of using the right to pre-emptive self-defence. And, in the spirit of the need to avoid future problems and the preventive, partnership approach that should be put in place wherever possible, identified in the previous chapter, any such involvement should include a framework for partnership arrangements.

In addition to these conditions, and consistent with traditional notions of Just War theory, any action should meet the tests associated with the traditional understanding of the right to self-defence. However, there must be modification of those terms. While proportionality will continue to be defined by context, as has always been the case, necessity and immediacy must be re-calibrated. Proportionality will need to be gauged to particular threats. If Saddam's personality was, ultimately, the biggest threat posed by his regime and the only way to disarm the regime and enforce compliance was large-scale combined arms engagement, then other cases might require a more limited, raiding approach, whether by air, sea or land – that is, quick missions, in and out, to eliminate part of a developing weapons programme, for example. Thus proportionality in the conduct of operations, as always, will be determined by the nature of particular problems. One size does not fit all when it comes to military operations, however clumsy armed force is as an instrument. The one additional condition might be the sensitivity over issues of necessity and immediacy, given that these need to be interpreted in new ways. In terms of Just War theory, *jus in bello* sensitivity – rightful conduct of war – might well be greater, given increased fragility regarding immediacy and necessity in terms of *jus ad bellum*, that is, just cause for resorting to armed force.

While traditionally necessity has been taken to be something akin to the domestic equivalent of an assailant's hands being around the throat, leaving no option but to use force to ensure survival, September 11 made clear that there could be circumstances in which waiting until the hands were at the throat might be too late. Necessity had to be understood as covering action prior to a clear physical assault, without which security would be threatened. For example, as North Korea demonstrated, to a considerable extent while the US focus was on Iraq, once 'rogues' possessed a nuclear weapons capability, the options for dealing with them were constrained. This suggested that there could be questions over WMD/I where a pre-emptive stitch in time would save considerably more than nine stitches when it was already too late. Similarly, the interpretation of immediacy needed to be extended. Immediacy has to be recast to complement the understanding of necessity: it needs temporal and spatial change to permit longer time frames and greater distances in defining the point at which a threat would be too close to be averted. Defining those temporal and spatial points, as well as the necessity of action, is not easy and, almost inevitably without transparent hard evidence for public presentation prior to defensive action (and even possibly after it, given the nature of many threats), such action will be contentious. Whatever the precise detail at any time, the measure of immediacy has to be 'before it is too late'. There will clearly be an onus on those taking action in self-defence, as with the Iraq case, as far as possible to demonstrate their just cause and to legitimate their action, *ex post facto*. Nonetheless, however contentious, even if the evidence cannot be adduced either before or after the action, such action might be necessary, before threats are too close or it is too late.

The foregoing discussion has highlighted the problems associated with pre-emptive self-defence, as well as reaffirming the necessity for it. Because pre-emptive self-defence is necessary, it is ultimately inevitable. And because it is inevitable, it is also inevitable that eventually it will become an accepted part of the legal-political framework for using force in international society. It is desirable that the necessary and inevitable should happen sooner rather than later and that they should be founded on greater agreement than disagreement on what is acceptable. In this context, I take the rare step of disagreeing, at least to some degree, with Adam Roberts. He states that there is 'no prospect of general agreement to a new set of black-letter rules regarding the circumstances in which the use of force may be legitimate'.[38] It is true that no 'black-letter' general agreement by treaty, or amendment of treaties, is likely in the short term. Any such agreement can usually be expected to take decades to achieve, although agreement and subsequent ratification of the Statute for the International Criminal Court (ICC) took a remarkably short time, with the Statute agreed only five years after the idea was reawakened and ratified only another four years later.[39] However, while the ICC holds open the prospect even of a more general and inclusive agreement more speedily agreed, this is not the only way in which a change in the rules – or perhaps more accurately, in the interpretation of the rules – might be achieved. The point is to bring the scope of the right to self-defence into line with its conceptual stable-mate, 'threats to international peace and security'. Given the manner in which that change was made by the first ever summit meeting of the Heads of

State and Government of the United Nations Security Council, it does not seem unreasonable that the Security Council could not work towards consensually issuing an equivalent statement, lending its legal and political authority, regarding the scope of the right to self-defence. In its resolutions regarding terrorism and the right to self-defence, the Security Council has already played a similar role in extending the scope of that right, which, as noted earlier, has been expeditiously, it seems, accepted into the customary framework of international law. There seems no reason why a similar step could not be taken regarding the necessary and inevitable, but very dangerous and contentious, further enhancement of the right to self-defence to include pre-emption. In taking such a step, the Security Council might also be balancing recognition of the possibility of pre-emption where it has not yet acted, for whatever reason (perhaps, excepting a veto by a country invoking the right to pre-emptive self-defence), and reaffirming its own authority, to some extent. However, any such move would require careful consideration by the members of the Security Council. It would need to take account of the preventive and potentially healing possibilities of partnership and the full sense of responsibility that any country taking pre-emptive action would need to demonstrate. It would need to take account of the various conditions and considerations above. And it would need to keep in mind prudential care for the basic tenets of international law and politics, as well as respect for them, to ensure that the scope for pre-emptive self-defence is constrained as far as possible so as to preclude, or deter, abuse. But, whatever the fine-tuning, one way or another, it would have to acknowledge a right to pre-emptive self-defence – a right that would inevitably be asserted and shaped, in any case.

## Conclusion

A re-conceptualization of self-defence is required that balances partnership and pre-emption. Both elements reflect the imperatives of responding to twenty-first-century security concerns. Those concerns reflect the nature of contemporary international order, where layers of stability have been created in an integrated world, made by the West, in which openness in trade and values are essential to states. In this world, the range of threats to peace and stability, as well as of direct physical threats characteristic of that world involving non-state actors and rogue states, are not consistent with the old state-centred world and its approaches to security. The nature of security challenges in the twenty-first century requires new approaches. This was recognized by the UN Security Council in 1992, when it redefined the meaning of 'threats to international peace and security', one of the two key terms governing the use of force in the international system. That redefinition reflected and gave rise to a spate of Security Council-sponsored activity that both tackled problems that would previously have been unidentified or untouchable and used an often inventive set of measures to address those problems. But that shift was not accompanied by a commensurate shift regarding the other key term governing the use of force in international life – the right to self-defence. As I have argued in this volume, that shift is necessary and should entail scope for pre-emption – indeed, this cannot be avoided. The only question is on which terms and with which limits it will emerge.

The shift to pre-emption is only one of the responses to the security challenges to the West. In this volume, through the theoretical prism of Constructivist Realism, I have shown that changes in the organizational arrangements for Western defence have occurred and will continue in relation to circumstances. Beyond this, I have argued that defence of the West requires a policy of partnership and pre-emption. This is the product of using Constructivist Realism in conjunction with a close analysis of empirical issues and developments. A benefit of this theoretical approach is that it permits this analysis, where other approaches cannot. Constructivist Realism, in which interests are constructed through the attribution of value, interaction with others and structure, and are governed by necessity, on the one hand, and values constitute interests through those same processes, on the other, offers the right lens. It solves the problem of rationality in using Constructivist approaches and it tackles the rigidity of using Realism.[40] The Realist idea of self-help as necessary – and so rational – remains true, whether imposed by human nature or structure. However, traditional Realism can no longer provide an explanation, given the nature of the system, of threats within it and, so, of rational action in the new security environment. Constructivist Realism squares the circle: achieving the imperative objective of states (Realist self-help) in the international system requires co-operation (Constructivist interaction and discourse). It does not bind states together artificially in either competitive or alliance arrangements, but it allows both for appropriate action and adaptation to do whatever is necessary to deal with threats. It permits both partnership and pre-emption.

Both partnership and pre-emption are different aspects of a strategy that recognizes that anticipation is central to the twenty-first-century security environment. This is because the nature of international order and of the overwhelming majority of threats associated with that order, which will disrupt the stability upon which the West depends, requires early action. Stability is better preserved through early action to prevent, rather than responding to challenges once order has been interrupted. Partnership is the key means – active, not declaratory – by which to ensure stability in the international system, fostering stability where there is fragility and weakness, making sure that the latter qualities do not emerge where they are not already present.

Partnership is also vital in two other ways. First, it is an essential requirement of any post-conflict environment if the need for stability in international order is to be met. Secondly, however, it should also be a condition of any pre-emptive Western action. The price of pre-emption should include the responsibility to transform hostile action as soon as possible into partnership. This is because pre-emption, which is also about taking preventive action of a kind before it is too late, is a contentious concept. It is a necessary development to cover the inevitable cases where the UN Security Council is unable to act, but states face threats to their peace and security. The problems that surround pre-emption need to be addressed, if necessary action is to be seen as legitimate. The key to this is to ensure that the necessary change in the scope of the right to self-defence is limited by relevant conditions and agreements, if at all possible. Perhaps the most likely way in which this can be achieved is through a statement by the Heads of State and Government of the UN Security Council, as discussed above. But this is not necessarily the only way. Whatever the way, because pre-emption is both necessary and inevitable, a change of rules is required.

In the end, while rules have to change, it is essential to recognize that adherence to and observance of the rules – an essential feature of the Western construct – have to be maintained. It can make no sense to defend the West in such a manner as to lose the essence of Western values. This is even truer domestically than it is internationally. This is because armed self-defence is not likely to be the most relevant approach most of the time in defending the West. In particular, there are two other strands to defence in practice – both of which also raise questions over upholding the essence of the values being protected.

The first of these concerns the use of intelligence. In the end, perhaps the only way in which the September 11 attackers could have been stopped is by knowing exactly who they were – or at least one of them. This is perhaps far more important than knowing what they were planning to do exactly. However, new approaches to public security within Western societies, where those who are latent suicide–mass murderers are largely invisible, may also mean a focus on the communities in which they live. That may result in aggravated inter-communal relations. There are severe problems here. Domestic laws may have to be changed to permit actions by the authorities; attention to particular communities may serve to generate antagonisms and in part to do the work of those who, for example, lay claim to the one truth of Islam (falsely, in my view), by leading those with other perspectives to conclude that 'perhaps those guys were right' all along. This has to be avoided as far as possible.

Defending the West is to define the West. The question of defining the West is very much a question of who needs to be protected and who supports the kinds of development needed to ensure defence of the West. And, in contrast, it is a question of who feels threatened by those steps necessary to defending the West. But there is more to this than a simple binary division might suggest. This is because there is a competition for hearts and minds that on some issues occurs at the core of multi-cultural Western societies. On the one hand, where there really is no compromise, then particular measures have to be taken within Western communities, as well as in the wider world. This can even mean setting aside some of the key Western principles, in very selected circumstances and carefully selected ways – for example, the difficult and contentious step of permitting indefinite detention without charge, a direct challenge to the principle of *habeas corpus*, historically established as the right to the person, if no charge is laid. However, where overriding security imperatives necessitate sidestepping that principle and this can be established to the satisfaction of an appropriate judge, the needs of protecting society from real threats must take precedence. This is not a step that can be taken lightly. There is a fine line between protecting society and its values, on the one hand, and destroying them by breaching core principles, on the other. This is true in principle. However, the problem with breaching core principles is not only one of principle.

In tackling the needs of Western security, maintaining principles has a practical ramification. History, as well as common sense, shows that anything but the most judicious use of detention and surveillance powers (and, indeed, even the most judicious) can result in counter-productive outcomes, which might include serving to recruit support for opponents, while undermining and dissipating support for government action. This does significant damage, in terms of socio-political legitimacy and so support for any government's strategy. In the context of Washington's 'War on Terror', the necessary detention of individuals deemed to be unlawful combatants for security purposes at Camp Delta, the US Naval facility at Guantanamo Bay in Cuba, has played this role. It has been a lightning rod for liberal dissenting opinion within the US and around the world, as well as for those opposed to the US who seek to use its own standards against it. While Camp Delta serves a necessary purpose, in security terms, conditions there appear relatively good, and the legalities involved are technically sound, it creates a poor image and has a politically adverse effect around the world. One of the chief elements here, for all sides, is that if liberty and freedom are the principles and qualities that can be held to define the Western way, then breaching them in face of a threat, without the greatest care, is to concede vital ground to the enemy in an ideological struggle. The point here is not to avoid taking necessary action. It is to remain focused on the point of defending the West. This includes identifying measures to ensure community cohesion and certainly limit inter-communal tension.[41] It also includes ensuring defence of the freedom to practise any faith, or hold any belief, so long as it brings no harm to others, whether Islam, Hinduism, various Christianities, some other religion, or some secular ideology. There is no West if diversity and openness are not preserved, or if patterns of inter-communal integration and balancing are not maintained and developed.

The second way in which to ensure defence of the West, therefore, is to adapt for domestic contexts notions of partnership which have relevance on the international stage. The West can ultimately be defended only if core values of openness and integration can be preserved – even if in limited ways, for limited periods they may be constrained. This means significant proaction on the part of Western governments to ensure social and community cohesion. The test is to find ways within society to ensure that communities are not alienated and certainly are not demonized. In this context, it is important to avoid anything that could give succour to those who talk of divisions that amount to a 'clash of civilizations'. Indeed, that term is nonsense: civilizations, by definition, cannot clash. But civilization and anti-civilization can, as can politicized cultures. It is important to avoid confusion between civilizations and cultures – for there may be clashes, larger and smaller, where cultures are politicized. Defending the West is about internal security in both the objective terms of counter-intelligence agencies preventing attacks and disruption and the subjective, cathectic sense of making people feel secure.

Partnership at the domestic level and at the international level are not enough. Pre-emptive self-defence is also required. Redefinition of defence is necessary, commensurate with that made by the UN Security Council, regarding the scope of threats to international peace and security. Pre-emption is necessary. But the introduction of pre-emption should be accompanied by appropriate reinterpretation of the rules. Yet acceptance of a new interpretation might take time. For comparative example, during the early 1990s the majority of commentators and actors were slow to accept that circumstances had changed, and, at the time, regarded the various radical actions authorized by the UN Security Council as being contraventions of the UN Charter. However, during the Kosovo operations in early 1999 it was noticeable that many of the same figures who had condemned the UN Security Council-authorized action concerning Iraq, and Bosnia and Hercegovina in the first half of the decade, alleging that it was in breach of the UN Charter and Article 51, had changed their stance. Instead, they objected to the Kosovo action on the grounds that it was not authorized under Chapter VII. The same happened over Iraq during 2003. At the moment where the story appeared to have moved on, the critics had only just caught up with the main events of the last chapter. Therefore, it may also take time before any expansion in the scope of self-defence is broadly recognized or understood, during which time there will be charges, counter-charges and uncertainty.

If the implication of an expanded concept of threats to international peace and security is an enlarged notion of self-defence, then it would be better to acknowledge this with an internationally agreed normative template. International law and international society are, indeed, 'what states make them', and normative changes should be made with clear understanding of political consequences. The needs of self-defence have, in reality, shifted as radically as the requirements of international order. This might best be handled by open and common recognition of the implied revolution in the concept of self-defence and a commitment to ensure that acceptance of this change is managed. Given the legitimacy it bestows and the desirability of and need for early action, this should as far as possible be done by the UN Security Council, rather than forced upon precedent-setting state action by the threat of veto. Whether this occurs or not, the revolution in the meaning of self-defence implied by the equivalent revolution concerning the governing notion of threats to international peace and security is an unavoidable issue.

The new approach to self-defence requires national and international support at some stage, even if action without support might be needed along the way as part of the pragmatic-theoretical discourse of ideas and events by which a new understanding of self-defence will be constructed. One part of that process is establishing the limits of the concept, for the period ahead. But the starting point is to recognize the need to go beyond the traditional taboo of anticipatory self-defence. The early twenty-first century is an era in which action can be and might have to be pre-emptive and prompt; otherwise it could be too late.

# NOTES

## Chapter 1    Introduction

1   The characters mentioned in the following paragraphs are fictitious and resemblance to any person, living or dead, is entirely coincidental. However, all are composites with traits drawn from individuals I have known.
2   *Daily Telegraph*, 17 July 2002.
3   *The National Security Strategy of the United States of America*, http://usinfo.state.gov/topical/pol/terror/secstrat.htm.
4   Rt. Hon. Geoff Hoon, Secretary of State for Defence, 'September 11: A New Chapter for the Strategic Defence Review', Speech, King's College London, 5 Dec. 2001, http://www.kcl.ac.uk/phpnews/wmview.php?ArtID=105.
5   *National Security Strategy*.
6   Al-Qa'ida might also be transliterated as 'al-Qaeda'. The former is preferred in the present volume, on two grounds, although the latter appears to have greater currency, particularly among journalists and their editors. The first is that it is the form used in official documents by governments where English is the main language. The second is that I am advised by colleagues with strong linguistic competence that, in a difficult field, the transliteration system used in this formulation is more authoritative and accurate. Similarly, therefore, I use this system throughout, where relevant – notably, to refer to Usama bin Ladin, who might also be transliterated as Osama ben Laden (and often, inconsistently, as Osama bin Laden). The use of Usama bin Ladin also correlates with use of the acronym-cumdiminutive 'UBL', widely used by those working in official capacities and a useful shorthand, including in the present context.
7   It must be taken as one of the many effects of American dominance of international discourse that references to this event are conventionally

consistent with American day/month usage, rather than the date order found in Europe and elsewhere.

8   *The UK Government Dossier on Iraq's Weapons of Mass Destruction*, 24 Sept. 2002, had that name and focus – and no mention of al-Qa'ida – because British intelligence did not regard the evidence of links as adding up to a serious threat at that stage, although, of course, the potential for a nightmare coalition could not be ruled out.

9   Samuel P. Huntington, *The Clash of Civilizations: The Remaking of World Order* (London: Free Press, 2002). Huntington's discussion of the West is strong and impressive, but ultimately his use of the word 'civilization' alongside it is more troubling, both in terms of the word itself and the connotation central to his thesis of clashing civilizations, and in terms of the sharp exclusion it permits and provokes. This is why a more reflexive approach is adopted here.

10   This is the fundamental point concerning all philosophical enquiry and intellectual examination. Definition always relies in part on identifying that which is not part of that definition. So, we know black for what it is, but also in distinction from its opposite, white, and in contrast to the range of shades that can occur. Or we recognize and make sense of 'inside' only by reference to 'outside', and so on. By this measure, 'the West' would cease to be a meaningful term if it were not to be contrasted with an alternative, although it is conceivable that such an alternative need not be contemporaneous.

11   Huntington, *Clash*, p. 47, cites William E. Naff, 'Reflections on the Question of "East and West" from the Point of View of Japan', *Comparative Civilizations Review*, 13–14 (fall 1985 and spring 1986).

12   Lower-case 'west' and 'east' are used to denote the geographical points, while upper-case 'West' and 'East' denote political, cultural or strategic concepts.

13   Kenneth Clark, *Civilisation* (London: BBC and John Murray, 1969), p. 1.

14   Huntington, *Clash*, p. 72.

15   William H. McNeill, *The Rise of the West: A History of the Human Community with a Retrospective Essay* (Chicago: University of Chicago Press, 1991); McNeill, *The Pursuit of Power: Technology, Armed Forces and Society* (Oxford: Basil Blackwell, 1983).

16   It is assumed that the Islamist conception of 'the West' is not fixed, just as the sense of 'the West' used in this volume is reflexive and open. It is also assumed that more than one Islamist conception of the West is possible, therefore, and that such conceptions can exist side by side and overlap. Finally, it should not be assumed that any Islamist idea of 'the West' necessarily coincides with any Western understanding.

17   Huntington, *Clash*.

18   Samuel P. Huntington, *The Soldier and the State: The Theory and Politics of Civil–Military Relations* (Cambridge, Mass.: Belknap Press of Harvard University Press, 1957) and Huntington, *Political Order in Changing Societies* (New Haven: Yale University Press, 1968).

19  I acknowledge that Huntington discusses a strong literature that refers to particular 'civilizations' and often compares them. This justifies his use of the term that far. However, the use of 'civilization' as a noun linked to particular labels referring to the contemporary era is problematic, in that it is seemingly unreflexive, static and quasi-unitary, not permitting the real scope for plurality and change that is essential to understanding what the West is, especially in terms of its security. Huntington's view, as well as using civilization in an unhelpful way and possibly not doing good service to the West in terms of its openness and flexibility, can also give the dangerous impression that the 'rest', especially the nascent clash with 'Islamic civilization' that he identifies, are homogeneous in a way that the West is not. I say this despite the care and appropriate qualifications Huntington offers at times, including the recognition of diversity of cultures and 'sub-civilizations'. However, the treatment of quite different conflicts such as Chechnya and Bosnia as focal points for an umbrella 'Muslim' label backed by relatively limited degrees of support caricatures Islamic movements. He rightly identifies views expressed by some Muslims that do not take account of realities of engagement (and neither it seems does Huntington). These include the untenable view that the West somehow fights against Muslims and not against Christians – whereas actions over Bosnia and Kosovo against Serbian forces directly contradict this, while support of Kuwait and Iraqi Kurds are clearly examples of 'the West' siding with Muslims, albeit against others who might be labelled Muslims. However, it is to Huntington's credit throughout that he always seeks to recognize the way others see the West, no matter how the West sees itself. Huntington, *Clash*, pp. 45–6, 277–8 and 285–9.

20  Huntington, *Clash*, p. 41.

21  Christopher Coker, 'Nato as a Postmodern Alliance', in Sabrina Ramet and Christina Ingebretsen (eds), *Coming in from the Cold War: Changes in US–European Interactions since 1980* (Lanham, Md: Rowman and Littlefield, 2002).

22  Ken Booth and Tim Dunne, 'Worlds in Collision', in Booth and Dunne (eds), *Worlds in Collision: Terror and the Future of Global Order* (London: Palgrave, 2002), p. 7, refers to the views of Ziahuddin Sardar, in pointing out that terrorist acts lie 'outside the faith and reasoning of Islam'.

23  See Guilan Denoeux, 'The Forgotten Swamp: Navigating Political Islam', *Middle East Policy*, 9, 2 (June 2002), pp. 56–81; Ibrahim A. Harawan, *The Islamist Impasse*, Adelphi Paper 314 (Oxford: Oxford University Press for the IISS, 1997); Fred Halliday, *Two Hours that Shook the World: September 11, 2001* (London: Saqi Books, 2002), p. 43.

24  Ziahuddin Sardar and Meryl Wyn Davies, *Why Do People Hate America?* (Cambridge: Icon Books, 2003).

25  Robert Kagan, *On Paradise and Power: America and Europe in the New World Order* (London: Atlantic Books, 2003).

26  James Gow, *Triumph of the Lack of Will: International Diplomacy and the Yugoslav War* (New York: Columbia University Press, 1997), pp. 298–9.
27  On the future of the transatlantic relationship, see Beatrice Heuser, *Transatlantic Relations: Sharing Ideals and Costs*, Chatham House Paper (London: Pinter Cassell, 1996).
28  Huntington, *Clash*, p. 321.

# Chapter 2    Theory

1  Terms such as Constructivist Realism are capitalized throughout clearly to denote the use of a specific label.
2  Alexander Wendt, *The Social Theory of International Relations* (Cambridge: Cambridge University Press, 1999).
3  Hans J. Morgenthau, *Politics among Nations: The Struggle for Power and Peace*, brief edn (New York: McGraw-Hill, 1993).
4  Ibid.
5  E. H. Carr, *The Twenty Years' Crisis 1919–1939* (London: Macmillan, 1941).
6  Chris Brown, *Understanding International Relations*, 2nd edn (London: Palgrave, 2001); original emphasis.
7  For a limited number of surveys of the variety of views encompassed by Liberalism, Idealism and their variants see e.g.: Michael P. Doyle, *Ways of War and Peace: Realism, Liberalism, and Socialism* (New York: W. W. Norton, 1997); Joshua S. Goldstein, *International Relations*, 3rd edn (New York: Longman, 1999), ch. 3; Tim Dunne, 'Liberalism', in John Baylis and Steve Smith (eds), *The Globalization of World Politics: An Introduction to International Relations* (Oxford: Oxford University Press, 2001); Scott Burchill, 'Liberalism', in Scott Burchill et al., *Theories of International Relations*, 2nd edn (London: Palgrave, 2001).
8  Immanuel Kant, *Perpetual Peace*, in *Kant's Political Writings*, ed. H. Reiss, tr. H. Nisbett (Cambridge: Cambridge University Press, 1970); see also W. B. Gallie, *Philosophers of Peace and War: Kant, Clausewitz, Marx, Engels and Tolstoy* (Cambridge: Cambridge University Press, 1978).
9  Karl Marx and Friedrich Engels, *The Communist Manifesto*, in *Collected Works* (London: Lawrence and Wishart, 1980). See also Andrew Linklater, 'Marxism', in Burchill et al., *Theories*, ch. 5.
10  However, it should be noted that the relative failure of Marxism as an explanatory force in international relations gave rise to a new wave of radical critiques of the international system and its structure. While not all involved were post-Marxists, to some extent there was a trend for those 'opposing' the prevailing order and who might have been expected to opt for a Marxist approach at one time to engage with any or all of a variety of alternative approaches. These include the 'structuralist', 'critical' and 'postmodern' perspectives, as well as often, though not necessarily,

kindred approaches, such as 'feminism' (which formed a variety of strands). For an overview, see Burchill et al., *Theories*; Steve Smith, Ken Booth and Marysia Zalewski (eds), *International Theory: Positivism and Beyond* (Cambridge: Cambridge University Press, 1996); Goldstein, *International Relations*, pp. 114–34.

11 Martin Wight, *International Theory: The Three Traditions*, ed. Gabrielle Wight and Brian Porter (London: Leicester University Press for the RIIA, 1994).

12 Hugo Grotius, *De Jure Belli ac Pacis*, tr. Francis W. Kelsey (Oxford: Clarendon, 1925); Hedley Bull, *The Anarchical Society: A Study of Order in World Politics* (London: Macmillan, 1977). Among the other key authors in this field, as noted by Chris Brown, *Understanding* (p. 54), are: Martin Wight, Adam Watson, R. J. Vincent, Robert Jackson, James Mayall, Tim Dunne and Nicholas Wheeler.

13 Students, in my experience, often refer to Bull's work using one or other of these categories, depending on their individual reading and the particular aspect of his work that concerns them.

14 Bull, *Anarchical Society*. To be clear, as 'oxymoron' has come into increasing usage, albeit with a decidedly wrong meaning attached to it, I use the word in its conventional literary (and dictionary) sense to mean an apparent contradiction in terms – i.e. something that actually makes sense, despite juxtaposing two contrasting terms. It is not, therefore, a contradiction in terms – and nor is it a paradox.

15 Goldstein, *International Relations*, for example, only has one reference to Bull (p. 77) and that is a footnote reference in the context of discussing Realism and the notion of 'anarchy' that appears in Bull's title.

16 Among the most prominent writers in this context are Joseph Nye and Robert Keohane.

17 Wendt has been the major proponent of this approach. Others include Christian Reus Smit, 'Constructivism', in Burchill et al., *Theories*, and Friedrich Kratochwil, *Rules, Norms and Decisions* (Cambridge: Cambridge University Press, 1989).

18 Grotius, *De Jure Belli*; Bull, *Anarchical Society*.

19 Wendt, *Social Theory*, p. xiii.

20 George Schöpflin, *Nations, Identity, Power* (London: Hurst and Co., 2000).

21 See Steve Smith, 'Reflectivist and Constructivist Approaches to International Theory', in Baylis and Smith (eds), *Globalization*, ch. 11.

22 In his landmark article 'Anarchy is What States Make it: The Social Construction of Power Politics', *International Organization*, 46, 2 (1992), the main message is placed in the title. The very intention in taking the Social Constructivist approach is to open up the possibility of change – there may be anarchy in the international system, which Wendt accepts, but it only needs to present a competitive security dilemma if states choose to make it such through their interaction.

23 See Reus Smit, 'Constructivism', in Burchill et al., *Theories*, pp. 222–3, and Smith, 'Reflectivist', in Baylis and Smith (eds), *Globalization*, ch. 11.

24  See Smith, 'Reflectivist'; see also Brown, *Understanding*, pp. 52–4, which discusses the difference between 'brute facts' and 'social facts'.

25  While I have developed Constructivist Realism as a concept, I am informed that I am not the first to use it – my supreme-being leader and mentor Lawry Freedman tells me that Peter Katzenstein informally told him that he was a 'constructivist realist' at a conference in the mid-1990s, although the term was not used beyond this, or developed as a concept. I am glad to note that although Professor Sir Lawrence says he did not know what Katzenstein meant, *de facto* this provides an embryonic precursor for the concept, which implicitly and unreflexively might be said to have underpinned our work over the years (for example, my discussion of the way in which the interaction of actors and existing structures with the events in the former Yugoslavia and their own actions, shared interests and values resulted in an international use of force and full engagement, each decision governed by necessity, paving the way for further necessary action when not enough to achieve success – Gow, *Triumph of the Lack of Will: International Diplomacy and the Yugoslav Crisis* (New York: Columbia University Press, 1997), pp. 298–9). In a co-authored article that marked the fiftieth anniversary of the journal in which it appeared, Katzenstein and his collaborators review the history and development of the field over the lifetime of the journal, concluding that, at the end of that period, the major debate in international relations is between 'rationalism' and 'constructivism'. Peter Katzenstein, Robert O. Keohane and Stephen Krasner, 'International Organization and the Study of World Politics', *International Organization*, 50, 4 (1999).

26  Wendt, 'Anarchy', p. 424.

27  Barry Buzan, Ole Weaver and Jaap de Wilde, *Security: A New Framework for Analysis* (Boulder, Colo.: Lynne Rienner, 1998), p. 30.

28  Ibid., p. 47 n. 7.

29  Ibid., p. 31.

30  Sabrina P. Ramet, 'The United States and Europe: Toward Greater Cooperation or a Historic Parting? – An Idealist Perspective', in Sabrina Ramet and Christina Ingebretsen (eds), *Coming in from the Cold War: Changes in US–European Interactions since 1980* (Lanham, Md: Rowman and Littlefield, 2002).

31  In their brief introduction to the notion of social constructivism, this position is acknowledged by Terry Terriff, Stuart Croft, Lucy James and Patrick M. Morgan, *Security Studies Today* (Cambridge: Polity, 1999).

32  Kenneth N. Waltz, *Theory of International Politics* (Reading, Mass.: Addison Wesley, 1979).

33  See e.g. Michael E. Brown (ed.), *Ethnic Conflict and International Security* (Princeton: Princeton University Press, 1993).

34  Barry Posen, 'The Security Dilemma and Ethnic Conflict', *Survival*, 35 (1993), p. 27.

35  See Martin van Creveld, *On Future War* (aka *The Transformation of War*) (London: Brassey's, 1991).

36  Carl von Clausewitz, *On War*, ed. Anatol Rapoport (Harmondsworth: Penguin, 1968); for excellent readings of Clausewitz, see Beatrice Heuser, *Reading Clausewitz* (London: Pimlico, 2002), Jan Willem Honig, 'Interpreting Clausewitz', *Security Studies*, 3, 3 (spring 1994) and 'Introduction', in Carl von Clausewitz, *On War*, tr. J. J. Graham (New York: Barnes and Noble, 2004); and Raymond Aron, *Penser la guerre: Clausewitz*, vol. 1 (Paris: Gallimard, 1976).

37  This is a topic addressed in a forthcoming book, *Nationalism and Security*, which I am co-authoring with Wolfgang Danspeckgrüber.

38  John Mearsheimer, *The Tragedy of Great Power Politics* (New York: W. W. Norton, 2001).

39  Joseph S. Nye, *The Paradox of American Power: Why the World's Only Superpower Can't Go Alone* (Oxford: Oxford University Press, 2002), p. x, points out that the final report of a commission on national security led by two former US Senators warned that there would be attacks on American soil in which large numbers of people might die.

40  Samuel P. Huntington, *The Clash of Civilizations: The Remaking of World Order* (London: Free Press, 2002), p. 321. Huntington's use of civilization and his argument are accepted and assumed for the present purpose, although it is more reflexively approached in the discussion of defining the West in chapter 1. For a superlative exposition of the Huntingtonian thesis and its internal contradictions and false steps in argument, see Lavina Rajendram, 'Does the Clash of Civilisations Paradigm Provide a Persuasive Explanation of International Politics after September 11th?', *Cambridge Review of International Affairs*, 15, 2 (2002), pp. 217–32.

41  I am indebted to Chris Mackmurdo throughout this discussion for the time he spent as a sounding board and springboard for ideas, but in particular for helping me to make the link between the theoretical approach and the empirical nature of post-Waltzian security challenges. He also made the intriguing and correct observation that the problems here might be informed by understanding of the dialogue between John Locke and George (Bishop) Berkeley (on which see the discussion by Bryan Magee and Michael Ayers in Magee (ed.), *The Great Philosophers* (London: BBC, 1987), Dialogue 6.

42  Nye, *Paradox*.

# Chapter 3  Order

1  See: Paul Fifoot, 'Functions and Powers, and Inventions: UN Action in Respect of Human Rights and Humanitarian Intervention', in Nigel Rodley (ed.), *To Loose the Bands of Wickedness: International Intervention in Defence of Human Rights* (London: Brassey's, 1992); Jarat Chopra and T. C. Weiss, 'Sovereignty is No Longer Sacrosanct: Codifying Humanitarian Intervention', *Ethics and International Affairs*, 6 (1992), pp. 95–117; Gregory H. Fox, 'New Approaches to International Human

Rights: The Sovereign State Revisited', in Sohail H. Hashmi (ed.), *State Sovereignty: Change and Assistance in International Relations* (University Park: Pennsylvania State University Press, 1997); Rein Müllerson, *Ordering Anarchy* (The Hague: Martinus Nijhoff, 2000).

2   James A. Baker III with Thomas M. Franck, *The Politics of Diplomacy: Revolution, War and Peace, 1989–1992* (New York: G. P. Puttnam, 1996), claimed that in a three- and a half-year period, while he was pathfinder-in-chief, the 'very nature' of the international system was transformed.

3   One of the prime and most influential examples here is Robert Kaplan, 'The Coming Anarchy', *Atlantic Monthly*, 273 (Feb. 1994), pp. 44–76. See also Zbigniew Brzezinski, *Out of Control: Global Turmoil on the Eve of the Twenty-first Century* (New York: Scribner's, 1993).

4   Henry Kissinger, *Diplomacy* (London and New York: Simon and Schuster, 1995), p. 806.

5   Collective security must be understood as a particular concept, based on the mission to prevent or limit war in the international state system. It is intended to operate according to a mechanism where all states have a vested interest in peace and so agree that should any one of their number forget or overlook this vested interest and commit an act of aggression against another state, all states would join together to restore the *status quo ante*. This was the idea that underpinned the creation of the United Nations and which came closest to reality in practice after Iraq invaded Kuwait in 1990. Collective security is sometimes used to refer to collective defence arrangements such as NATO, given that the Alliance is collective and concerned with security. However, given the specificity of the concept of collective security, it is preferable to avoid such usage. For discussion of the concept, see Ines L. Claude Jr, *Power in International Relations* (New York: Random House, 1962).

6   G. John Ikenberry, 'The Myth of Post-Cold War Chaos', *Foreign Affairs*, 75, 3 (May–June 1996), p. 81.

7   Ken Booth, 'Human Wrongs and International Relations', *International Affairs*, 71, 1 (Jan. 1995), p. 117.

8   The following passage draws on James Gow, 'A Revolution in International Affairs?', *Security Dialogue*, 30, 3 (Sept. 2000).

9   Daniel Philpott, 'Westphalia, Authority and International Society', in Robert Jackson (ed.), *Sovereignty at the Millennium* (Oxford: Blackwell Publishers for the Political Studies Association, 1999), pp. 155–6, identifies 'constitutional revolutions' which are radical changes to one or more of what he terms the three faces of sovereignty.

10  Michael Ross Fowler and Julie Marie Bunck, *Law, Power, and the Sovereign State: The Evolution and the Application of the Concept of Sovereignty* (University Park: Pennsylvania State University Press, 1995), p. 12, quoted in Stephen D. Krasner, *Sovereignty: Organized Hypocrisy* (Princeton: Princeton University Press, 1999), p. 16.

11  Krasner, *Sovereignty*, pp. 9–25, emphasizes two versions of sovereignty, what he calls international legal sovereignty and what he terms

Westphalian sovereignty, but he omits to note that these are merely two faces of the same coin.

12  See e.g. Gidon Gottlieb, *Nation against State: A New Approach to Ethnic Conflicts and the Decline of Sovereignty* (New York: Council on Foreign Relations Press, 1993).

13  Cf. Gene M. Lyons and Michael Mastanduno (eds), *Beyond Westphalia? State Sovereignty and International Intervention* (Baltimore: Johns Hopkins University Press, 1995).

14  See Ikenberry, 'Myth'.

15  For a summary of such views in the first half of the twentieth century, see Alfred Cobban, *The Nation-state and National Self-determination* (London: Collins, 1969), p. 134.

16  Georg Sørensen, 'Sovereignty: Change and Continuity in a Fundamental Institution', in Jackson (ed.), *Sovereignty*, pp. 168–82.

17  See Harvey Starr, *Anarchy, Order and Integration: How to Manage Interdependence* (Ann Arbor: University of Michigan Press, 1997), p. 86.

18  See e.g. James Mayall, *Nationalism and International Society* (Cambridge: Cambridge University Press, 1990), pp. 26–7 and 36–7, and Cobban, *Nation-state*, pp. 40–1.

19  This is the key point of Krasner, *Sovereignty*.

20  Alexander Wendt, 'Anarchy is What States Make of it: The Social Construction of State Politics', *International Organization*, 46, 2 (1992), pp. 391–425.

21  See James Gow, 'Stratified Stability: Interpreting International Order', in Michael Clarke (ed.), *Brassey's Defence Yearbook 1997* (London: Brassey's, 1997), pp. 349–65.

22  'Annual Report to UN General Assembly', UN doc. SG/SM/7136 and GA/9596, 20 Sept. 1999.

23  The term was introduced by Jacob Bronowski, to explain the process by which order emerges in the physical world; Bronowski, *The Ascent of Man* (London: Book Club Associates, 1977), pp. 348–9.

24  There are points of correspondence with the attention to 'interconnections' and stability in Robert Jervis, *System Effects: Complexity in Political and Social Life* (Princeton: Princeton University Press, 1999).

25  This and all quotations in the following paragraphs are taken from Bronowski, *Ascent*, pp. 348–9.

26  Ernest Gellner, *Nations and Nationalism* (Oxford: Basil Blackwell, 1983).

27  Hedley Bull, *The Anarchical Society: A Study of Order in World Politics* (London: Macmillan, 1977).

28  Similar notions are liberty and justice – see W. B. Gallie, *Philosophy and the Historical Understanding* (London: Chatto and Windus, 1964), ch. 8.

29  Alan James, 'Sovereignty in Eastern Europe', *Millennium: Journal of International Studies*, 20, 1 (1991).

30  See Robert H. Jackson, *Quasi-States: Sovereignty, International Relations and the Third World* (Cambridge: Cambridge University Press, 1990)

and Barry Buzan, *People, States and Fear: An Agenda for International Security Studies in the Post-Cold War Era* (Hemel Hempstead: Harvester-Wheatsheaf, 1991), pp. 67–9.

31   Gordon Pocock, 'Nation, Community, Devolution and Sovereignty', *Political Quarterly*, 61, 3 (1990), p. 323. It should be noted that in Pocock's original he refers to sovereignty as a 'power'. However, this is a misconception: power can assist in the exercise of sovereign rights, but sovereignty is in principle about right, not capacity – a distinction in many ways key to the argument that Jackson makes in *Quasi-states*, distinguishing states endowed with formal sovereign rights, but only limited capacities to exercise those rights, often resulting in situations where the rights tend to be overridden by power concerns.

32   The case for purely legal conceptions of sovereignty is made by Fox, 'Approaches'; Fox draws on Ian Brownlie, *Principles of Public International Law*, 4th edn (Oxford: Clarendon, 1990).

33   See Mayall, *Nationalism*, p. 28.

34   Benedict Kingsbury, 'Claims by Non-state Groups in International Law', *Cornell International Law Journal*, 25 (1992).

35   See James Gow, *Triumph of the Lack of Will: International Diplomacy and the Yugoslav War* (New York: Columbia University Press, 1997), ch. 4.

36   'Statement of the Heads of State and Government of the United Nations Security Council', UN doc. S/23500, 31 Jan. 1992.

37   The Libyan case concerned the extradition of suspected terrorists to either the US or the UK from Libya in connection with the Lockerbie bombing incident (Resolution 748, 1992). Tripoli's failure to hand over the two suspects was taken by the Security Council to constitute a threat to international peace and security. This seemed to be straining the limits of the Security Council's power – even appearing to be an abuse, given that the US and the UK were Permanent Members of the Security Council. However, Libya's challenge to this action at the International Court of Justice resulted in a finding that the Council was supreme – in effect, sovereign: it defined international law regarding matters of international peace and security when it took action under Chapter VII. This confirmed both the Security Council's powers and set a tide mark for the meaning of the key phrase 'threat to international peace and security': it could even mean the presence of two individuals within a country. Libya's appeal to the International Court of Justice was rejected on the grounds that, in matters of international peace and security, the Security Council held the trump cards.

38   See Security Council Resolutions 1076, 1189, 1193, 1214 and especially 1267 and 1269 (15 and 19 Oct. 1999 respectively) on Afghanistan; 1070 on Sudan; 1199, 1203 and 1244 on Kosovo; 1264 and 1272 on East Timor; and 1031, 1088, 1174 and 1247 on Bosnia and Hercegovina.

39   NATO Secretary General Lord (George) Robertson. Interview with Jonathan Dimbleby, London Weekend Television, 11 June 2000, 1310 hrs.

## Chapter 4   Threats

1   This chapter is based on my general understanding of the concerns of Western governments and my judgement of the threats that the West faces. It is based on work done over more than a decade, including contributions to the development of the UK *Strategic Defence Review* in 1997–8 and the *Strategic Context Paper* in 2000. The work here and the judgements are my own, but in some cases are comparable to a range of official positions (although in some the views expressed here exceed those found in government documentation). See *The National Security Strategy of the United States of America*, http://usinfo.state.gov/ topical/pol/terror/secstrat.htm; *Strategic Defence Review Presented to Parliament by the Secretary of State for Defence by Command of Her Majesty* (London: Stationery Office, July 1998); *Strategic Context Paper* (London: Stationery Office, 2000); European Union Institute of Security Studies, *A Secure Europe in a Better World* (Paris, Dec. 2003).

2   Jessica Stern, 'The Protean Enemy', *Foreign Affairs*, 82, 4 (2003).

3   Philip Bobbit, *The Shield of Achilles* (London: Allen Lane, 2002), p. 820.

4   For a brief explanation of the Clausewitzian trinity, as used here, see ch. 2.

5   The prohibition on the use of chemical and biological weapons appears to be the only categorical position in the laws of war, where provisions are generally subject to the conditions of necessity and proportionality. Reflecting other agreements, this is stipulated in the *Statute of the International Criminal Court* (Article 8, Paragraph 2 (xvii), (xviii), (xx), which came into effect for States Parties to it on 1 July 2002, www.icc-cpi.int/ library/basicdocuments/rome_statute(e).html.

6   It might be noted that in the mid-1990s US officials were using the term 'rogue state', but that the terminological discussion and the potential confusion and negative implications of the label led the US State Department to use 'states of particular concern' instead by the end of that decade. However, the term 'rogue' continued generally to be used and recognized, and on this basis is used here.

7   David Victor and Nadejda M. Victor, 'Axis of Oil?', *Foreign Affairs*, 82, 2 (March–April 2003), p. 55.

8   The following is based on Mark Stenhouse and Bruce George, *NATO and Mediterranean Security: The New Central Region*, London Defence Studies 22 (London: Brassey's for the Centre for Defence Studies, 1994), pp. 5–13.

9   *Daily Telegraph*, 11 Dec. 2002.

10  See Stuart Croft, 'European Integration, Nuclear Deterrence and Franco-British Co-operation', *International Affairs*, 72, 4 (Oct. 1996), pp. 771–87.

11  Roberto Zadra, *European Integration and Nuclear Deterrence after the Cold War*, Chaillot Paper 5 (Paris: WEU Security Studies Institute, 1992).

12   *Strategic Defence Review*, para. 13.
13   Kenneth M. Pollack, 'Securing the Gulf', *Foreign Affairs*, 82, 4 (2003), p. 3.

# Chapter 5   Alliance

1   Christopher Coker, 'Nato as a Postmodern Alliance', in Sabrina Ramet and Christina Ingebretsen (eds), *Coming in from the Cold War: Changes in US–European Interactions since 1980* (Lanham, Md: Rowman and Littlefield, 2002).

2   There is a wealth of literature on NATO. Jan Willem Honig, *NATO: An Institution under Threat?* (New York: Institute for East–West Security Studies, Occasional Paper Series, 1991), remains the best study prior to the late 1990s, when an outpouring of volumes on Alliance transformation and enlargement appeared. A selection of the work available includes: Terry Terriff, Stuart Croft, E. Krahmann, Mark Webber and Jolyon Howorth, 'NATO's Next Enlargement', *International Affairs*, 78, 4 (2002); Paul Cornish, 'European Security: The End of Architecture and the New NATO', *International Affairs*, 72, 4 (1996); Ted Carpenter (ed.), *NATO Enters the 21st Century* (London: Frank Cass, 2001); André Dumoulin, *L'IESD, entre le nouveau concept stratégique de l'OTAN, la guerre au Kosovo et le Sommet de Cologne* (Liège: Centre d'Etudes de Defense, CAPRI, 2000); Christopher Coker, *Globalisation and Insecurity in the Twenty-first Century: NATO and the Management of Risk*, Adelphi Paper 345 (Oxford: Oxford University Press for the IISS, 2002); Jeffrey Simon, *NATO Enlargement: Opinions and Options* (Washington, DC: National Defense University Press, 1996).

3   The 'mostly' qualifying 'unimaginable' should be noted: those interested should look to NATO official Jamie Shea's *NATO 2000* (London: Brassey's, 1990), published ten years earlier, outlining a development of the Alliance not unlike much of that which occurred.

4   On the European Union and defence and security, see: Jolyon Howorth, *European Integration and Defence: the Ultimate Challenge?*, Chaillot Paper 43 (Paris: Institute for Security Studies, 2000); Jolyon Howorth, 'ESDP and NATO: Wedlock or Deadlock?', *Cooperation and Conflict*, 38, 3 (2003); Alison Bailes, 'The Institutional Reform of ESDP and Post-Prague NATO', *International Spectator*, 38, 3 (2003), pp. 31–46; Michael Clarke and Paul Cornish, 'The European Defence Project and the Prague Summit', *International Affairs*, 78, 4 (2002); Philip H. Gordon, 'Their Own Army? Making European Defence Work', *Foreign Affairs*, 79, 4 (2000); François Heisbourg, 'Europe's Strategic Ambitions: The Limits of Ambiguity', *Survival*, 42, 2 (2000); François Heisbourg (ed.), *European Defence: Making it Work*, Chaillot Paper 42 (Paris: Institute for Security Studies, 2000).

5   'Berlin Plus Agreement', www.nato.int/shape/news/2003/shape_eu/
    se030822a.htm at 19 Feb. 2004; *NATO Briefing*, Oct. 2003, p. 5; 'Speech
    by NATO Secretary General, Jaap de Hoop Scheffer at the Munich
    Security Conference', 7 Feb. 2004, www.nato.int/docu/speech/2004/
    s040207a.htm at 19 Feb. 2004.
6   Beatrice Heuser, *Reading Clausewitz* (London: Pimlico, 2002).
7   Jonathan Eyal, 'Ten Commandments to Cleanse the Guilt in Bosnia',
    *World Today*, 52, 12 (Dec. 1996), pp. 300–1; James Gow, *Triumph of the
    Lack of Will: International Diplomacy and the Yugoslav War* (New York:
    Columbia University Press, 1997).
8   See James Gow, *The Serbian Project and its Adversaries: A Strategy of
    War Crimes* (London: Hurst and Co., 2003).
9   The following draws on draft work: James Gow and Fotini Bellou,
    'Leadership and Legitimacy, Image and Intervention', *Civil Wars*, 6, 2
    (2003). The notion of leadership image was developed by Bellou, 'Amer-
    ican Leadership Image and the Yugoslav Crisis, 1991–1997', PhD thesis,
    King's College London, 2000.
10  Joseph S. Nye, *The Paradox of American Power: Why the World's Only
    Superpower Can't Go Alone* (Oxford: Oxford University Press, 2002).
11  European Union Institute of Security Studies, *A Secure Europe in a Better
    World* (Paris, Dec. 2003).

## Chapter 6    Partnership

1   Robert Kagan, *On Paradise and Power: America and Europe in the New
    World Order* (London: Atlantic Books, 2003). Kagan's core concern is
    preparedness to use force. However, the same continuity can be seen in
    terms of diplomacy and partnership, as the US Secretary of State made
    apparent – see Colin Powell, 'A Strategy of Partnerships', *Foreign Affairs*,
    83, 21 (Jan.–Feb. 2004).
2   A small example of the potential for difficulty could be found prior to
    the 1999 accession. The Czech Republic was embarrassed on the eve of
    joining the Alliance when its security service revealed the identity and
    much of the sensitive work regarding, *inter alia*, Iraq that the British
    Secret Intelligence Service officer posted to Prague had been carrying
    out. *Daily Telegraph*, 4 Feb. 1999.
3   Madeleine K. Albright, 'The Testing of American Foreign Policy', *For-
    eign Affairs*, 77, 6 (Nov.–Dec. 1998), p. 52; see also 'NATO: Preparing
    for the Washington Summit', *Dispatch* [US Department of State]
    (Dec. 1998).
4   *Strategic Defence Review Presented to Parliament by the Secretary of
    State for Defence by Command of Her Majesty* (London: Stationery
    Office, July 1998).
5   Powell, 'Strategy of Partnerships', p. 26.
6   *Strategic Defence Review*, para. 30.

7   Albright, 'Testing', p. 53.
8   This part of the analysis benefited from the insightful advice of Clelia Rontonnyanni, Russia and Eurasia Programme, Royal Institute of International Affairs.
9   This analysis is based on a variety of interviews, almost all confidential, with both Russian and Western officials.
10  While not wholly inconsistent with the multifaceted political-military approach laid out in the EU's strategy document this is not explicitly envisaged: European Union Institute of Security Studies, *A Secure Europe in a Better World* (Paris: Dec. 2003), p. 12.
11  Steven Kull, *A Study of Public Attitudes on European-American Issues, Part Two: Americans on the NATO Operation in Bosnia* (Washington, DC: Program on International Policy Attitudes, March 1998, also available at http://www.pipa.org (8 May 1998), where cognate research by the program can be found. See also Kull, *Seeking a New Balance: A Study of American and European Public Attitudes on Transatlantic Issues* (Washington, DC: Program on International Policy Attitudes, June 1998).

# Chapter 7   Pre-emption

1   I first identified this conceptual implication in the late 1990s, while holding visiting positions at the Woodrow Wilson International Center for Scholars, the Institute of War and Peace Studies, Columbia University, and the Center of International Studies, Princeton University. The conceptual case for a revolution in self-defence was first published in my article 'A Revolution in International Affairs?', *Security Dialogue*, 30, 3 (2000), resting on the logic extending from the UN Security Council's redefinition of threats to peace and security – some way before the discussion on pre-emptive self-defence that developed with the advent of the George W. Bush Presidency in the US and the September 11 attacks.
2   Lee Feinstein and Anne-Marie Slaughter, 'A Duty to Prevent', *Foreign Affairs*, 83, 1 (Jan.–Feb. 2004).
3   I have ample evidence for this both from discussion with friends and colleagues, and from the reaction of readers of both the original manuscript for this volume and earlier attempts to address the problem conceptually, including review and publication of my article 'A Revolution in International Affairs?'
4   There were two discrete senses in which this could be understood. The first concerned the more general question of solving problems and preventing disruption in international order, in the interests of states and the system itself. The second, narrower, sense involved the emergence of 'neo-conservative' thinking in the United States, which sought not only to make the world work, but to make it work in a particular way by exporting a particular ideological and political programme to the world

as a whole. This second sense of 'setting the world right' became more pronounced when George W. Bush became US President, and formed an Administration in which strong neo-conservative thinkers and politicians had influence – most notably, Paul Wolfowitz, one of US Defense Secretary Donald Rumsfeld's senior deputies, the chief ideologue and architect of US policy on Iraq. See Bob Woodward, *Bush at War: Inside the Bush White House* (London: Simon and Schuster, 2002) and Eric Laurent, *La Guerre de Bush: les secrets inavouables d'un conflit* (Paris: Plon, 2003), pp. 122–51 *passim*, and Eric Laurent, *Le Monde secret de Bush: la religion, les affaires, les réseaux occultes* (Paris: Plon, 2003), tr. as *Bush's Secret World* (Cambridge: Polity, 2004), chs. 7 and 10.

5   For example, the overwhelming majority of participants at seminars at the Institute of Contemporary Arts, London and the Institute for Defence Studies, Lisbon in spring 2003 (where I was making presentations on the topic) took the view that there was no legal basis for action whatsoever.

6   See e.g. the discussions by Adam Roberts, 'Law and the Use of Force after Iraq', and Mats Berdal, 'The UN Security Council: Ineffective but Indispensable', *Survival*, 45, 2 (summer 2003).

7   Although Security Council Resolution 1441 appears to be necessary to confirm the currency and status of Resolutions 678 and 687, and this was a position taken by the UK and others, the formal US position expressed in a letter dated 20 March 2003 to the Secretary-General by its Permanent Representative to the UN Security Council rested only on the relationship between 687 and 678. This is cited by Adam Roberts, 'Law and the Use of Force', pp. 40 and 55 n. 16.

8   Interview with a British government official, March 2003.

9   George W. Bush, 'Remarks by the President in Address to the Nation, The Cross Hall' ('President Says Saddam Hussein Must Leave Iraq within 48 Hours'), 17 March 2003, www.whitehouse.gov/news/releases/3002/03/20030317-7.html at 5 Feb. 2004.

10  *CNN International*, 15 Aug. 2002.

11  This is contrary to the pessimistic reactions of some commentators. See e.g. Michael Glennon, 'Why the Security Council Failed', *Foreign Affairs*, 82, 3 (May–June 2003).

12  Nicholas J. Wheeler, *Saving Strangers: Humanitarian Intervention in International Society* (Oxford: Oxford University Press, 2000); cf. the ultra-conservative view of Ian Brownlie, *International Law and the Use of Force by States* (Oxford: Clarendon, 1963), as cited by Rein Müllerson, '*Jus ad Bellum*: Plus ça Change (le Monde) Plus C'est la Même Chose (Le Droit)?', *Journal of Conflict and Security Law*, 7, 2 (2002).

13  Jean Anouilh, *Becket ou l'honneur de Dieu* (Paris: Collection Folio, 1978), p. 66.

14  *The National Security Strategy of the United States of America*, http://usinfo.state.gov/topical/pol/terror/secstrat.htm, p. 15.

15  The quintessential conservative legal position is that expressed by Ian Brownlie, who in his standard texts for international lawyers stipulates a highly restrictive interpretation as being authoritative, in which almost no use of force is allowed. See Brownlie, *International Law* and *Principles of Public International Law*, 4th edn (Oxford: Clarendon, 1990). Müllerson reports that Brownlie reasserted this position during 2001 in a lecture delivered at the HEI in Geneva, in '*Jus ad Bellum*', pp. 149–50. See also the strict discussion offered by Michael Glennon, *Limits of Law, Prerogatives of Power: Interventionism after Kosovo* (New York: Palgrave, 2001), pp. 21–4.

16  Christopher Greenwood, 'International Law and the "War against Terrorism"', *International Affairs*, 78, 2 (2002), pp. 301–17; Michael Byers, 'Terrorism, Defence and International Law: Unleashing Force', *World Today*, 27, 12 (Dec. 2001), pp. 20–2.

17  See Marjorie Whiteman (ed.), *Digest of International Law*, vol. 12 (Washington, DC: US Department of State, 1971), pp. 42–77.

18  I am grateful to Vesko Popovski for engaging me in discussion on this point and helping me to clarify my thinking.

19  Vesselin Popovski, 'The UN Security Council and the International Constitution', unpublished draft work, 2000.

20  Yoram Dinstein, *War, Aggression and Self-Defence*, 3rd edn (Cambridge: Grotius, 2001), p. 228.

21  As noted above, this is the position taken by the central text in the field, Brownlie, *International Law*.

22  Oscar Schachter, 'The Right of States to Use Armed Force', *Michigan Law Review*, 82 (1984).

23  David Rodin, *War and Self-Defence* (Oxford: Clarendon, 2002), pp. 111–12.

24  E. J. P. Myjer and N. D. White, 'An Unlimited Right to Self-Defence?', *Journal of Conflict and Security Law*, 7, 1 (2002).

25  Müllerson, '*Jus ad Bellum*', p. 175 n. 80.

26  This is argued fully by Müllerson, '*Jus ad Bellum*'. It is more briefly confirmed with authority by Michael Byers, 'Terror and the Future of International Law', in Ken Booth and Tim Dunne, *Worlds in Collision: Terror and the Future of Global Order* (London: Palgrave, 2002), pp. 121–2 and Roberts, 'Law and the Use of Force', p. 51.

27  I have always assumed that the fourth airliner, which crashed in Pennsylvania, was also headed for a target in Virginia. The strategic character and logic of the attacks suggests this. Two planes struck at the centre of economic power, hitting the World Trade Center in New York City. And one plane struck at one part of the core of US security, the Pentagon, in Virginia. It seems to me that the fourth plane was intended for the CIA headquarters in Langley, Virginia – the other core part of America's security capability. This seems to make far more strategic sense than suggestions that it was destined for either the President's

retreat at Camp David in Maryland – a favourite suggestion in the days after the attack – or the White House, about which there was also much speculation at the time.

28  Roberts, 'Law and the Use of Force', p. 48.
29  Cf. the discussion of this in ch. 2.
30  Response to questions, 'Spinning Hutton: In Search of the Big Picture', European Research Institute, University of Birmingham, 20 Feb. 2004.
31  *UK Government Dossier on Iraq's Weapons of Mass Destruction* (London: Stationery Office, 24 Sept. 2002).
32  'Transcript: David Kay at Senate Hearing', *CNN.com*, www.cnn.com/2004/US/01/28/kay.transcript/index.html, at 4 Feb. 2004.
33  Interview on *ABC World News Tonight*, 5 Feb. 2004.
34  CIA Director George Tenet, FBI Director Robert Mueller and DIA Director Admiral Lowell Jacoby.
35  Martha Raddatz, *ABC World News Tonight*, 23 Feb. 2004.
36  *ABC World News Tonight*, 23 Feb. 2004.
37  Beatrice Heuser, *Reading Clausewitz* (London: Pimlico, 2002).
38  Roberts, 'Law and the Use of Force', p. 51.
39  Vesselin Popovski, 'The International Criminal Court', *International Relations*, 15, 3 (Dec. 2000).
40  Credit must go to Chris Mackmurdo for this insight.
41  Cf. the discussion in ch. 1.

# BIBLIOGRAPHY

Ajami, Fouad, 'The Falseness of Anti-Americanism', *Foreign Policy*, 138 (Sept.–Oct. 2003).

Albright, Madeleine K., 'Bridges, Bombs or Bluster?' *Foreign Affairs*, 82, 5 (Sept.–Oct. 2003).

Albright, Madeleine K., 'NATO: Preparing for the Washington Summit', *Dispatch* [US Department of State] (Dec. 1998).

Albright, Madeleine K., 'The Testing of American Foreign Policy', *Foreign Affairs*, 77, 6 (Nov.–Dec. 1998).

Albright, Madeleine K., 'United Nations', *Foreign Policy*, 138 (Sept.–Oct. 2003).

Allin, Dana, *NATO's Balkan Interventions*, Adelphi Paper 347 (Oxford: Oxford University Press for the IISS, 2002).

'Annual Report to UN General Assembly', UN doc. SG/SM/7136 and GA/ 9596/20, Sept. 1999.

Anouilh, Jean, *Becket ou l'honneur de Dieu* (Paris: Collection Folio, 1978).

Aron, Raymond, *Penser la guerre: Clausewitz*, vol. 1 (Paris: Gallimard, 1976).

Asmuth, Ronald D., 'Rebuilding the Atlantic Alliance', *Foreign Affairs*, 82, 5 (Sept.–Oct. 2003).

Bailes, Alison, 'The Institutional Reform of ESDP and post-Prague NATO', *International Spectator*, 38, 3 (2003), pp. 31–46.

Baker, James A., III, with Thomas M. Franck, *The Politics of Diplomacy: Revolution, War and Peace, 1989–1992* (New York: G. P. Puttnam, 1996).

Baylis, John, and Steve Smith (eds), *The Globalization of World Politics: An Introduction to International Relations* (Oxford: Oxford University Press, 2001).

Bellou, Fotini, 'American Leadership Image and the Yugoslav Crisis, 1991–1997', PhD thesis, King's College London, 2000.

Berdal, Mats, 'The UN Security Council: Ineffective but Indispensable', *Survival*, 45, 2 (summer 2003).

Best, Geoffrey, *War and Law since 1945* (Oxford: Clarendon, 1997).
Biddell, Stephen, 'Afghanistan and the Future of Warfare', *Foreign Affairs*, 82, 2 (2003).
Bobbit, Philip, *The Shield of Achilles* (London: Allen Lane, 2002).
Bono, G., *NATO's Peace Enforcement Tasks and Policy Communities: 1990–1999* (Aldershot: Ashgate, 2003).
Boot, Max, 'The New American Way of War', *Foreign Affairs*, 82, 4 (July–Aug. 2003).
Booth, Ken, 'Human Wrongs and International Relations', *International Affairs*, 71, 1 (Jan. 1995).
Booth, Ken, and Tim Dunne, 'Worlds in Collision', in Booth and Dunne (eds), *Worlds in Collision: Terror and the Future of Global Order* (London: Palgrave, 2002).
Booth, Ken, and Tim Dunne, *Worlds in Collision: Terror and the Future of Global Order* (London: Palgrave, 2002).
Bronowski, Jacob, *The Ascent of Man* (London: Book Club Associates, 1977).
Brown, Chris, *Sovereignty, Rights and Justice: International Political Theory Today* (Cambridge: Polity, 2002).
Brown, Chris, *Understanding International Relations*, 2nd edn (London: Palgrave, 2001).
Brown, Michael E. (ed.), *Ethnic Conflict and International Security* (Princeton: Princeton University Press, 1993).
Brownlie, Ian, *International Law and the Use of Force by States* (Oxford: Clarendon, 1963).
Brownlie, Ian, *Principles of Public International Law*, 4th edn (Oxford: Clarendon, 1990).
Brzezinski, Zbigniew, *Out of Control: Global Turmoil on the Eve of the Twenty-first Century* (New York: Scribner's, 1993).
Burchill, Scott, et al., *Theories of International Relations*, 2nd edn (London: Palgrave, 2001).
Bull, Hedley, *The Anarchical Society: A Study of Order in World Politics* (London: Macmillan, 1977).
Buzan, Barry, *People, States and Fear: An Agenda for International Security Studies in the Post-Cold War Era* (Hemel Hempstead: Harvester-Wheatsheaf, 1991).
Buzan, Barry, Ole Weaver and Jaap de Wilde, *Security: A New Framework for Analysis* (Boulder, Colo.: Lynne Rienner, 1998).
Byers, Michael, 'Terror and the Future of International Law', in Ken Booth and Tim Dunne (eds), *Worlds in Collision: Terror and the Future of Global Order* (London: Palgrave, 2002).
Byers, Michael, 'Terrorism, Defence and International Law: Unleashing Force', *World Today*, 27, 12 (Dec. 2001).
Carpenter, Ted (ed.), *NATO Enters the 21st Century* (London: Frank Cass, 2001).
Carr, E. H., *The Twenty Years' Crisis 1919–1939* (London: Macmillan, 1941).

Chopra, Jarat, and T. C. Weiss, 'Sovereignty is No Longer Sacrosanct: Codifying Humanitarian Intervention', *Ethics and International Affairs*, 6 (1992), pp. 95–117.

Clark, Kenneth, *Civilisation* (London: BBC and John Murray, 1969), p. 1.

Clarke, Michael, and Paul Cornish, 'The European Defence Project and the Prague Summit', *International Affairs*, 78, 4 (2002).

Claude, Ines L. Jr, *Power in International Relations* (New York: Random House, 1962).

Clausewitz, Carl von, *On War*, ed. Anatol Rapaport (Harmondsworth: Penguin, 1968).

Cobban, Alfred, *The Nation-state and National Self-determination* (London: Collins, 1969).

Cohen, Elliott A., 'A Tale of Two Secretaries', *Foreign Affairs*, 81, 3 (2002).

Coker, Christopher, *Globalisation and Insecurity in the Twenty-first Century: NATO and the Management of Risk*, Adelphi Paper 345 (Oxford: Oxford University Press for the IISS, 2002).

Coker, Christopher, 'Nato as a Postmodern Alliance', in Sabrina Ramet and Christina Ingebretsen (eds), *Coming in from the Cold War: Changes in US–European Interactions since 1980* (Lanham, Md: Rowman and Littlefield, 2002).

Cooper, Robert, *The Breaking of Nations: Order and Chaos in the Twenty-first Century* (London: Atlantic Books, 2003).

Corbin, Jane, *The Base: al-Qaeda and the Changing Face of Global Terror* (London: Simon and Schuster, 2002).

Cornish, Paul, 'European Security: The End of Architecture and the New NATO', *International Affairs*, 72, 4 (1996).

Cornish, Paul, 'NATO: The Practice and Politics of Transformation', *International Affairs*, 80, 1 (Jan. 2004).

Cox, Michael, 'Martians and Venusians in the New World Order', *International Affairs*, 79, 3 (May 2003).

Creveld, Martin van, *On Future War* (aka *The Transformation of War*) (London: Brassey's, 1991).

Crocker, Chester D., 'Engaging Failing States', *Foreign Affairs*, 82, 5 (2003).

Croft, Stuart, 'European Integration, Nuclear Deterrence and Franco-British Co-operation', *International Affairs*, 72, 4 (Oct. 1996).

Crowe, Brian, 'A Common European Foreign Policy after Iraq?', *International Affairs*, 79, 3 (May 2003).

Daalder, Ivo H., 'The End of Atlanticism', *Survival*, 45, 2 (summer 2003).

Denoeux, Guilan, 'The Forgotten Swamp: Navigating Political Islam', *Middle East Policy*, 9, 2 (June 2002).

Dinstein, Yoram, *War, Aggression and Self-Defence*, 3rd edn (Cambridge: Grotius, 2001).

Doyle, Michael P., *Ways of War and Peace: Realism, Liberalism, and Socialism* (New York: W. W. Norton, 1997).

Dumoulin, André, *L'IESD, entre le nouveau concept stratégique de l'OTAN, la guerre au Kosovo et le Sommet de Cologne* (Liège: Centre d'Etudes de Défense, CAPRI, 2000).

Dunne, Tim, 'Liberalism', in John Baylis and Steve Smith (eds), *The Globalization of World Politics: An Introduction to International Relations*, 2nd edn (Oxford: Oxford University Press, 2001).

Emmerson, Donald K., 'Americanising Asia?' *Foreign Affairs*, 77, 3 (May–June 1998).

European Union Institute of Security Studies, *A Secure Europe in a Better World* (Paris, Dec. 2003).

Eyal, Jonathan, 'NATO's Enlargement: Anatomy of a Decision', *International Affairs*, 73, 4 (1997).

Eyal, Jonathan, 'Ten Commandments to Cleanse the Guilt in Bosnia', *World Today*, 52, 12 (Dec. 1996).

Lee, Feinstein, and Anne-Marie Slaughter, 'A Duty to Prevent', *Foreign Affairs*, 83, 1 (Jan.–Feb. 2004).

Fifoot, Paul, 'Functions and Powers, and Inventions: UN Action in Respect of Human Rights and Humanitarian Intervention', in Nigel Rodley (ed.), *To Loose the Bands of Wickedness: International Intervention in Defence of Human Rights* (London: Brassey's, 1992).

Freedman, Lawrence D., 'War', *Foreign Policy*, 137 (July–Aug. 2003).

Freedman, Lawrence, *Deterrence* (Cambridge: Polity, 2004).

Fox, Gregory H., 'New Approaches to International Human Rights: The Sovereign State Revisited', in Sohail H. Hashmi (ed.), *State Sovereignty: Change and Assistance in International Relations* (University Park: Pennsylvania State University Press, 1997).

Fuller, Greg, 'The Future of Political Islam', *Foreign Affairs*, 81, 2 (March–April 2002).

Gallie, W. B., *Philosophers of Peace and War: Kant, Clausewitz, Marx, Engels and Tolstoy* (Cambridge: Cambridge University Press, 1978).

Gallie, W. B., *Philosophy and the Historical Understanding* (London: Chatto and Windus, 1964).

Gellner, Ernest, *Nations and Nationalism* (Oxford: Basil Blackwell, 1983).

Glennon, Michael, *Limits of Law, Prerogatives of Power: Interventionism after Kosovo* (New York: Palgrave, 2001).

Glennon, Michael, 'Why the Security Council Failed', *Foreign Affairs*, 82, 3 (May–June 2003).

Goldstein, Joshua S., *International Relations*, 3rd edn (New York: Longman, 1999).

Gordon, Philip H., 'Their Own Army? Making European Defence Work', *Foreign Affairs*, 79, 4 (2000).

Gottlieb, Gidon, *Nation against State: A New Approach to Ethnic Conflicts and the Decline of Sovereignty* (New York: Council on Foreign Relations Press, 1993).

Gow, James, 'A Revolution in International Affairs?' *Security Dialogue*, 30, 3 (Sept. 2000).

Gow, James, *The Serbian Project and its Adversaries: A Strategy of War Crimes* (London: Hurst and Co., 2003).

Gow, James, 'Stratified Stability: Interpreting International Order', in Michael Clarke (ed.), *Brassey's Defence Yearbook 1997* (London: Brassey's, 1997).

Gow, James, *Triumph of the Lack of Will: International Diplomacy and the Yugoslav War* (New York: Columbia University Press, 1997).

Gow, James, and Fotini Bellou, 'Leadership and Legitimacy, Image and Intervention', *Civil Wars*, 6, 2 (2003).

Greenwood, Christopher, 'International Law and the "War against Terrorism"', *International Affairs*, 78, 2 (2002).

Grotius, Hugo, *De Jure Belli ac Pacis*, tr. Francis W. Kelsey (Oxford: Clarendon, 1925).

Hagman, Hans. Christian, *European Crisis Management and Defence: The Search for Capabilities*, Adelphi Paper 353 (Oxford: Oxford University Press for the IISS, 2002).

Halliday, Fred, *Two Hours that Shook the World: September 11, 2001* (London: Saqi Books, 2002).

Harawan, Ibrahim A., *The Islamist Impasse*, Adelphi Paper 314 (Oxford: Oxford University Press for the IISS, 1997).

Hashmi, Sohail H. (ed.), *State Sovereignty: Change and Assistance in International Relations* (University Park: Pennsylvania State University Press, 1997).

Haslam, Jonathan, *No Virtue Like Necessity: Realist Thought in International Relations since Machiavelli* (New Haven: Yale University Press, 2002).

Hassner, Pierre, *La Terreur et l'Empire: la violence et la paix II* (Paris: Seuil, 2003).

Hassner, Pierre, and Roland Marchal, *Guerres et sociétés: État et violence après la Guerre Froide* (Paris: Karthala, 2003).

Hassner, Pierre, and Justin Vaïse, *Washington et le monde* (Paris: CERI/ Autrement, 2003).

Heisbourg, François, 'Europe's Strategic Ambitions: The Limits of Ambiguity', *Survival*, 42, 2 (2000).

Heisbourg, François (ed.), *European Defence: Making it Work*, Chaillot Paper 42 (Paris: Institute for Security Studies, 2000).

Heuser, Beatrice, *Reading Clausewitz* (London: Pimlico, 2002).

Heuser, Beatrice, *Transatlantic Relations: Sharing Ideals and Costs*, Chatham House Paper (London: Pinter Cassell, 1996).

Hippel, Karin von, *Democracy by Force: US Military Intervention in the Post-Cold War World* (Cambridge: Cambridge University Press, 2000).

Hirst, Paul, *War and Power in the 21st Century* (Cambridge: Polity, 2001).

Hoffmann, Stanley, 'Clash of Globalizations', *Foreign Affairs*, 81, 4 (2002).

Hoffmann, Stanley, 'US–European Relations: Past and Future', *International Relations*, 79, 5 (2003).

Holsti, K. J., *International Politics: A Framework for Analysis*, 5th edn (Englewood Cliffs, NJ: Prentice-Hall, 1988).

Honig, Jan Willem, 'Interpreting Clausewitz', *Security Studies*, 3, 3 (spring 1994).

Honig, Jan Willem, 'Introduction', in Carl von Clausewitz, *On War*, tr. J. J. Graham (New York: Barnes and Noble, 2004).

Honig, Jan Willem, *NATO: An Institution under Threat?* (New York: Institute for East–West Security Studies, Occasional Paper Series, 1991).

Hoon, Geoff, Secretary of State for Defence, 'September 11: A New Chapter for the Strategic Defence Review', Speech, King's College London, 5 Dec. 2001, http://www.kcl.ac.uk/phpnews/wmview.php?ArtID=105.

Howard, Michael, George J. Andreopolous and Mark R. Shulman, *The Laws of War: Constraints on War in the Western World* (New Haven: Yale University Press, 1994).

Howorth, Jolyon, 'Britain, France and the European Defence Initiative', *Survival*, 42, 2 (2000).

Howorth, Jolyon, 'ESDP and NATO: Wedlock or Deadlock?' *Cooperation and Conflict*, 38, 3 (2003).

Howorth, Jolyon, *European Integration and Defence: The Ultimate Challenge?* Chaillot Paper 43 (Paris: Institute for Security Studies, 2000).

Huntington, Samuel P., *The Clash of Civilizations: The Remaking of World Order* (London: Free Press, 2002).

Huntington, Samuel P., *Political Order in Changing Societies* (New Haven: Yale University Press, 1968).

Huntington, Samuel P., *The Soldier and the State: The Theory and Politics of Civil–Military Relations* (Cambridge, Mass.: Belknap Press of Harvard University Press, 1957).

Ikenberry, G. John, 'The Myth of Post-Cold War Chaos', *Foreign Affairs*, 75, 3 (May–June 1996).

Jackson, Robert H., *Quasi-states: Sovereignty, International Relations and the Third World* (Cambridge: Cambridge University Press, 1990).

James, Alan, 'Sovereignty in Eastern Europe', *Millennium: Journal of International Studies*, 20, 1 (1991).

Jervis, Robert, 'Compulsive Empire', *Foreign Policy*, 137 (July–Aug. 2003).

Jervis, Robert, *System Effects: Complexity in Political and Social Life* (Princeton: Princeton University Press, 1999).

Kagan, Robert, *On Paradise and Power: America and Europe in the New World Order* (London: Atlantic Books, 2003).

Kant, Immanuel, *Perpetual Peace*, in *Kant's Political Writings*, ed. H. Reiss, tr. H. Nisbett (Cambridge: Cambridge University Press, 1970).

Kaplan, Robert, 'The Coming Anarchy', *Atlantic Monthly*, 273 (Feb. 1994), pp. 44–76.

Kaztenstein, Peter, Robert O. Keohane and Stephen Krasner, 'International Organization and the Study of World Politics', *International Organization*, 50, 4 (1999).

Kingsbury, Benedict, 'Claims by Non-state Groups in International Law', *Cornell International Law Journal*, 25 (1992).

Kellner, Douglas, *From 9/11 to Terror War: The Dangers of the Bush Legacy* (Boulder, Colo.: Rowman and Littlefield, 2003).

Kissinger, Henry, *Diplomacy* (London and New York: Simon and Schuster, 1995).

Krasner, Stephen D. (ed.), *Problematic Sovereignty: Contested Rules and Political Possibilities* (New York: Columbia University Press, 2001).

Krasner, Stephen D., *Sovereignty: Organized Hypocrisy* (Princeton: Princeton University Press, 1999).

Kratochwil, Friedrich, *Rules, Norms and Decisions* (Cambridge: Cambridge University Press, 1989).

Kull, Steven, *A Study of Public Attitudes on European–American Issues, Part Two: Americans on the NATO Operation in Bosnia* (Washington, DC: Program on International Policy Attitudes, March 1998).

Kull, Steven, *Seeking a New Balance: A Study of American and European Public Attitudes on Transatlantic Issues* (Washington, DC: Program on International Policy Attitudes, June 1998).

Laurent, Eric, *La Guerre de Bush: les secrets inavouables d'un conflit* (Paris: Plon, 2003).

Laurent, Eric, *Le Monde secret de Bush: la religion, les affaires, les réseaux occultes* (Paris: Plon, 2003); Eng. tr. *Bush's Secret World* (Cambridge: Polity, 2004).

Leffler, Melvin P., '9/11 and the Past and Future of American Foreign Policy', *International Affairs*, 79, 5 (2003).

Leonard, Mark, 'Diplomacy by Other Means', *Foreign Policy*, 132 (Sept.–Oct. 2002).

Levite, Ariel E., and Elizabeth Sherwood-Randall, 'The Case for Discriminate Force', *Survival*, 44, 4 (winter 2002–3).

Linklater, Andrew, 'Marxism', in Burchill et al., *Theories*, ch. 5.

Litwak, Robert S., 'The New Calculus of Pre-emption', *Survival*, 44, 4 (winter 2002–3).

Lynch, Mark, 'Taking Arabs Seriously', *Foreign Affairs*, 82, 5 (2003).

Lyons, Gene M., and Michael Mastanduno (eds), *Beyond Westphalia? State Sovereignty and International Intervention* (Baltimore: Johns Hopkins University Press, 1995).

McNeill, William H., *The Pursuit of Power: Technology, Armed Forces and Society* (Oxford: Basil Blackwell, 1983).

McNeill, William H., *The Rise of the West: A History of the Human Community with a Retrospective Essay* (Chicago: University of Chicago Press, 1991).

Magee, Bryan (ed.), *The Great Philosophers* (London: BBC, 1987), Dialogue 6.

Mallaby, Sebastian, 'The Reluctant Imperialist', *Foreign Affairs*, 81, 2 (March–April 2002).

Manuel, Anja, and P. W. Singer, 'A New Model Afghan Army?', *Foreign Affairs*, 81, 4 (2002).

Mathiopolus, Margarita, and Istvan Gyarmati, 'St Malo and Beyond: Toward European Defence', *Washington Quarterly*, 22, 4 (1999).

Marx, Karl, and Friedrich Engels, *The Communist Manifesto*, in *Collected Works* (London: Lawrence and Wishart, 1980).

Mayall, James, *Nationalism and International Society*, Cambridge Studies in International Relations 10 (Cambridge: Cambridge University Press, 1990).

Mayall, James, *World Politics: Progress and its Limits* (Cambridge: Polity, 2000).

Mazower, Mark, *Dark Continent: Europe's Twentieth Century* (London: Penguin, 1998).

Mearsheimer, John, *The Tragedy of Great Power Politics* (New York: W. W. Norton, 2001).

Messervy-Whitting, Graham, 'The European Union's Nascent Military Staff', *RUSI Journal*, 145, 6 (2000).

Migdal, Joel S., *Strong Societies and Weak States: State–Society Relations and State Capabilities in the Third World* (Princeton: Princeton University Press, 1998).

Miller, John, Michael Stone and Chris Mitchell, *The Cell: Inside the 9/11 Plot and Why the FBI and CIA Failed to Stop it* (New York: Hyperion, 2002).

Moravcsik, Andrew, 'Striking a New Transatlantic Bargain', *Foreign Affairs*, 82, 4 (2003).

Morgenthau, Hans J., *Politics among Nations: The Struggle for Power and Peace*, brief edn (New York: McGraw-Hill, 1993).

Müllerson, Rein, '*Jus ad Bellum*: Plus ça Change (le Monde) Plus C'est la Même Chose (Le Droit)?', *Journal of Conflict and Security Law*, 7, 2 (2002).

Müllerson, Rein, *Ordering Anarchy* (The Hague: Martinus Nijhoff, 2000).

Myjer, E. J. P., and N. D. White, 'An Unlimited Right to Self-Defence?', *Journal of Conflict and Security Law*, 7, 1 (2002).

*The National Security Strategy of the United States of America*, http:// usinfo.state.gov/topical/pol/terror/secstrat.htm.

Nye, Joseph S., *The Paradox of American Power: Why the World's Only Superpower Can't Go Alone* (Oxford: Oxford University Press, 2002).

Nye, Joseph S., 'US Power and Strategy after Iraq', *Foreign Affairs*, 82, 4 (July–Aug. 2003).

O'Brien, Kevin, 'AIDs and African Armies', *The Atlantic Monthly* (July–Aug. 2003).

O'Hanlon, Michael E., 'A Flawed Masterpiece', *Foreign Affairs*, 81, 3 (2002).

Patten, Chris, 'Democracy Doesn't Flow from the Barrel of a Gun', *Foreign Policy*, 138 (Sept.–Oct. 2003).

Philpott, Daniel, 'Westphalia, Authority and International Society', in Robert Jackson (ed.), *Sovereignty at the Millennium* (Oxford: Blackwell Publishers for the Political Studies Association, 1999).

Pocock, Gordon, 'Nation, Community, Devolution and Sovereignty', *Political Quarterly*, 61, 3 (1990).

Pollack, Kenneth M., 'Next Stop Baghdad?', *Foreign Affairs*, 81, 2 (March–April 2002).

Pollack, Kenneth M., 'Securing the Gulf', *Foreign Affairs*, 82, 4 (2003).

Popovski, Vesselin, 'The International Criminal Court', *International Relations*, 15, 3 (Dec. 2000).

Posen, Barry, 'The Security Dilemma and Ethnic Conflict', *Survival*, 35, 2 (1993).

Powell, Colin, 'A Strategy of Partnerships', *Foreign Affairs*, 83, 21 (Jan.–Feb. 2004).

Rajendram, Lavina, 'Does the Clash of Civilisations Paradigm Provide a Persuasive Explanation of International Politics after September 11th?' *Cambridge Review of International Affairs*, 15, 2 (2002).

Ramet, Sabrina P., 'The United States and Europe: Toward Greater Cooperation or a Historic Parting? – An Idealist Perspective', in Sabrina Ramet and Christina Ingebretsen (eds), *Coming in from the Cold War: Changes in US–European Interactions since 1980* (Lanham, Md: Rowman and Littlefield, 2002).

Ramet, Sabrina, and Christina Ingebretsen (eds), *Coming in from the Cold War: Changes in US–European Interactions since 1980* (Lanham, Md: Rowman and Littlefield, 2002).

Rashid, Ahmed, 'The Taliban: Exporting Extremism', *Foreign Affairs*, 78, 6 (Nov.–Dec. 1999).

Roberts, Adam, 'Law and the Use of Force After Iraq', *Survival*, 45, 2 (summer 2003).

Rodin, David, *War and Self-Defence* (Oxford: Clarendon, 2002).

Rotberg, Robert I., 'Failed States in a World of Terror', *Foreign Affairs*, 81, 4 (2002).

Rubin, James P., 'Stumbling into War', *Foreign Affairs*, 82, 5 (2003).

Rumsfeld, Donald H., 'Transforming the Military', *Foreign Affairs*, 81, 3 (2002).

Sardar, Ziahuddin, and Meryl Wyn Davies, *Why Do People Hate America?* (Cambridge: Icon Books, 2003).

Sayyid, Bobby, *A Fundamental Fear: Eurocentrism and the Emergence of Islamism* (London: Zed Books, 1996).

Schachter, Oscar, 'The Right of States to Use Armed Force', *Michigan Law Review*, 82 (1984).

Schelling, Thomas, 'What Makes Greenhouse Sense?', *Foreign Affairs*, 81, 3 (2002).

Schöpflin, George, *Nations, Identity, Power* (London: Hurst and Co., 2000).

Shea, Jamie, *NATO 2000* (London: Brassey's, 1990).

Simon, Jeffrey, *NATO Enlargement: Opinions and Options* (Washington, DC: National Defense University Press, 1996).

Slaughter, Anne-Marie, 'Mercy Killings', *Foreign Policy*, 136 (May–June 2003).

Smit, Christian Reus, 'Constructivism', in Scott Burchill et al., *Theories of International Relations*, 2nd edn (London: Palgrave, 2001).

Smith, Julie, 'The Future of Europe and the Transatlantic Relationship: Introduction', *International Affairs*, 79, 5 (Oct. 2003).

Smith, Steve, Ken Booth and Marysia Zalewski (eds), *International Theory: Positivism and Beyond* (Cambridge: Cambridge University Press, 1996).

Smith, Steve, 'Reflectivist and Constructivist Approaches to International Theory', in Baylis and Smith (eds), *Globalization*.

Sørensen, Georg, 'Sovereignty: Change and Continuity in a Fundamental Institution', in Robert Jackson (ed.), *Sovereignty at the Millennium* (Oxford: Blackwell Publishers for the Political Studies Association, 1999).

'Speech by NATO Secretary General, Jaap de Hoop Scheffer at the Munich Security Conference', 7 Feb. 2004.

Starr, Harvey, *Anarchy, Order and Integration: How to Manage Interdependence* (Ann Arbor: University of Michigan Press, 1999).

'Statement of the Heads of State and Government of the United Nations Security Council', UN doc. S/23500, 31 Jan. 1992.

*Statute of the International Criminal Court*, www.icc-cpi.int/library/basicdocuments/rome_statute(e).html.

Steinberg, James B., 'An Elective Partnership: Salvaging Transatlantic Relations', *Survival*, 45, 2 (summer 2003).

Stenhouse, Mark, and Bruce George, *NATO and Mediterranean Security: The New Central Region*, London Defence Studies 22 (London: Brassey's for the Centre for Defence Studies, 1994).

Stevenson, Jonathan, 'How Europe and America Defend Themselves', *Foreign Affairs*, 82, 2 (2003).

Stern, Jessica, 'The Protean Enemy', *Foreign Affairs*, 82, 4 (2003).

*Strategic Context Paper* (London: Stationery Office, 2000).

*Strategic Defence Review Presented to Parliament by the Secretary of State for Defence by Command of Her Majesty* (London: Stationery Office, July 1998).

Talbott, Strobe, 'War in Iraq, Revolution in America', *International Affairs*, 79, 5 (2003).

Terriff, Terry, Stuart Croft, E. Krahmann, Mark Webber and Jolyon Howorth, 'NATO's Next Enlargement', *International Affairs*, 78, 4 (2002).

Teriff, Terry, Stuart Croft, Lucy James and Patrick M. Morgan, *Security Studies Today* (Cambridge: Polity, 1999).

Tharoor, Shashi, 'Why America Still Needs the United Nations', *Foreign Affairs*, 82, 5 (2003).

*UK Government Dossier on Iraq's Weapons of Mass Destruction* (London: Stationery Office, 24 Sept. 2002).

Victor, David, and Nadejda M. Victor, 'Axis of Oil?', *Foreign Affairs*, 82, 2 (March–April 2003).

Waltz, Kenneth N., *Theory of International Politics* (Reading, Mass.: Addison Wesley, 1979).

Wendt, Alexander, 'Anarchy is What States Make of it: The Social Construction of State Politics', *International Organization*, 46, 2 (1992), pp. 391–425.

Wendt, Alexander, *The Social Theory of International Relations* (Cambridge: Cambridge University Press, 1999).

Wheeler, Nicholas J., *Saving Strangers: Humanitarian Intervention in International Society* (Oxford: Oxford University Press, 2000).

Whiteman, Marjorie (ed.), *Digest of International Law*, vol. 12 (Washington, DC: US Department of State, 1971).

Wight, Martin, *International Theory: The Three Traditions*, ed. Gabrielle Wight and Brian Porter (London: Leicester University Press for the RIIA, 1994).

Woodward, Bob, *Bush at War: Inside the Bush White House* (London: Simon and Schuster, 2002).

Yost, David, *NATO Transformed: The Alliance's New Roles in International Security* (Washington, DC: United States Institute of Peace Press, 1998).

Zadra, Roberto, *European Integration and Nuclear Deterrence after the Cold War*, Chaillot Paper 5 (Paris: WEU Security Studies Institute, 1992).

# INDEX